The
Princeton
Review

PrincetonReview.com

LAW SCHOOL ESSAYS

THAT MADE

A DIFFERENCE

BY ERIC OWENS AND THE STAFF OF
THE PRINCETON REVIEW

Random House, Inc.
New York

The Princeton Review, Inc
111 Speen St., Suite 550
Framingham, MA 01701
E-mail: bookeditor@review.com

ISBN: 978-0-375-42786-2
ISSN: 2155-8299

Senior VP; Publisher: Robert Franek
Editor: Laura Braswell
Production: Best Content Solutions, LLC
Production Editor: Kristen O'Toole

Printed in the United States of America on partially recycled paper.

9 8 7 6 5 4 3 2 1

ACKNOWLEDGMENTS

Special thanks to Ian Van Tuyl, Rob Tallia, and David Adam Hollander, Esq., who provided me with a solid foundation from which my understanding of the law school application process grew.

I also wish to thank John Katzman and Rob Franek for their support of my work and ideas.

I am grateful to my editor, Laura Braswell, for her counsel during my work on the manuscript.

CONTENTS

Introduction 1
   How to Use This Book 2
   Law School Admissions: A Brief Overview 3
   The Law School Application Process: A Crash Course 5
   Writing a Great Personal Statement 9
   Addenda 40

Q & A with Admissions Officers 43

The Applicants 77
   American University Washington College of Law 80
   Boston College Law School 83
   Boston University School of Law 86
   Columbia University School of Law 91
   Cornell University School of Law 98
   Duke University School of Law 101
   Emory University School of Law 106
   Fordham University School of Law 111
   The George Washington University Law School 119
   Georgetown University Law Center 132
   Harvard University Law School 138
   Indiana University—Bloomington School of Law 171
   New York University School of Law 174
   Northwestern University School of Law 180
   Rutgers University, The State University of New Jersey
      School of Law—Camden 189
   South Texas College of Law 195
   University of Alabama 199
   University of Chicago Law School 215
   University of Colorado—Boulder School of Law 222
   University of Houston Law Center 224
   University of Michigan Law School 227
   University of New Mexico School of Law 240
   University of Ottawa Faculty of Law 246
   University of Pennsylvania Law School 249
   University of St. Thomas School of Law 265
   University of Texas at Austin School of Law 271

University of Virginia School of Law...275

University of Wisconsin Law School...277

Vanderbilt University Law School...284

Yale University Law School...287

About the Author.. **295**

Introduction

HOW TO USE THIS BOOK

The first part of this book—you are reading it now—addresses how to write a great personal statement for your application to law school. There's no magic recipe, of course; nevertheless, if you follow our advice about what to put in and what to leave out, we're confident that you'll end up with a memorable personal statement that will differentiate you from the larger applicant pool and make you a more competitive candidate.

The second part consists of interviews with the deans and directors of admissions at eight of the most selective law schools in the nation. Read what they have to say about the role that personal statements play in the admissions process. Their statements lend a human perspective to the sometimes harrowing law school admissions process.

The third part contains several unedited, unexpurgated personal statements written and submitted by actual law school applicants to a variety of selective law schools. You'll find that not every sentence is eloquent, nor every comma perfectly placed. These are the essays as they were submitted, read, and ultimately accepted. We think they're all solid. Some are excellent. More important, they've all passed the ultimate test for law school application soundness—their authors gained acceptance into at least one of the top law schools to which they applied.

It's important to note that the statements you'll find in these pages were written by students of diverse backgrounds and objectives. As with most collections of prose by a group of authors, this compilation may contain interesting or unexpected juxtapositions of ideas. The applicants whose work is featured in this book wrote about a variety of topics, including their relationships with family members, experiences in the working world, and difficulties with physical disabilities. There are some essays with somber themes and others that are more upbeat. You'll find accounts of achievement and stories of failure. These essays reveal a range of creativity and cleverness with the written word. Some are so good that they will intimidate you; others may hardly impress you. Some are strange; others will perhaps strike you as commonplace. No single type of essay is better than any other. We think you'll find, as we have, that the most memorable essays illuminate their writers. They are believable and perhaps relatable—but above all else, they're sincere.

Ideally, these personal statements will inspire you; supply you with paradigms for narrative and organizational structures; and teach you themes, illustrious words and phrases, and ways to express yourself that you hadn't considered, which will help you write exactly what you wish to communicate.

Of course, the personal statement doesn't stand alone. It has a place within the larger admissions context, and in this book, we show you the whole picture—including LSAT scores, undergraduate GPAs, work history, extracurricular involvement, and a complete list of admissions decisions for every single applicant whose essay you'll read. In this way, we hope to provide you with a thorough understanding of the relative selectivity of each of the top law schools featured and of the admissions context in which the personal statement comes into play.

Finally, though it goes without saying: Don't plagiarize the personal statements in this book. That's worth repeating: **Do not plagiarize the statements you read in this book.** Different law schools ask different questions. Some simply ask for a personal statement. Others want you to answer several short essay questions in addition to writing a personal statement. Requested lengths will vary. We encourage you to note buzzwords, structures, and themes that you like. But draw the line at copying paragraphs, sentences, or even phrases. There's a chance you'll get caught and won't get into law school at all. Penalties notwithstanding, plagiarism is simply wrong, so don't do it. Period.

LAW SCHOOL ADMISSIONS: A BRIEF OVERVIEW

Law school admissions counselors say that they do not use a formula to determine which applicants to accept or reject. Insofar as nobody plugs all the parts of your application into a mathematical equation that generates decisions, it's true that there is no formula.

In the grand scheme of things, however, getting into law school comes down to a very basic set of requirements. Wherever you apply, your application will be divided into three roughly equal parts: your undergraduate grades (and your graduate school grades, if applicable); your LSAT score; and "the subjective stuff," which consists of your personal statement, your professional experience, and all the other intangibles that can't be measured numerically. It is this third part that keeps the law school admissions process from becoming an entirely predictable quantitative assessment.

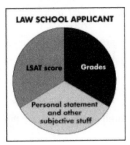

THE ADMISSIONS INDEX

When evaluating your application, law schools will usually combine your grades and your LSAT score into an "index." The index is a number (which varies from school to school) that is made up of a weighted combination of your UGPA (undergraduate grade point average) multiplied by your LSAT score. Your LSAT score is often weighted more heavily than your UGPA. (After all, the LSAT serves as a standard by which admissions officers can reliably—if, some may argue, arbitrarily—compare the performance of one candidate with that of the applicant pool at large.) While the process differs from one school to another, it is generally the case that your index will put you into one of the three categories described below.

(Probably) Accepted. A select few applicants who have high LSAT scores and stellar GPAs are admitted virtually automatically. If your index is very, very strong as compared with the median or target index of the school to which you are applying, then you're as good as in.

(Probably) Rejected. If your index is very weak compared with the median or target index of the school to which you are applying, then you are probably going to be rejected without much to-do. When admissions officers consider an application with a weaker index, they'll be on the lookout for something outstanding or unique (like, say, **a truly outstanding personal statement**).

Well . . . maybe. The majority of applicants fall somewhere in the middle; the indexes of applicants in this group are right around the medians or target indexes of the schools to which they apply. Applicants in this category have satisfactory LSAT scores and GPAs, but the numbers are not high enough to merit virtually automatic admission. Many people fall into this category because they apply to schools they think they have at least a shot of getting into based on their grades and LSAT scores. That is to say, law school applicants tend to self-select. Harvard, for example, probably doesn't see many applicants who earned a 140 on the LSAT. What determines the fate of candidates whose applications hang in the balance? Well, law schools often consider the competitiveness of the undergraduate program. On the one hand, someone with a 3.3 GPA in an easy major at a school from which everybody graduates with a 3.3 or higher will face an uphill battle. On the other hand, someone with the same GPA in a difficult major from a school that has a reputation for being stingy with A's is in better shape. Admissions officers will also pore over the personal statement, letters of recommendation, and resume for reasons to admit, reject, or waitlist "well . . . maybe" candidates.

Non-quantitative factors are particularly important at law schools that receive applications from thousands of numerically qualified applicants. "Top Ten" law schools that receive ten or fifteen applications for every offer of admission that they make have no choice but to "look beyond the numbers." These elite schools may have thousands of fully qualified applicants, but only a few hundred precious spots in their first-year classes. Their admissions offices will almost certainly have to turn away plenty applicants with near-perfect LSAT scores and impressive college grades; the subjective stuff of applicants who advance past the initial cut will be scrutinized.

Somewhat less competitive schools also seek to identify capable individuals, some of whom may have relatively unimpressive GPAs and LSAT scores. The importance of the other components of the application (the personal statement perhaps chief among them) is greatly magnified for these students, as they must demonstrate their probable success in law school in more subjective ways.

THE LAW SCHOOL APPLICATION PROCESS: A CRASH COURSE

It's time-consuming, and it's not known for being fun. The LSAT alone can easily consume eighty or more hours of prep time, and a single application form may take as long as thirty hours if you take great care with the essay questions (as you should). You don't want to sabotage your efforts because of last-minute sloppiness, nor do you want to let this already tedious process become a gigantic burden. Our advice: Start early, and pace yourself.

WHEN TO APPLY

It really, **really** varies. If you apply to Stanford, your application must be postmarked no earlier than September 1 and no later than February 1. If you apply to Duke, January 1 is your final deadline for submitting all materials. Boston College accepts applications for regular admission from mid-September until March 1, but the folks in admissions "urge you to submit your application well before the March 1 deadline." The University of Tennessee advises that you "complete your application file as soon as possible." Applications received before February 15 will be afforded something called "priority consideration" at Tennessee, while applications received after March 1 will be considered late and will probably not be reviewed at all. At Loyola University Chicago School of Law, you must submit everything by April 1.

As a general rule, the longer you wait to apply to a school—regardless of its deadline—the worse your chances of getting into that school will be. No efficient admissions staff is going to wait for all the applications to arrive before starting to make selections. If you're reading this in December and hope to get into a law school for the fall but haven't done anything about it, you're not in the most favorable position. If you're happy with your LSAT score, you're in a somewhat better position. Your applications, however, will get to the law schools after the optimum time and may appear a bit rushed. The best course of action is to start early in the year, methodically take care of one thing at a time, and **finish by December**.

Early notification options. Many schools have early notification options, so you may know by the holiday season if you've been accepted. Naturally, early notifications entail early applications. For example, early admissions applicants at Duke University School of Law must have taken the LSAT no later than June, and all application materials must be received no later than November 1. Boston College has an Early Notification program for applicants who submit applications by November 1 and whose files are complete by November 26. Loyola University Chicago also has an early notification program; applicants must submit all materials by January 15.

Applying early is a good idea for a few reasons. It can give you an indication of your chances of gaining admission to other schools; it can also relieve the stress of waiting until April (or June or August) to learn where you'll be spending the next three years of your life. Also, it's better to get waitlisted in December than in April (or whenever you would be notified for regular admission); if there is a "tie" among applicants on the waiting list, they'll probably admit whoever applied first. Of course, not every school has the same early admissions options. Some schools don't offer an early admissions option at all.

Rolling admissions. "Rolling admissions" refers to a first-come-first-served admissions policy. Many law schools evaluate applications and notify applicants of admissions decisions throughout the course of several months (ordinarily from late fall to midsummer). Obviously, if you apply to one of these schools, it is vital that you apply as early as possible because there will be more places available at the beginning of the process than there will be later on.

Applying online (versus the old-school-typewriter-snail-mail-method). We recommend that you apply online. It's easier, and most schools prefer to receive electronic applications. While you aren't likely to be penalized for using a typewriter and snail mail, why should you spend extra time on that?

THE BIG HURDLES

The application process is, as we mentioned, demanding. In that sense, it's an appropriate introduction to law school. Here are a few key tasks you will have to undertake as part of that process.

Take the LSAT. The Law School Admission Test (LSAT) is a roughly four-hour exam. The LSAT is given in February, June, October (or, occasionally, late September), and December. It's divided into five thirty-five-minute multiple-choice sections and one thirty-minute writing section (which is neither given a numerical score by the Law School Admission Council (LSAC) nor always taken into consideration by law schools). All ABA-approved and most non-ABA-approved law schools in the United States and Canada require an LSAT score from each and every applicant.

LSAT Q & A

Q. Is there a limit to the number of times I can take the LSAT?

A. You may take the LSAT three times in any two-year period, and all scores remain on your record for five years.

Q. What happens if I have multiple LSAT scores?

A. Most top law schools average multiple LSAT scores.

Q. How many times should I take the LSAT?

A. If possible, just once. It is better to have one score that shows true ability than it is to have two that may elicit questions or compel interpretation.

Q. Can I cancel my scores?

A. Yes, you may cancel your scores—before you see them, of course. You can cancel your LSAT scores at the test center by completing the score cancellation section of the LSAT answer sheet. You can also cancel your scores by sending a written cancellation request to LSAC within five days of taking the test. Note, however, that score reports will reflect that your score was cancelled at your request.

Q. What is considered a good LSAT score?

A. A score that gets you into the schools to which you apply (and that you hope ultimately to attend) is a good LSAT score. In terms of what is considered "good" in general, more than 50 percent of test takers receive scores between 145 and 159, though this range represents less than one-quarter of the possible scaled scores. A score of about 160 or above would put you in an elite group.

Q. How far in advance do I need to register to take the LSAT?

A. Registration deadlines are typically one month before the test date, and late registration deadlines are typically three weeks before the test date. That said, if you want to secure a place at a particular testing site, you should plan to register as early as possible. Otherwise, you may have to commute to take the LSAT.

Q. How much does the LSAT cost?

A. It costs $127 to take the LSAT and receive one free score report. The late registration fee is an additional $66. Further, subscription to the Law School Data Assembly Service (LSDAS), which costs $121, is required to apply to most law schools. Law school reports—which include test scores, LSAT writing sample copies, transcripts, undergraduate academic summaries, and letters of recommendation—cost $12 each. Applying to law school isn't cheap; but neither is attending law school. You'll reap the rewards in the quality of education you receive and of course in your future career as an attorney.

Complete applications from six or seven schools. Fairly early—like in July—select a couple of "reach" schools, a couple of schools to which you have a good shot at being accepted, and a couple of "safety" schools to which you are highly likely to be accepted. Your safety schools—if they are indeed true safety schools—will probably accept you quickly. It may take a while to get a final decision from the other schools, but you won't be totally panicked because you'll know your safety schools are there for you. If, for whatever reason, your UGPA or LSAT score is extremely low, you should apply to several safety schools.

Write your personal statement. Many schools will have open-ended prompts that simply say, in one variation or another, "Tell us about yourself." It's critical, however, that you personalize each essay for every single law school to which you apply. In addition, some schools will ask you to write a few shorter essays along with your primary personal statement—yet another reason to select your schools fairly early.

Obtain two or three recommendations. Some schools require you to submit two recommendations, both of which must be academic. Other schools request more than two recommendations and want at least one of them to be from someone who knows you outside of traditional academic circles. (A handful of schools don't ask for recommendations at all, but this is the exception, not the rule.) As part of your LSDAS file, LSAC will accept up to three letters of recommendation on your behalf and will send those letters to all of the schools to which you apply.

Update/create your resume. Most law school applications request a copy of your resume. Make sure yours is up-to-date and suitable for submission to an academic institution. Put your academic credentials and experience first—no matter what they are and no matter how much professional experience you have. The resume functions as a supplement to the rest of the material; it's probably the simplest part of the application process.

Get your academic transcripts sent to the LSDAS. When you subscribe to the Law School Data Assembly Service, you must request that the registrar at every undergraduate, graduate, and professional school that you ever attended send to them an official transcript. Do not attempt to send your own transcripts anywhere; law schools will consider them to be unofficial transcripts and **not** accept them. For this reason, it is imperative that you **make your transcript requests in August.** If you're applying for early decision, start sending for transcripts as early as May. Law schools will not make a decision without a complete file, and the LSDAS will not send your information to law schools without your transcripts. Undergraduate institutions occasionally delay the transcript process—sometimes even when students go there personally and pay them to provide the LSDAS with their records. Give yourself some time to fix any problems that may arise.

Write any necessary addenda. An addendum is a brief letter written to explain a deficient portion of your application. If your personal and academic life has been fairly smooth, you won't need to include any addenda with your application. If, however, you were ever arrested, put on academic probation, or have a low grade point average, you may need to write an addendum to explain the circumstances of your situation. Other legitimate addenda topics are a low or discrepant LSAT scores, DUI/DWI suspensions, or any time gap in your academic or professional career. (See page 26 for more on addenda.)

Send in your seat deposit. Once you are accepted to a particular school, that school will ask you to send in a deposit. A typical fee runs for $250 or more. This amount will be credited to your first-term tuition once you register for classes.

Do any other stuff. The law school application process is extensive, and accordingly, you may find that there are additional tasks beyond those just outlined. (You may wish to request a fee waiver, for example.) Keep a list of everything you need to take care of, and check off tasks as you accomplish them. Obtain a copy of the LSAC's **LSAT/LSDAS Registration and Information Book,** which is an invaluable resource for law school applicants. It has the forms you'll need, a sample LSAT, admissions information, the current Law Forum schedule, and sample application schedules. You can also find everything you'll need at www.lsac.org.

WRITING A GREAT PERSONAL STATEMENT

The personal statement often presents the only opportunity for you to differentiate yourself from the greater pool of applicants and to show that you can string more than a few sentences together. Sure, there's an essay on the LSAT, but it won't be taken anywhere nearly as seriously as your personal statement (though if it differs too substantially in quality and style from your personal statement, it may raise a few red flags for admissions officers).

Your personal statement—together with your grades and LSAT score—is critically important to your law school application. Your statement should be about two or three pages in length (or the length specified in the prompt to which you are responding), and it should amount to something significantly more profound than "A six-figure salary really appeals to me," or "Being a lawyer seems like a solid career move." Your statement should provide the reader with insights into who you are—where you come from, where you're going, and why you've chosen this path to get there—concisely and eloquently. You can accomplish this if you invest time and thought. Keep reading; we'll show you how.

PERSONAL STATEMENT THEORY: EIGHT ESSENTIALS

1. Be professional, and always consider your audience. In your personal statement, you want to present yourself as intelligent, professional, mature, and persuasive. These are the qualities law schools seek in applicants. Moreover, these are the qualities that make good lawyers. The personal statement of a law school application (unlike the college application essay, for example) is not the place to discuss what your trip to Europe meant to you, describe your wacky chemistry teacher, or try your hand at verse. While you want to stand out, you definitely don't want to be considered immature or inappropriate.

Keep in mind the perspective of the reader as you craft your essay. Ultimately, you are offering a portrait of yourself in words to someone who doesn't know you and who may never meet you, but who nevertheless has the power to make a very important decision about the course of your life. Remember that it's a real person who will read your personal statement. Keep this person interested. Make them curious. Make them smile. Engage them intellectually. Properly orient this person so that he or she is at no point distracted from the content of your essay.

2. Demonstrate motive, and create a frame within which the reader can place you. It's usually important to show why you want to go to law school. While you do not have to make your motivation for attending law school the central focus of your essay, you do want the admissions staff to come away with some understanding of why you want to commit three years of your life to codes and case law and to the practice of law many years thereafter.

Put yourself in a genuine context by explaining how your education, your personal and professional experiences, and the world around you have influenced you and your decision to attend law school. Give the admissions officers a frame of reference and real insight into the person you've become as a result of the experiences you've had. (If you do this well, the reader will understand why you want to attend law school without you having to explicitly state it.) Be open about yourself. Don't just ramble on with clichés and platitudes. The more personal and individualized your personal statement is, the better received it will be. In a nutshell, admissions

officers want you to communicate (in a clear, concise, grammatically accurate way) who you really are and what has made you the person you are today. They look for introspection and your ability to reflect intellectually upon yourself and upon the experiences that helped to develop your attitudes and beliefs. Admissions officers seek out individuals who understand their own strengths, weaknesses, and limitations. They look for people who are aware of their own pasts and who have learned from their own mistakes. They look for candidates who have grown intellectually and professionally and who want to grow some more.

3. Write clearly and succinctly, and get to the point within three pages unless there are unusual circumstances. Like any good writing, your law school application should be unambiguous and concise. Cut out excessive verbiage. Eschew obfuscation. Clarity and conciseness are usually the products of much careful reading, rereading (and rereading and rereading), and rewriting. Without question, repeated critical revision is the surest way to trim, fine-tune, and improve your prose.

Don't be long-winded and boring. Admissions officers don't typically like long personal statements. Most people who have unusual circumstances are those who are in their thirties or forties (or fifties or sixties) and therefore have more life experience. Unless you have particularly unusual circumstances that warrant (and merit) a longer essay, keep it brief. Moreover, regardless of the length, make certain that your personal statement is concise.

Details, Details, Details

We cannot stress enough the importance of proofreading. If in the personal statement that you submit to one school, you mention another, you will (rightfully) be pegged as careless in your attention to detail. Such imprecision can render your entire application unsuccessful. Lawyers need to be conscientious and circumspect—and so do you.

4. Tell the truth, and find your unique angle. Candor is the product of proper motivation. Honesty, sincerity, and authenticity cannot be superimposed after the fact; your writing must be candid from the outset. Do not try to fake candor (even if it's almost convincing). No matter how good your insincere personal statement may be, we're quite confident that an honest

Don't Write Defensively

Don't apologize for not being extraordinary enough (whatever that means), for taking the admissions officer's time, or for not being sufficiently creative or interesting. If you're hoping that such professed humility will somehow excuse you from having to hold your reader's interest or if you think it hasn't all been professed with varying degrees of *faux*-mility before, you are sadly mistaken. Don't apologize for what you *aren't*; tout all that you *are*. Every experience has something valuable and interesting to teach you. We recommend that you forego the defensive in favor of the interesting. You (not to mention the admissions officer reading your personal statement) will be much more satisfied with the result.

and authentic personal statement will be even better.

The admissions people read tons of really boring essays about "how great I am" and "why I think there should be justice for everyone." Strive to find an angle that is interesting and unique to you. If what you write isn't interesting to you, we promise that it won't be even remotely interesting to an admissions officer. Not only will a unique and interesting essay be more effective; it will also be far more enjoyable to write. Who are you? Why are you different? What distinguishes you from others? Sometimes applicants want to answer this question in a superficial way. They want to say, for example, "I am an Asian American from Missouri." Expressed in such a general way, your background provides almost no insight into your character. If you choose to talk about your background in the context of how it has shaped your perspective and influenced your choices, that's a different story. If you go this route, however, remember to be highly specific; you do not want to be thought of as an applicant who was trying to fit into a preconceived notion of identity. Finally, you almost never need to mention the honors and awards you've received. After all, there's a place for those on almost every law school application.

5. Devise a well-conceived narrative, and remember that good writing can (and will) be easily understood. Structural soundness is the product of a well-crafted outline. It really pays to sketch out the general themes of your personal statement first; worry about filling in the particulars later. Pay especially close attention to the structure of your personal statement and to the fundamental message it communicates. Your personal statement should flow seamlessly from beginning to end. Use paragraphs properly, and make sure the paragraphs are in logical order. The sentences within each paragraph should be complete and also in logical order.

You want to get your point across, not bury it in words. Your prose should be clear and direct. Don't say in ten words what you can just as satisfactorily communicate in five—unless you have another clearly identifiable and worthy stylistic objective. If an admissions officer has to struggle to figure out what you are trying to say, you'll be in trouble. Since legal writing courses make up a significant part of most law school curricula, you will have a serious edge if you can demonstrate that you already possess impressive writing skills.

6. Avoid gimmicks, yet make yourself stand out. Do not make your personal statement into a poem, an epic, or anything besides standard prose. Anything other than standard prose is highly ineffective.

A solid, well-crafted essay will impress any admissions officer; however, if it reads like all the others, that admissions officer may not remember you. Yours will be just another personal statement, and as a result, you will present yourself as just another applicant. You don't want to be just another applicant, so seek to write something better than just another personal statement. You will be competing against thousands of well-qualified applicants for admission. Your primary task in writing your application is to separate yourself from the crowd. Admissions committees will read innumerable applications from bright twenty-two-year old candidates with good grades. Particularly if you are applying directly from college or if you have been out of school for a very short time, you must do your best to make sure the admissions committee doesn't lump you in with everyone else of similar age and credentials. Your essay presents an opportunity to put your unique set of credentials into context and distinguish yourself. Seize this opportunity! Keep in mind, however, that cheap tricks and gimmicks will make you stand out in a bad way. Sincerity is key here.

7. Customize your statement for each school. You'll probably need to write only one basic personal statement, but you must make absolutely sure to make it specific (even if it's only ever-so-slightly specific) to each law school to which you apply. Law school admissions officers see a number of essays that have been written for some school other than theirs, and they hate that. Don't send the personal statement you wrote for your Fordham application to the University of Michigan. Pay extremely close attention to what each school is asking in the prompt for its personal statement because there are probably some subtle (if not blunt) differences. Track each personal statement to make sure it goes to the right place.

> ### To Be or Not To Be?
> Whenever possible, choose a verb that suggests a causal relationship instead of the linking verb *to be*. (The mantra: Don't equate when you can relate.) If someone *is* something, include that information in a modifier. Instead of, for example, "Jane Smith is a varsity basketball player," try, "A varsity basketball player, Jane Smith wins because she takes risky shots." Whenever possible, use the active voice in your sentences. Convey key information directly and succinctly.

8. Proofreading is absolutely essential—and so is total grammar and spelling accuracy. A thoughtful essay that offers true insight will stand out unmistakably; but if that essay is riddled with poor grammar and misspelled words, it will not receive serious consideration. Proofread your personal statement. Then proofread it again; then proofread it some more. Have three or four people read your personal statement from beginning to end and critique it. Read it aloud (this really helps!). Ask friends, boyfriends, girlfriends, professors, brothers, sisters—anybody—to read your essay and comment on it. Do whatever it takes to make sure your personal statement is compelling, clear, concise, candid, and structurally sound.

It is critical that your essay be 100 percent grammatically correct. We just can't stress this enough. Do not misspell anything; use awkwardly constructed sentences, run-on sentences, or wrong verb tenses; misplaced modifiers; or make a single error in punctuation. Make use of your spelling and grammar checks, but do not trust them to catch everything. Go back and read (and reread) your essay to ensure that you are submitting an example of your absolute best work.

In fact, making sure your writing is 100 percent grammatically accurate is so important that we've devoted a whole section to a review of the essential rules of good grammar and style. Even great writers can occasionally use a primer in the mechanics of good writing, and in order to crank out a great application essay you're going to need to be able to apply all of these rules, with panáche.

GOOD GRAMMAR = GOOD FORM

Think of each essay you write as a building. If it doesn't have structural integrity, law school admissions officers will tear through it with a wrecking ball.

Let's face it: You can write the most rip-roaring yarn this side of Clive Cussler, but without grammatical accuracy, it'll fall apart. A thoughtful essay that offers true insight will not receive serious consideration if it's riddled with poor grammar and misspelled words. It's critical that you avoid grammatical errors. We can't stress this enough. Misspellings, awkward constructions, run-on sentences, and misplaced modifiers cast doubt on your efforts, not to mention your intelligence.

Most Common Grammar Mistakes

Chances are you know the difference between a subject and a verb. So we won't spend time here reviewing the basic components of English sentence construction (however, if you feel like you could use a refresher, check out our book, *Grammar Smart.*) Instead we will focus on problems of usage.

Below is a brief overview to the seven most common usage errors among English speakers. These are errors we all make (some more than others) and knowing what they are will help you snuff them out in your own writing.

Mistake #1: Misplaced Modifier

A modifier is a descriptive word or phrase inserted into a sentence to add dimension to the thing it modifies. For example:

> *Because he could talk*, Mr. Ed was a unique horse.

A Good Book

Buy and read *The Elements of Style*, by William Strunk, Jr. and E. B. White. We can't recommend it highly enough. This little book is a requisite investment for any writer (and believe us, you'll be doing plenty of writing as a law student and practicing attorney). You will constantly refer to it, and your writing will improve as a result.

Because he could talk is the modifying phrase in the sentence. It describes a characteristic of Mr. Ed. Generally speaking, a modifying phrase should be right next to the thing it modifies. If it's not, the meaning of the sentence may change. For example:

Every time he goes to the bathroom outside, John praises his new puppy for being so good.

Who's going to the bathroom outside? In this sentence, it's John! There are laws against that! The descriptive phrase *every time he goes to the bathroom outside* needs to be near *puppy* for the sentence to say what it means.

When you are writing sentences that begin with a descriptive phrase followed by a comma, make sure that the thing that comes after the comma is the person or thing being modified.

Mistake #2: Pronoun Agreement

As you know, a pronoun is a little word that is inserted to represent a noun (*he, she, it, they, etc*). Pronouns must agree with their nouns: The pronoun that replaces a singular noun must also be singular, and the pronoun that replaces a plural noun must be plural.

During your proofreading, be sure your pronouns agree with the nouns they represent. The most common mistake is to follow a singular noun with a plural pronoun (or vice versa), as in the following:

If a writer misuses words, they will not do well on the state exam.

The problem with this sentence is that the noun ("writer") is singular, but the pronoun ("they") is plural. The sentence would be correctly written as follows:

If a writer misuses words, he or she will not do well on the state exam.

Or

If writers misuse words, they will not do well on the state exam.

This may seem obvious but it is also the most commonly violated rule in ordinary speech. How often have you heard people say, *The class must hand in their assignment before leaving.* Class is singular. But *their* is plural. Class isn't the only tricky noun that sounds singular but is actually plural. Following is a list of "tricky" nouns—technically called collective nouns. They are nouns that typically describe a group of people but are considered singular and therefore need a singular pronoun:

Family

Jury

Group

Team

Audience

Congregation

United States

If different pronouns are used to refer to the same subject or one pronoun is used to replace another, the pronouns must also agree. The following pronouns are singular:

Either

Neither

None

Each

Anyone

No one

Everyone

If you are using a pronoun later in a sentence, double-check to make sure it agrees with the noun/pronoun it is replacing.

Mistake #3: Subject-Verb Agreement

The rule regarding subject-verb agreement is simple: singular with singular, plural with plural. If you are given a singular subject (*he, she, it*), then your verb must also be singular (*is, has, was*).

Sometimes you may not know if a subject is plural or singular, making it tough to determine whether its verb should be plural or singular. (Just go back to our list of collective nouns that sound plural but are really singular).

Subjects joined by *and* are plural:

Bill and Pat *were* going to the show.

However, nouns joined by or can be singular or plural—if the last noun given is singular, then it takes a singular verb; if the last noun given is plural, it takes a plural verb.

Bill or Pat *was* going to get tickets to the show.

When in doubt about whether your subjects and verbs agree, trim the fat! Cross out all the prepositions, commas, adverbs, and adjectives separating your subject from its verb. Stripping the sentence down to its component parts will allow you to quickly see whether your subjects and verbs are in order.

Mistake #4: Verb Tense

As you know, verbs come in different tenses—for example, *is* is present tense, while was is past tense. The other tense you need to know about is "past perfect."

Past perfect refers to some action that happened in the past and was completed (perfected) before another event in the past. For example:

I had already begun to volunteer at the hospital when I discovered my passion for medicine.

You'll use the past perfect a lot when you describe your accomplishments to admissions officers. For the most part, verb tense should not change within a sentence (e.g., switching from past to present).

Mistake #5: Parallel Construction

Remember this from your SATs? Just as parallel lines line up with one another, parallelism means that the different parts of a sentence line up in the same way. For example:

Jose told the career counselor his plan: he will be taking the GMAT, attend business school, and become a CEO.

In this sentence, Jose is going to *be taking*, *attend*, and, *become*. The first verb, *be taking* is not written I the same form as the other verbs in the series. In other words, it is not parallel. To make this sentence parallel, it should read:

Jose told the career counselor his plan: he will take the GMAT, attend business school, and become a CEO.

It is common to make errors of parallelism when writing sentences that list actions or items. Be careful.

Mistake #6: Comparisons

When comparing two things, make sure that you are comparing what can be compared. Sound like double-talk? Look at the following sentence:

Larry goes shopping at Foodtown because the prices are better than Shoprite.

Sound okay? Well, sorry—it's wrong. As written, this sentence says that the prices at Foodtown are better than Shoprite—the entire store. What Larry means is that the prices at Foodtown are better than the *prices* at Shoprite. You can only compare like things (prices to prices, not prices to stores).

The English language uses different comparison words when comparing two things than when comparing more than two things. Check out these examples:

more (for two things) vs. **most** (for more than two)
Ex.: Given Alex and David as possible dates, Alex is the *more* appealing of the two.
In fact, of all the guys I know, Alex is the *most* attractive.

less (for two things) vs. **least** (for more than two)
Ex.: I am *less* likely to be chosen than you are.
I am the *least* likely person to be chosen from the department.

better (for two things) vs. **best** (for more than two)
Ex.: Taking a cab is *better* than hitchhiking.
My organic chemistry professor is the *best* professor I have ever had.

between (for two things) vs. **among** (for more than two)
Ex.: Just *between* you and me, I never liked her anyway.
Among all the people here, no one likes her.

Keep track of what's being compared in a sentence so you don't fall into this grammatical black hole.

Mistake #7: Diction

Diction means choice of words. There are tons of frequently confused words in the English language. They can be broken down into words that sound the same but mean different things (*there, they're, their*), words and phrases that are made up (*irregardless*) and words that are incorrectly used as synonyms (*fewer, less*).

Words that sound the same but mean different things are homonyms. Some examples are:

there, they're, their: *There* is used to indicate a location in time or space. *They're* is a contraction of "they are." *Their* is a possessive pronoun.

effect/affect: *Effect* is the result of something. *Affect* is to influence or change something.

conscience/conscious: *Conscience* is Freudian, and is a sense of right or wrong. *Conscious* is to be awake.

principle/principal: *Principle* is a value. *Principal* is the person in charge at a school.

eminent/imminent: *Eminent* describes a person who is highly regarded. *Imminent* means impending.

Imaginary words that don't exist but tend to be used in writing include:

Alot: Despite widespread use, *alot* is not a word. *A lot* is the correct form.

Irregardless: *Irregardless* is not in anybody's dictionary—it's not a real word. *Regardless* is the word that you want.

Sometimes people don't know when to use a word. How often have you seen this sign?

Express checkout: Ten items or less.

Unfortunately, supermarkets across America are making a blatant grammatical error when they post this sign. When items can be counted, you must use the word *fewer*. When something cannot be counted, you would use the word *less*. For example:

If you eat fewer French fries, you can use less ketchup.

Here are some other words people make te mistake of using interchangeably:

number/amount: Use *number* when referring to something that can be counted. Use *amount* when it cannot.

aggravate/irritate: *Aggravate* and *irritate* are not synonymous. To *aggravate* is to make worse. To *irritate* is to annoy.

disinterested/uninterested: *Disinterest* means impartiality; absence of strong feelings about something, good or bad. To be *uninterested*, on the other hand, indicates boredom.

Diction errors require someone to cast a keen, fresh eye on your essay because they trick your ear and require focused attention to catch.

Here's a handy chart to help you remember the most common grammar usage errors:

GRAMMAR CHART

Grammatical Category	What's the Rule?	Bad Grammar	Good Grammar
Misplaced Modifier	A modifier is word or phrase that describes something and should go right next to the thing it modifies.	1. Eaten in Mediterranean countries for centuries, **northern Europeans** viewed the tomato with suspicion. 2. A **former greens keeper** now about to become the Masters champion, **tears** welled up in my eyes as I hit my last miraculous shot.	1. Eaten in Mediterranean countries for centuries, the tomato was viewed by **the tomato** with suspicion by Northern Europeans. 2. **I was a former greens keeper** who was now about to become the Masters champion; **tears** welled up in my eyes as I hit my last miraculous shot.
Pronoun Agreement	A pronoun must refer unambiguously to a noun and it must agree in number with that noun.	1. Although **brokers** are not permitted to know executive access **codes**, **they** are widely known. 2. The **golden retriever** is one of the smartest breeds of dogs, but **they** often **have** trouble writing **personal statements** for law school admission. 3. Unfortunately, both **candidates** for whom I worked sabotaged their own **campaigns** by accepting a **contribution** from illegal **sources.**	1. Although **brokers** are not permitted to know executive access **codes, the codes** are widely known. 2. The **golden retriever** is one of the smartest breeds of dogs, but often **it has** trouble writing **a personal statement** for law school admission. 3. Unfortunately, both **candidates** for whom I worked sabotaged their own **campaigns** by accepting **contributions** from illegal **sources.**
Subject-Verb Agreement	The subject must always agree in number with the verb. Make sure you don't forget what the subject of a sentence is, and don't use the object of a preposition as a subject.	1. **Each** of the men involved in the extensive renovations **were** engineers. 2. Federally imposed **restrictions** on the ability to use certain information **has** made life difficult for Martha Stewart.	1. **Each** of the men involved in the extensive renovations **was** engineers. 2. Federally imposed **restrictions** on the ability to use certain information **have** made life difficult for Martha Stewart.

Grammatical Category	What's the Rule?	Bad Grammar	Good Grammar
Verb Tense	Always make sure your sentences' tenses match the time frame being discussed.	1. After he finished working on his law school essays he **would go** to the party.	1. After he finished working on his law school essays he **went** to the party.
Paralell Construction	Two or more ideas in a single sentence that are parallel need to be similar in grammatical form.	1. The two main goals of the Eisenhower presidency were a **reduction** of taxes and **to increase** military strength. 2. **To provide a child** with the skills necessary for survival in modern life is **like guaranteeing their** success.	1. The two main goals of the Eisenhower presidency were **to reduce** taxes and **to increase** military strength. 2. **Providing children** with the skills necessary for survival in modern life is **like guaranteeing their** success.
Cmparisons	You can only compare things that are exactly the same.	1. The **rules** of written English are **more stringent** than spoken **English.** 2. The **considerations** that led many colleges to impose admissions quotas in the last few decades are *similar to the quotas* imposed in the recent past by large businesses.	1. The rules of written English are **more stringent than those of** spoken English. 2. The **considerations** that led many colleges to impose admissions quotas in the last few decades **are similar to those** that led large businesses to impose quotas in the recent past.
Diction	There are many words that sound the same but mean different things.	1. Studying had a very positive **affect** on my score. 2. My high SAT score has positively **effected** the outcome of my college applications.	1. Studying had a very positive **effect** on my score. 2. My high SAT score has positively **affected** the outcome of my college applications.

Using Punctuation Correctly

Now that we've got that covered, it's time to talk about punctuation. As a member of the LOL generation you might be great at turning punctuation into nonverbal clues, but colons and parentheses have other uses besides standing in as smiley faces at the end of your texts.

A formal essay is not like the notes you take in econometrics. "W/" is not an acceptable substitute for *with*, and neither is "b/c" for *because*. Symbols are also not acceptable substitutes for words (@ for *at*, & for *and*, etc.). (In fact, try to avoid the use of "etc."; it is not entirely acceptable in formal writing. Use "and so forth" or "among others" instead.) And please don't indulge in any "cute" spelling ("nite" for *night*, "tho" for *though*). This kind of writing conveys a message that you don't care about your essay. Show the admissions officers how serious you are by eliminating these shortcuts.

The overall effectiveness of your business school application essay is greatly dependent on your ability to use punctuation wisely. Here's what you need to know:

Commas (,)

Very few people understand every rule for proper comma use in the English language.

This lack of understanding leads to two disturbing phenomena: essays without commas and essays with commas everywhere. Here is a quick summary of proper comma use:

Use Commas to Set Off Introductory Elements.

- Breezing through my application essay, I wondered if everyone were as well prepared as I.

- Incidentally, I got a 750 on the GMAT.

- Before you jump to any conclusions, I was only taking a mote out of her eye.

Use Commas to Separate Items in a Series.

- She made hot chocolate, cinnamon toast, scrambled eggs with cheese, and coffee cake.

[Note: There's always great debate as to whether the final serial comma (before the *and*) is necessary. In this case, the comma must be added; otherwise, there will be a question about the contents of the scrambled eggs. In cases where no such ambiguity exists, the extra comma seems superfluous. Use your best judgment. When in doubt, separate all the items in a series with commas.]

Use Commas Around a Phrase or Clause that Could Be Removed Logically from the Sentence.

- The Analytical Writing section, the first section of the GMAT, always makes my palms sweat.

- Xavier, the student whose test was interrupted by marching band practice, would have liked to have had ear plugs.

Use a Comma to Separate Coordinate (Equally Important) Adjectives. *Do Not* Use a Comma to Separate Noncoordinate Adjectives.

- It was a dark, stormy night.

- It was messy triple bypass.

Do Not Use a Comma to Separate a Subject and a Verb.

- Incorrect: My new GMAT study group, meets at the local café.

- Correct: My new GMAT study group meets at the local café.

Do Not Use a Comma to Separate Compound Subjects or Predicates.

(A compound subject means two "do-ers"; a compound predicate means two actions done.)

- Incorrect: My best friend Xavier, and his brother Lou always tell me the truth about my practice essays.

- Correct: My best friend Xavier and his brother Lou always tell me the truth about my practice essays.

- Incorrect: Because of the strange tickling in the back of my throat, I stayed in bed, and gave myself a break from studying.

- Correct: Because of the strange tickling in the back of my throat, I stayed in bed and gave myself a break from studying.

Colons (:)

Use a colon to introduce an explanation or a list.

- "I think you judge Truman too charitably when you call him a child: He is more like a sweetly vicious old lady." *Tennessee Williams*

- "When I am dead, I hope it may be said: 'His sins were scarlet, but his books were read.'" *Hilaire Belloc*

- "Everything goes by the board to get the book written: honor, pride, decency..." *William Faulkner*

Semicolons (;)

Use a semicolon to join related independent clauses in a single sentence (a clause is independent if it can logically stand alone).

- "An artist is born kneeling; he fights to stand." *Hortense Calisher*

- "Why had I become a writer in the first place? Because I wasn't fit for society; I didn't fit into the system." *Brian Aldiss*

Dashes (—)

Use a dash for an abrupt shift. Use a pair of dashes (one on either side) to frame a parenthetical statement that interrupts the sentence. Dashes are more informal than colons.

- "Like a lot of what happens in novels, inspiration is a sort of spontaneous combustion—the oily rags of the head and heart." *Stanley Elkin*

- "Writers should be read—but neither seen nor heard." *Daphne du Maurier*

- "Of all the cants which are canted in this canting world—though the cant of hypocrites may be the worst—the cant of criticism is the most tormenting." *Laurence Sterne*

Exclamation Points (!)

Use exclamation points sparingly. Try to express excitement, surprise, or rage in the words you choose. A good rule of thumb is *one* exclamation point per essay, at the most.

- "You don't know what it is to stay a whole day with your head in your hands trying to squeeze your unfortunate brain so as to find a word.... Ah! I certainly know the agonies of style." *Gustave Flaubert*

Question Marks (?)

Use a question mark after a direct question. Don't forget to use a question mark after rhetorical questions (ones that you make in the course of argument that you answer yourself).

- "Why shouldn't we quarrel about a word? What is the good of words if they aren't important enough to quarrel over? Why do we choose one word over another if there isn't any difference between them?" *G. K. Chesterton*

Quotation Marks (" ")

Use quotation marks to indicate a writer's exact words. Use quotation marks for titles of songs, chapters, essays, articles, or stories—a piece that is part of a larger whole. Periods and commas always go inside the quotation mark. Exclamation points and question marks go inside the quotation mark when they belong to the quotation and not to the larger sentence. Colons, semicolons, and dashes go outside the quotation mark.

- "That's not writing, that's typing." *Truman Capote* on Jack Kerouac

WRITING CLEARLY

Now that you've gotten a refresher in the building blocks of good writing, it's time to talk about the other half of the equation: style. If grammar and punctuation represent the mechanics of your writing, style represents the choices you make in sentence structure, diction, and figures of thought that reveal your personality to admissions officers. We can't recommend highly enough that you read *The Elements of Style*, by William Strunk Jr., E. B. White, and Roger Angell. This little book is a great investment. Even if you've successfully completed a course or two in composition without it, it will prove invaluable and become your new best friend—and hopefully also your muse.

ELIMINATING WORDINESS

Remember: Good writing is writing that's easily understood. You want to get your point across, not bury it in words. Make your prose clear and direct. **If an admissions officer has to struggle to figure out what you're trying to say, there's a good chance he or she might not bother reading further.** Abide by word limits and avoid the pitfall of overwriting. Here are some suggestions that will help clarify your writing by eliminating wordiness:

Address One Idea at a Time

Don't try to put too much information into one sentence. If you're ever uncertain whether a sentence needs three commas and two semicolons or two colons and a dash, just make it into two separate sentences. Two simple sentences are better than one long convoluted one. Which of the following examples seems clearer to you?

Example #1:

Many people, politicians for instance, act like they are thinking of the people they represent by the comments made in their speeches, while at the same time they are filling their pockets at the expense of the taxpayers.

Example #2:

Many people appear to be thinking of others, but are actually thinking of themselves. For example, many politicians claim to be thinking of their constituents, but are in fact filling their pockets at the taxpayers' expense.

Use Fewer Words to Express an Idea

In a 500-word essay, you don't have time to mess around. In an attempt to sound important, many of us "pad" our writing. Always consider whether there's a shorter way to express your thoughts. We are all guilty of some of the following types of clutter:

Cluttered	Clear
due to the fact that	because
with the possible exception of	except
until such time as	until
for the purpose of	for
referred to as	called
at the present time	now
at all times	always

Test Yourself: Eliminating Wordiness Exercise

Another way in which unnecessary words may sneak into your writing is through the use of redundant phrases. Pare each phrase listed below down to a single word:

cooperate together_____

resulting effect_____

large in size_____

absolutely unprecedented_____

disappear from sight_____

new innovation_____

repeat again_____

totally unique_____

necessary essentials_____

Use Fewer Qualifiers

A qualifier is a little phrase we use to cover ourselves. Instead of plainly stating that "Former President Reagan sold arms in exchange for hostages," we feel more comfortable stating "*It's quite possible* that former President Reagan *practically* sold arms in *a kind* of exchange for people who were *basically* hostages." Over-qualifying weakens your writing. Prune out these words and expressions wherever possible:

kind of	basically
a bit	practically
sort of	essentially
pretty much	in a way
rather	quite

Another type of qualifier is the *personal qualifier*, where instead of stating the truth, I state the truth "in my opinion." Face it: Everything you state (except perhaps for scientific or historical facts) is your opinion. Personal qualifiers like the following can often be pruned:

to me

in my opinion

in my experience

I think

it is my belief

it is my contention

the way I see it

Use Fewer Adverbs

If you choose the right verb or adjective to begin with, an adverb is often unnecessary.

Use an adverb only if it does useful work in the sentence. It's fine to say "the politician's campaign ran smoothly up to the primaries," because the adverb "smoothly" tells us something important about the running of the campaign. The adverb could be eliminated, however, if the verb were more specific: "The politician's campaign sailed up to the primaries." The combination of the strong verb *and* the adverb, as in "the politician's campaign sailed smoothly up to the primaries," is unnecessary because the adverb does no work. Here are other examples of unnecessary adverbs:

very unique

instantly startled

dejectedly slumped

effortlessly easy

absolutely perfect

totally flabbergasted

completely undeniable

Test Yourself: Eliminating Wordiness Exercise (part 2)

Rewrite these sentences to make them less wordy.

1. It can be no doubt argued that the availability of dangerous and lethal guns and firearms are in part, to some extent, responsible for the undeniable explosion of violence in our society today.

_____

_____

_____

_____

2. Why is it always imperative and necessary for the teaching educational establishment to subdue and suppress the natural spirits and energies of adolescents in scholarly settings?

_____

_____

_____

_____

3. It seems to me that I believe one must not ignore the fact that Hamlet was a heroic character as well as a tragic and doomed character fated to suffer.

_____

_____

_____

_____

4. No one would deny the strong and truthful fact that young teenage pregnancy is on the rise and is increasing at unbelievable rates each and every single day of the year.

_____

_____

_____

_____

ELIMINATING FRAGMENTS AND RUN-ONS

Sentences with too few words are just as annoying to admissions officers as those with too many.

A fragment is an unfinished sentence. It may lack a subject or verb, or it may be a dependent clause. Use this test for sentence fragments: can the fragment logically stand alone, without the previous or following sentences?

- Fragment: My pencil broke during the last five minutes of the test. Pieces rolling beneath my chair.

- Correct Sentence: My pencil broke during the last five minute of the test, and the pieces rolled beneath my chair.

A run-on is an instance where two sentences run together when they should be separate. Sometimes the author forgets the necessary conjunction or the proper punctuation. Sometimes the two sentences are simply too long to fit together well.

- Run-on: Regardless of the weather, I will go spear fishing in Bali the water is as clear as glass.

- Correct Sentences: Regardless of the weather, I will go spear fishing in Bali where the water is as clear as glass.

Make sure your sentences don't contain these fatal errors.

Limiting Your Use of Passive Voice

Consistently writing in the active voice and limiting your use of the passive voice can make your writing more forceful, authoritative, and interesting. Look at the sentences below. They convey essentially the same basic idea, but they have very different effects on the reader.

- The Tobacco Industry deliberately withheld data about the dangers of second-hand smoke.

- Data about the dangers of second-hand smoke were deliberately withheld [by the Tobacco Industry].

The first sentence is in the active voice; the second, in the passive voice. The active voice has a clear subject-verb relationship which illustrates that the subject is doing the action. A sentence is in the passive voice when the subject of the sentence, instead of acting, is acted upon. By distancing the subject from the verb, the passive voice makes it appear that the action is being done to the subject. The passive voice uses a form of be (is, am, are, was, were, been) plus the main verb in past participle form. The "do-er" of a passive voice sentence is either absent or relegated to the end of the sentence in a "by" phrase.

Test Yourself: Eliminating the Passive Voice Exercise

Put each of the following sentences into the active voice:

1. The Constitution was created by the Founders to protect individual rights against the abuse of federal power.

_____

_____

_____

_____

2. Information about the Vietnam War was withheld by the government.

_____

_____

_____

_____

3. The right to privacy was called upon by the Supreme Court to form the foundation of the Roe v. Wade decision.

_____

_____

_____

_____

4. Teachers in many school districts are now often required by administrators to "teach to the test."

_____

_____

_____

_____

5. Residents of planned communities are mandated by Block Associations to limit the number of cars parked in their driveways.

_____

_____

_____

_____

6. Mistakes were made by the President.

_____

_____

_____

_____

7. The gaze of the tiny porcupine was captured by the headlights of the oncoming Range Rover.

_____

_____

_____

_____

USING NONSEXIST LANGUAGE

Pronoun agreement problems often arise because the writer is trying to avoid a sexist use of language. Because there is no gender-neutral singular pronoun in English, many people use _they_, as in the incorrect sentence above. But there are other, more grammatically correct ways of getting around this problem.

One common, albeit quite awkward, solution is to use _he/she_ or _his/her_ in place of _they_ or _their_. For example, instead of writing, "If someone doesn't pay income tax, then they will go to jail," you can write, "If someone doesn't pay income tax, then he or she will go to jail." A more graceful (and shorter) alternative to _he/she_ is to use the plural form of both noun and pronoun: "If people don't pay income tax, they will go to jail." Using nonsexist language also means finding alternatives for the word _man_ when you are referring to humans in general. Instead of _mankind_ you can write _humankind_ or _humanity_, instead of _mailman_, you can use _mail carrier_, rather than stating that something is _man-made_ you can call it _manufactured_ or _artificial_.

There are a number of good reasons for you to use nonsexist language. For one thing, it is coming to be the accepted usage; that is, it is the language educated people use to communicate their ideas. Many publications now make it their editorial policy to use only non-gendered language. In addition, nonsexist language is often more accurate. Some of the people who deliver mail, for example, are female, so you are not describing the real state of affairs by referring to all of the people who deliver your mail as _men_ (since it is no longer universally accepted that _man_ refers to all humans). Finally, there is a good chance that at least one of your readers will be female, and that she—or, indeed, many male readers—will consider your use of the generic "he" to be a sign that you either are not aware of current academic conventions or do not think that they matter. It is best not to give your readers that impression.

Use of non-sexist language can feel awkward at first. Practice until it comes to seem natural; you may soon find that it is the old way of doing things that seems strange.

STYLE CHART

Style Category	What's the Rule?	Bad Style	Good Style
Wordiness	Sentences should not contain any unnecessary words.	1. The medical school is accepting applications **at this point in time.**	1. The medical school is accepting applications **now.**
		2. She carries a book bag that is made out of leather **and textured.**	2. She carries a **textured, leather** book bag.
Fragments	Sentence should contain a subject and a verb and express a complete idea.	1. And I went to the library.	1. I went to class and I went to the library.
Run-ons	Sentences that consist of two independent clauses should be joined by the proper conjunction.	1. The test has a lot of difficult information **in it, you should** start studying right away.	1. The test has a lot of difficult information **in it, and you should** start studying right away.
Passive/Active Voice	Choose the active voice, in which the subject performs the action.	1. **The ball was hit by the bat.**	1. **The bat hit the bat.**
		2. **My time and money were wasted** trying to keep www.justdillpickles. com afloat single-handedly.	2. **I wasted time and money** trying to keep www.justdillpickles. com afloat single-handedly.
Nonsexist Language	Sentences should not contain any gender bias.	1. A professor should correct **his** students' papers according to the preset guidelines.	1. Professors should correct **their** students' papers according to the preset guidelines.
		2. From the beginning of time, **mankind** used language in one way or another.	2. From the beginning of time, **humans** used language in one way or another.
		3. Are there any **upperclassmen** who would like to help students in their Lit classes?	3. Are there any **seniors** who would like to help students in their Lit classes?

Personal Statement Strategy: Pitfalls to Avoid

Don't repeat information from other parts of your application. That is, don't repeat information from other parts of your application **unless** you can spin it to elucidate previously unmentioned facets of your personality and perspectives. The admissions staff already has your transcripts, LSAT score, and list of academic and extracurricular achievements. The personal statement is your **only** opportunity to present all the other aspects of yourself in a meaningful way. Even if you don't mind wasting your own time, admissions officers will mind if you waste theirs.

In general, avoid generalities. Admissions officers have to read an unbelievable number of boring essays. You will find it harder to be boring if you write about particulars. It's the details that stick in a reader's mind. As Ludwig Mies van der Rohe wrote, "God is in the details."

Stick to the length that is requested. It's only common courtesy, and doing so demonstrates that you follow instructions well.

Even if no length is requested, don't get carried away. Although some law schools do not set a limit on the length of the personal statement, you shouldn't consider such compositional freedom an opportunity to author your first tome. You can be certain that your statement will be at least glanced at in its entirety, but admissions officers are human, and their massive workloads may prevent them from spending more time considering one applicant (who wrote a longer essay, say) than another. You should limit yourself to two or three typed, double-spaced pages. Does this make your job any easier? Not at all. In fact, practical constraints on the length of your essay demand a higher degree of efficiency and precision. Your essay needs to convey what kind of thinking, feeling human being you are; and page limitations allow for absolutely no fat.

Follow the directions. Somebody put plenty of thought into the language a law school uses to explain what it is looking for in a personal statement. Make sure you give each law school to which you apply **exactly** what it wants.

Unless the directions ask you to, don't go on at length about your goals. Face it: You have only an imprecise idea of what law school will be like. Everybody's goals change throughout the years. Your goals are especially likely to change because law school will change you. As you change and grow, your goals will evolve, so leave the seventy-five-year plan out of your personal statement.

Maintain the proper tone. Your essay should be memorable without being outrageous and easy to read without being too formal or sloppy. When in doubt, err on the formal side.

Don't try to be funny unless what you have to say is actually funny. An applicant who can make an admissions officer laugh never gets lost in the shuffle. No one will be able to bear tossing your application into the "reject" pile if you're actually funny. But beware! Only a select few are able to pull off humor in this context.

Stay away from anything even remotely off-color. Avoid profanity. It's not a good idea to be irreverent in your law school application (although you will find at least one statement in this book that was both saucy and successful). Also, there are some things admissions officers don't need (or want) to know about you, so keep those things to yourself.

Circumvent political issues if possible. We can imagine a situation in which political issues may be unavoidable. If, for example, you worked as a paid consultant for a political campaign in the last presidential election, then it makes some sense to discuss politics because of the clear relationship to your experience and development. However, you don't want to write a polemic about your pet issue, no matter how near and dear it is to your heart.

> "The test of a first-rate intelligence is the ability to hold two opposed ideas in mind at the same time and still retain the ability to function."
>
> —F. Scott Fitzgerald

Admissions officers don't care about your particular political perspectives, as long as your viewpoints are thoughtful. They don't care if you are a Republican or a Democrat or about your position on the issue of gun control. The problem is that if you write about a political issue, you may come across as the type of person who is intolerant or unwilling to consider other viewpoints. In law school (and certainly in your career beyond law school), you will (more than) occasionally have to defend a position with which you disagree—and you don't want to seem like someone who is so impassioned as to be incapable of arguing both sides of an issue. If you opt to write about politics, be very careful. Again, if you worked on a political campaign or did other similar work, feel free to discuss it—just be sure to keep your discussion within the context of what you learned and how your experience shaped you to be the person you are today.

Consider your audience if you want to write about religion. As a general rule, don't make religion the focal point of your essay unless you're applying to a law school with a religious affiliation. Don't misunderstand us. Religion is not taboo. It's **totally fine** to mention religion in any personal statement; just put it in the context of the whole, dynamic person you are. The obvious exception is if you apply to a religiously affiliated school such as Baylor, Brigham Young, or Yeshiva University, since religion is very important at these institutions.

Put the fraternity bake sale behind you. The same goes for the juggling club juggle-a-thon and the like. It's definitely worth noting on your resume if you were the president of your sorority or of any such institutionally affiliated organization. That said, achievements in a Greek organization or any club or student group are not the kind of life-changing events that have made you the person you fundamentally are today. If you were the editor of the school paper and ended up in the middle of an important First Amendment debate or if you personally facilitated the temporary housing of more than two hundred victims of domestic abuse over a three-year period—well, that's different. Tread cautiously. Make sure what you did has had an actual impact on your life (and better yet, on the lives of others).

No gimmicks; no gambles. Avoid tricky stuff. You want to differentiate yourself but not because you are some kind of daredevil. Don't rhyme. Don't write a satire or mocked-up front-page newspaper article. Gimmicky personal statements mostly appear contrived, and as a result, they fall flat. More important, law schools don't like gimmicks. They don't like personal statements written as obituaries or philosophical dialogues in which students of Socrates answer "really profound questions." In addition to seeming contrived, such essays often fail to accomplish their primary purpose: illuminating **you** and your character.

Personal Statement Strategy: Subject Matter You Should Avoid

"My LSAT score isn't great, but I'm just not a good test taker." If you have a low LSAT score, avoid directly discussing it in your personal statement like the plague. Law school is a test-rich environment. In fact, grades in most law school courses are determined by a single exam at the end of the semester (and occasionally even at the end of the year). As a law student, you'll spend your Novembers and Aprils in a study carrel, cramming madly. Saying that you are not good at taking tests will do little to convince an admissions committee that you have the ability to succeed in law school once accepted. Moreover, the bar exam is a terrifically stressful two-day (if not longer) standardized test, which the admissions officers (not to mention the institution at large) hope that you'll pass on your first attempt.

Consider also that a low LSAT score speaks for itself—all too eloquently. It doesn't need you to speak for it too. The LSAT may be a flawed test, but don't argue the merits of the test to admissions officers because ordinarily it is the primary factor they use to make admissions decisions. We feel for you, but you'd be barking up the wrong tree there. Save any mention of a low LSAT score for an addendum. (See page 26.)

"My college grades weren't that high, but ..." This issue is a little more complicated than the low LSAT score. Law school admissions committees will be more willing to listen to your interpretation of your college performance, but only within limits. Keep in mind that law schools require official transcripts for a reason. Members of the admissions committee will be aware of your academic credentials even before they read your essay. **Just as is the case with low LSAT scores, your safest course of action is to save any explanation of low grades for an addendum.**

Make no mistake: If your grades are unimpressive, you should offer the admissions committee something else by which to judge your abilities. Again, the best argument for looking past your college grades is evidence of achievement in another area, whether it is in your LSAT score, extracurricular activities, overcoming economic hardship as an undergraduate, or career accomplishments.

"I've always wanted to be a lawyer." Many applicants seem to feel the need to point out in their personal statements that they really, really want to become attorneys. You know better, and you will do yourself a great service by avoiding such throwaway lines. Do not convince yourself in a moment of desperation that claiming to have known that the law was your calling since age six (when—let's be honest—you really wanted to be a firefighter) will somehow move your application to the top of the pile. The admissions committee is not interested in how much you want to practice law. They want to know **why**—not just **why** you want to become a lawyer, but **why** you are the person you've become.

"I want to become a lawyer to fight injustice." Let's be clear: If you really want to spend your life battling for cosmic justice, then by all means write your essay about it. Just keep in mind that there are many people who will address this topic as well. Although some of these people really **do** want to fight injustice, way down in the cockles of their hearts, most just say that because they want to look good and are in fact motivated by less altruistic desires to attend law school. Among the more than one million practicing lawyers in the United States, relatively few actually earn a living defending the indigent or protecting the civil rights of ordinary people. Tremendously dedicated attorneys who work for peanuts and take charity cases are few and far between. In fact, an overwhelming proportion of U.S. lawyers—74 percent or about 802,500 attorneys—are in private practice; whereas a meager few—1 percent or about 10,800 attorneys—work in legal aid or as public defenders.[1]

Here's the rub: Many essays about fighting injustice will appear bogus and insincere. Even if you are sincere, your essay may get tossed into the same pile as all the insincere ones. Admissions officers will take your professed altruistic ambitions (and those of the hundreds of other personal statements identical to yours) with a grain of salt.

---

[1] *The Lawyer Statistical Report.* American Bar Foundation, 2004. Available online at www.abanet. org/marketresearch/lawyerdem2004.pdf. (accessed December 9, 2007). American Bar Association, Chicago, IL 2005.

If you can in good conscience say that you are committed to a career in the public interest, you must show the committee something tangible on your application and in your essay that will allow them to see your statements as more than hollow assertions. **Speak from experience, not from desire.** This is where those details we've already discussed come into play. If you cannot show that you are already a veteran in the good fight, then don't claim to be. Also, do not be afraid of appearing morally moderate. If the truth is that you want the guarantee of the relatively good job that a law degree practically ensures, be forthright. Nothing is as impressive to the reader of a personal statement as the truth.

Our Position on Work Experience

Work experience in college. Most law school applications require you to list any part-time jobs you may have held while you were in college and how many hours per week you worked. If you had (or chose) to work your way through your undergraduate years, this should come as good news. Many law schools make it clear that they take your work commitments into consideration when evaluating your UGPA.

Work experience in real life. All law school applications ask you about your work experience beyond college. They will give you three or four lines on which to list such experience. Some schools invite you to submit a resume. If you have a very good one, you should really milk this opportunity for all that it is worth. Even if you don't have a marvelous resume, a few lines on the application and your resume are the only opportunities you'll have to discuss your post-college experience meaningfully—unless you choose to discuss professional experience in your personal statement as well.

Community service. An overwhelming majority of law schools single out community involvement as one of several influential factors in their admissions decisions. Law schools would like to admit applicants who demonstrate a long-standing commitment to something other than their own advancement.

It is certainly understandable that law schools wish to determine the level of such commitment before admitting an applicant, particularly since so few law students go on to practice public interest law. Be forewarned, however, that nothing—**nothing**—is so obviously bogus as an insincere statement of a commitment to public interest issues. Admissions committees are well aware that very few people take the time out of their lives to become significantly involved in their communities. If you aren't one of those people, trying to fake it can only hurt you.

If you have a legitimate history of community service and you choose to address community service in your personal statement, use it as a springboard for discussing who you are. Additionally, it is incredibly important to discuss actual experiences you have had and how they have affected your attitudes, beliefs, and life. Don't just discuss public service (or anything else) in the abstract.

Work experience and community service in your personal statement. The kind of job you've had or the kind of community service in which you have participated is not as important as you may think. The admissions committee is more interested in what you've made of that job and what it has made of you. If you choose to mention a job that you've held in your personal statement, then you'll probably want to offer credible evidence of your competence and, as a result, increased responsibility. More important, you should use your work experience to give the admissions officer a frame of reference about who you are. How did that job change you and help you grow as a person? What skills and ideas did you offer that uniquely and positively influenced the work you did? If possible, you may also want to relate (either explicitly or implicitly) your professional experience to your decision to attend law school.

ADDENDA

In addition to your personal statement, you may also opt to submit an addendum or two explaining certain unappealing aspects of your application, such as a low LSAT score, low grades, or an arrest. In some cases, you may be **required** to submit an addendum explaining an incident in your past.

Just the facts, and nothing but the facts. An addendum is absolutely not the place to go off on polemics about the fundamental unfairness of the LSAT or how that evil campus security officer was only out to get you when you were arrested. If possible, dryly point out that you have never done well on standardized tests, but that this tendency didn't stop you from maintaining a 3.8 grade point average in high school and a 3.6 GPA in college. Whatever the case, lay out the facts, but let your readers draw their own conclusions. Be brief and balanced. Be fair, elegant, honest. Do not launch into detailed descriptions. Explain the problem and state what you did about it. **Do not make excuses (even if they are completely legitimate excuses).** This is no time to whine.

The Low LSAT Addendum

If you have a low LSAT score, you may consider including an addendum that addresses it. You are never going to be able to mitigate a low LSAT score completely. The obvious and preferable alternative to an explicit discussion of a weak score is a personal statement that focuses on your strengths. If you really are bad at standardized test taking, you must be better at something else, or you wouldn't have gotten as far as you have. If you are a marvelous researcher, say so. If you are a wonderful writer, show it. There is no way to convince an admissions committee to overlook your LSAT score entirely. You may, however, present compelling reasons for them to look beyond it.

Multiple LSAT scores, and one good one. Let's say you took the LSAT twice. If you did much better in your second sitting than in your first, or vice versa, a brief explanation—if there is an explanation—couldn't hurt. If some adverse circumstance caused you to perform less than optimally, say so. Be honest. Be forthright. Get to the point quickly. Bear in mind that your explanation may mean little to the committee, which may have its own hard-and-fast rules for interpreting multiple LSAT scores.

> **Elegant**
>
> "*adj.* Characterized by or exhibiting refined, tasteful beauty of manner, form, or style."

> **Acceptable Explanations for Low LSAT Scores**
>
> (1) Death in the family or other serious family emergency; (2) stress over a work emergency; and/or (3) serious illness. Note: Number 2 may backfire. Why didn't you reschedule?

Good grades, but bad LSAT score. If you have a history of poor standardized test scores but good grades, state as much candidly and cordially in a short, sweet, nondefensive addendum. All you really have to say is: "Standardized test scores don't predict my academic performance, and here is some evidence to support my claim." If you have them, include copies of SAT or ACT score reports to substantiate your argument. It would be a nice touch if you could convince a college professor to write a letter on your behalf saying, "This student has always had high grades but poor standardized test scores, so please disregard the scores."

The Low Grades Addendum

If you have lower college grades because you had to work at a real job in addition to going to college because you had a child to feed or for some other legitimate reason, don't be afraid to say so. It is much easier to argue a less-than-stellar record than it is to justify a weak LSAT score. In fact, it's imperative that you address the reason for your low grades if that reason is noteworthy. Let's say, for example, that you started out as an aspiring electrical engineering major at Georgia Tech, promptly flunked out, and enrolled at Oglethorpe University, majored in English, and achieved a 4.0. Your cumulative UGPA is 2.85. You simply must write an addendum stating the facts of your situation fairly and honestly. There's a very good chance that you'll be pleasantly surprised at how easy it is to get admissions staffs to look beyond middling grades.

READY, SET, WRITE!

We've stressed the importance of demonstrating sincerity, honesty, and forthrightness; avoiding plagiarism, clichés, and generalizations; and writing effective personal statements. Now we're going to venture beyond the realm of abstraction and feature essays of law school applicants that made the grade at top law schools across the country. Read and take note of what you think works well. Feel free to draw inspiration from these essays—but do *not* draw content from them. Once you've gotten a clear sense of what a successful law school essay reads like, you should be ready to pick up your pen and write your own.

The Importance of Being Honest

Don't lie on your law school application. If they ask you if you've been arrested, and you have been arrested, you must tell the truth. It's true that you'll probably have no trouble concealing those crazy things you did as an undergraduate from law school admissions staffs. There is, however, this thing called the bar exam that you take when you graduate from law school. If the bar examiners find out you lied on your law school application, there is a high probability that you will never be allowed to practice law. After you complete three years of law school and spend untold thousands of dollars in a legal education, you don't want to be caught lying. It's not worth the risk. We promise. Plus, it's always good to be a person of integrity.

Q & A with Admissions Officers

We interviewed admissions officers at eight highly selective law schools. We asked them about their application processes in general and about the role of the personal statement in particular. They revealed how they and their staffs review applications; discussed essay themes, plagiarism, and supplementary materials; and offered writing tips to law school applicants. The following professionals gave generously their time and insights in answering our questions.

Edward Tom, Director of Admissions at Boalt Hall School of Law, University of California—Berkeley

Mark Hill, Senior Admissions Officer at Duke University Law School

Alison H. Price, Associate Dean and Director of Admissions at George Mason University School of Law

Robert Stanek, Associate Dean for Admission and Financial Aid at The George Washington University Law School

Andy Cornblatt, Assistant Dean of Admissions at Georgetown University Law Center

Don Rebstock, Associate Dean of Enrollment Management and Career Strategy at Northwestern University School of Law

Sarah C. Zearfoss, Assistant Dean of Admissions at the University of Michigan School of Law

Derek E. Meeker, Associate Dean for Admissions and Financial Aid at the University of Pennsylvania Law School

For ease of reading, we introduce the response of each admissions officer with the name of the institution that he or she serves.

WHICH THEMES CONTINUALLY APPEAR IN PERSONAL STATEMENTS?

Berkeley: Common themes are "Why I want to go to law school," or "I want to specialize in a particular area of the law." These and other themes haven't changed too much. But we know a lot of people change their minds about what they want to do with their law degrees, so applicants need to think more globally. Applicants [also] need to be strategic. An alternate and maybe better approach is to describe your life's journey and to define and describe the voice you have been developing along the way. This is a more generalized approach that can integrate your background, experiences, and academics if done well.

Duke: Study abroad, political internships, legal internships/work.

George Mason: Motivation for attending law school; applicant's life goals; personal experience that has affected, challenged, tested or otherwise influenced the applicant; resumé written out in complete sentences.

George Washington: The topic of the majority of personal statements is autobiographical. Other common themes include "Why I want to go to law school," "What I hope to do in the future," and "A significant moment in my life."

Georgetown: Most personal statements are autobiographical in part: for example, in describing an applicant's commitment to service. In addition, every year applicants comment on current national and world events and how these have affected their careers and goals. Occasionally candidates describe why they want to come to Georgetown. Often personal statements contain all of these themes together—just a mixture.

Northwestern: The most common personal statements tend to be chronologies of applicants' lives, tragedies people have faced, and the standard essay "Why I want to go to law school."

UPenn: The themes we encounter most often in personal statements include "why I want to be an attorney" or "why I want to go to law school"; international work, study, or travel experiences; overcoming hardship, disadvantages, or challenges; greatest accomplishments, including personal, professional, and academic accomplishments; and how the applicant would contribute to the diversity of the law school community or the legal profession based on factors and characteristics such as unique work or academic experience, race, culture, sexual orientation, age, socioeconomic background, and geography.

WHAT WRITING TIPS WOULD YOU OFFER TO YOUR APPLICANT POOL?

Berkeley: I look for quality of writing as well as substance. There should be no spelling or grammatical errors. If there are such errors, then I worry about how accurate you will be in future practice. Will you misplace a comma in a multimillion-dollar contract? Most importantly, write from the heart. It shows. Don't use a generic template, one written by someone else, or one lifted from a book. Any question about integrity is [damaging].

Duke: Give yourself plenty of time to edit and rewrite your personal statement. Think about what else is in your application (transcript, resumé, [and so on]), and use the personal statement to provide additional information, not repetition of what we know from other sources. Think about what other applicants [may] be saying, and try to set yourself apart from them. We don't have many preconceptions about the content of a personal statement, so write as yourself for yourself, not to what you think we want to hear. Pay as much attention to the style as to the substance of your essay; we are interested in your thought processes and how you express yourself as well as in what you have done.

George Mason: Be sure you are answering the questions that have been asked of you. Do not exceed the word limitation and follow directions, such as spacing or font requirements, carefully. Use topic sentences. Avoid overuse of the passive voice. Write concisely. Check grammar and punctuation, and do not rely on spell check. Solicit feedback from others, particularly if they do not know you well, to be sure that your message is clear and you have avoided grammatical errors.

George Washington: Proofreading is always recommended, yet often forgotten. Ultimately, [applicants] need to sit and think about how they want to portray themselves and what picture they want to draw. They can look to self-help books for stylistic guidance, but the personal statement should be sincere and personal; there's no formula that should be followed.

I would also read the personal statement aloud to someone. If it sounds good, then it's probably sound grammatically. The vocabulary, grammar, and writing style of the piece is a reflection of the applicant. If others help them in the process, that's fine; they can get some words of wisdom. But the help should be limited to advice. As far as asking someone else to read it, I'd recommend relying on someone they respect, such as a teacher or supervisor.

Georgetown: Applicants should be brief and focused. Part of the overall strategy is to write an essay keeping in mind what it would be like to be the reader. Our admissions committee is reading thousands of personal statements each year, so the notion of "the more, the better" defeats the purpose. I tell applicants to say what you have to say and no more. My experience tells me that two pages are usually sufficient.

The more personal, the better; an applicant's essay should be about himself/herself. Since most law schools do not have formal interviews as part of the admissions process, consider your personal statement to be your interview. When you fill out your application, surely you must, at some point, say to yourself, I have filled in the blanks, but I have so much more to say in this area. I would like to elaborate and emphasize certain things, but the application itself just does not allow me the opportunity. That, in my view, is precisely the use to which the personal statement should be put.

Northwestern: Stylistically, make sure they check it closely. I've seen many mess up with merges of law school names, [for example], "I want to go to X law school because...." Focus on one or two main points. Go to the bookstore to the management section about hiring people. There are questions in the backs of books you'll find there that you could answer.

My pet peeve is the generic personal statement. Applicants should tailor their statements to the school they are applying to. Show us that you did some homework on us.

We offer an open-ended question and two optional essays. The reason for the optional essay is because of the generic statements that we receive. The generic personal statement is based on the false assumption that all law schools are looking for the same thing.

UMichigan: The personal statement is not the time to use words you've never used before. After being in this job for a couple of years, I finally went into the Law School's archives, dug out my own personal statement from a decade before, and was horrified to realize that it read as if I'd drafted it with my nose in the thesaurus! It sounded so stilted and was clearly my idea at the time of what a lawyer ought to sound like. Instead of trying to impress someone with a vocabulary I didn't actually possess, I should have sought to write with clarity and precision.

What do you not like reading in an essay?

Berkeley: Another law school's name mistakenly placed in the body of the personal statement sent to me. Carelessness really is the kiss of death. Another pet peeve is the statement that contains a sentence that uses the word, "always," as in, "I have always been interested in law."

Duke: Gimmicks. Playing with the format (e.g., writing poetry, addressing your twenty-fifth reunion, formatting your essay as a court transcript) is only rarely done well, and most often such gimmicks make it hard for us to really get a sense of the applicant. Many applicants will frame their essays with a story about a relative or other figure who has inspired them. This can be okay, but the focus should be on the applicant, not on the other person. (Yes, your grandmother's adventures in emigrating from Russia are fascinating, but I'm considering admitting you, not her.)

George Mason: Personal statements that have simply turned the resumé into sentences; quotes from famous movies or pieces of literature; statements hat the applicant's parent, aunt (or insert any other friend or relative) has always told the applicant that they should be a lawyer; why an applicant wants to be a lawyer; excuses for low LSAT scores and/or grades; another law school's name where the name of my law school should be inserted.

George Washington: The worst offenses are misspellings, awkward constructions, and incomplete sentences. And, of course, I never like reading the statements of applicants who report that another school is the place they always wanted to attend.

As far as content goes—I don't like gimmicks. I don't like personal statements written as obituaries. I don't like dialogue-based personal statements. I prefer a straightforward narrative.

At GW we ask an open-ended question; the personal statement can be anything the applicant chooses. What applicants choose to write about tells us something important about their judgment.

Georgetown: In terms of grammar, I hate to see people bungle the English language.

In terms of content, applicants should not simply submit a paragraph form of the resumé. Candidates also should avoid expounding, for example, on theories of law and society and God and how they are all interrelated. It is possible that candidates may have something interesting to say on [this] topic, but the personal statement is not the place for it. I am more eager to read what they have to say about themselves as candidates for admission. This is your opportunity; the floor is yours.

Northwestern: The generic one. The straight chronology. Uses of humor that don't work. Stylistically, when people extend beyond two or three pages. Also, tiny fonts. And the ones where the applicant is clearly trying to "sound intelligent" by using obscure words.

UPenn: Explanations or excuses for poor grades or LSAT scores. If an applicant does have legitimate reasons for poor school or test performance, it may be helpful to explain the reasons to the admissions committee. But the place to do that is in an addendum (an additional memo) to the application, and not in the essay.

WHAT TOPICS WOULD YOU ADVISE STUDENTS AVOID USING?

Duke: Unless you have a particularly detailed case to make, "why law school" is generally not a productive topic. Especially for college seniors, these essays are usually too vague to be helpful and thus are not terribly distinctive. Many applicants like to debate and are interested in public policy—these are not bad reasons to want to go to law school, but they do not help us to distinguish one applicant from another. This topic is much more effective when the applicant has an extensive record that culminates in a particular interest in law (e.g., lots of environmental activism leading to the realization that a JD will help the applicant be more effective in promoting the cause he or she is interested in). That said, what an applicant wants to do in law school and thereafter is often best left out of the personal statement. We are more interested in where you have come from and how you have reached the point of applying to law school than in what you may do afterward (especially since such plans often change dramatically over the course of law school). Again, it's possible to make this case, but not every applicant can do so effectively.

George Mason: Controversial subjects (you never know who will be on an admissions committee); poor grades and test scores.

George Washington: I don't believe that there is any topic that must be avoided. However, I would try to be upbeat and positive in my delivery. Certainly, you should try to end the statement on a positive note.

UMichigan: I don't think there is any one topic I would advise students to avoid, but I think it is very important for students to keep some perspective, especially when talking about a difficult period or an obstacle they overcame. We see an enormous number of applications, and the chances are very good that whatever you have been through has been experienced (and written about) by others as well. That is not to say it isn't important or noteworthy—but don't make the mistake of thinking it is unique. And be sure to explain why it is relevant—what you learned, what the story demonstrates about you, and so on.

In general, for topics, I advise applicants to spend some time thinking about what it is that they would tell an admissions officer if they had ten minutes of his or her undivided attention—perhaps what led them to law school, what they intend to do with a law degree, why they would be interesting or valuable individuals to have in the class, why they think that they are particularly well-suited to the study of law, etc.

UPenn: Unless they have related experience, applicants should generally avoid writing on why they want to become attorneys and the types of law they want to practice. Few students applying directly from college have the experience and perspective to write a genuine and effective personal statement on this topic. For example, many applicants write about a desire to "do good" in the world and work in the public interest; yet they have little or no experience working with agencies that provide legal services to indigent or underrepresented members of society. If an applicant chooses to write on this topic, he or she should have the experience to back it up; otherwise, it may come off as unrealistic and disingenuous.

Applicants sometimes write about an influential person in their lives, which can be effective. I caution applicants, however, that the personal statement is for the admissions committee to get to know them. I have read personal statements after which I know far more about the person who influenced the applicant than I do about the applicant. An applicant can avoid that problem by, for example, describing how the person was influential, what the applicant learned from the person, and how the applicant plans to put those lessons into action.

When an applicant writes on a particular internship or job that was influential or a hardship or obstacle that the applicant has overcome, the applicant should take it to that next level. Tell us how you changed or grew as a result of the event or experience, and what you can contribute to the classroom or community based on that experience.

Finally, a note about study or travel abroad: It is extremely common, at least in Penn's applicant pool. If an applicant chooses to write about that experience, he or she should have something exceptional to say about it. For example, if the applicant had to overcome significant challenges in terms of assimilating to another culture, learning a new language, or engaging in substantive work or community service under challenging conditions, he or she could probably write an effective and interesting personal statement. But more general personal statements about "my summer abroad program" or the challenges of traveling for the first time in Europe should be avoided.

WHICH GRAMMATICAL MISTAKES MAKE YOU CRINGE?

Berkeley: Do not write your personal statement in the third person. Always use first person.

George Mason: Improper use of commas; overuse of passive voice; improper use of possessives ('s and s'); improper use of me, myself, and I.

UMichigan: Virtually all of them, particularly when they appear in the first line! I'm quite forgiving if a small error crops up on the second page, but if it comes in the first line, it's hard to overcome. That said, the confusion between its and it's, [subject]/verb agreement, and the confusion between I and me are particular sore points.

UPenn: All grammatical mistakes make me cringe. They detract from the smoothness and effectiveness of otherwise strong essays. And they can be avoided! Have as many people as possible proofread your essays and do not rely on spell check.

WHAT DO YOU LOVE TO SEE?

Berkeley: Explain how your experiences have helped and informed your maturation process and what you have learned about yourself and about others along the way. We're interested in more than just a list of experiences. Include a resumé—even if the application doesn't ask for one—as a way to chronologically sort your activities so that time is not wasted listing all of this in the body of the personal statement. Consider [including] an addendum to highlight specific topics such as an illness that caused your grades to slide, or a history of poor standardized test scores, in which case be sure to include copies of previous SAT or ACT scores.

Duke: Good writing. Maturity. Applicants who have a good sense of where they have been and where they might like to go. Good writing can do far more for an essay on a standard topic than an unusual topic can do for an essay with average writing. It's much easier to tell people what not do to because we see the same "mistakes" repeatedly. The inspired essays are in some sense unique, and it's hard to generalize from them.

George Mason: A personal statement that is tailored to my school and its unique curricular opportunities; a personal statement that focuses on only one accomplishment or experience which may or may not have been reflected on the resumé; a personal statement with a theme that is apparent at the beginning of the statement and at the end of the statement.

George Washington: I like to learn the history and background of the applicant. I prefer an autobiographical statement; I like to know what kind of person we're admitting to the law school.

Georgetown: I am impressed by a personal statement that conveys a sense of openness by an applicant who isn't afraid to give me a real sense of who he or she is. The key, in my view, is for candidates to stress their strengths without being obnoxious and deal with their weaknesses without being defensive. I know fully well that this is a lot easier to say than to do. I also look for essays in which the writer has given thought to the content and isn't just rambling on.

Northwestern: I like to see demonstrated research about a school. I actually like personal statements that will have a section where they rattle off kind of neat components of their [lives], things that are unique that you don't see in application but present life and tie into [a] theme. I also like to read about [a] significant thing in their [lives] and how it has changed and influenced them.

UMichigan: I love to see an essay that makes me feel, when I've finished reading it, that I just had a conversation with the applicant—something straightforward, direct, and engaging.

UPenn: Just tell us your story! Delve deeply and get as personal as you can. We want to know your dreams, your challenges, your accomplishments, your unique life experiences. What did you learn, how were you affected, how will you teach or affect others as a result...or what do you hope to learn or hope to teach? We want to know what you are going to add to our dynamic mix of students. Your resumé, transcript, and references will tell us a lot about your course work and academic abilities, your work experience, and your extracurricular and community activities. Don't rehash or repeat what we will learn from those materials—tell us something more.

WHAT BORES YOU?

Berkeley: Applicants sometimes provide a statement of purpose instead of a personal statement. We want to know something about the individual's background and personality.

Duke: Pure narrative is not effective. If you are telling us about your campaign for student body president (for instance), don't just tell us what happened. You should dig deeper to reflect on what the experience meant to you, how it changed you, what you might have done differently.

George Mason: Why an applicant wants to go to law school because we have seen almost every reason imaginable; statements based on quotations from historical figures or from movies or from great pieces of literature.

George Washington: After thirty-one years of doing this, there is a lot that bores me. But I try to read each file as I would like my application to be read. From an applicant's standpoint, I'm probably less interested in their goals than in their backgrounds. I fi nd goals and future plans less helpful in evaluating applicants because I've seen a lot of goals change over the years. Applicants don't always know what law school is like and only have a vague idea of what career opportunities they may have.

Northwestern: The chronology.

WHAT TOPICS ARE RISKY? WHEN DO SUCH TOPICS WORK?

Berkeley: Humor, poetry, writing about a family member or friend instead of yourself, and unusual formats, such as court transcripts, should not be used. Beautifully composed prose is best.

Duke: Humor is dicey. Several people will read an essay, and they may not all have the same sense of humor. Some people worry about political topics, but if the opinions are heartfelt and well argued, they should be fine.

George Mason: It is risky to write a fiction essay of any topic. It is risky to write your personal statement as poetry.

George Washington: It seems to be fashionable to discuss extremely personal experiences, and I think applicants take the term "personal" too literally. There are some things I don't need to know—and some things I'd rather not know—about an applicant.

Georgetown: I don't think there are any risky topics. However, in an effort to stand out, some applicants try to be clever and gimmicky with their personal statements, and most of these essays feel contrived and flat. If you try to gamble with a poem, for every one that works, ten are lame.

Northwestern: Humor and poetry are risky.

UMichigan: The "obstacles overcome" idea sketched out [earlier] is risky only because most people don't adequately explain the point they're trying to make—but it is definitely a subject worth addressing.

What's an example of a ridiculous achievement that you've seen referenced in an essay?

Berkeley: No response.

Duke: I don't like to see people coasting on high school experiences. There are exceptions; but in most cases, if you have accomplished something significant in high school, I'd expect to see you building on it in college rather than still citing it four (or more) years down the road.

George Washington: The ones that have the least impact, for me, are achievements in a fraternity or sorority. I'm sure a great effort was put forth, but somehow, raising money through bake sales is not something they should list as a great achievement in life.

UPenn: Getting to attend an NCAA Final Four basketball game—and missing classes to do it.

What experience would you like students to write about more often?

George Mason: I would like to see more students write about one accomplishment they have had, or one project they have undertaken, or one experience that they have had which changed them in some way, explaining that change. The personal statement is one of the best ways for a student to distinguish him or herself from the rest.

George Washington: The kind of experience that led to the formulation of the candidate's attitude and beliefs. The kind of things that made them the [people] they are today. That's who we'll be dealing with for the next three years, so that's the person I'd like to know. It can be an event, a general history—you can get at that person in a number of different ways—but ultimately, that's the person I'm trying to get to know.

Georgetown: I'm always interested in hearing about an applicant's background. I have noticed that some applicants are reluctant to discuss certain aspects of their backgrounds, such as a history of disadvantage, ethnic status, [and so on]. This is a mistake, plain and simple. No one is asking for lengthy stories or heroism in overcoming enormous obstacles. Information of this kind, however, is very valuable to the admissions committee, and in every instance, it can only work to the applicant's advantage.

What steps do you take to recognize and prevent plagiarism? Do you have an institutional policy on plagiarism?

Berkeley: We're aware of the various books, organizations, and sites that "help" with personal statements. We do have a policy on plagiarism and anytime it is determined, we report it to the LSAC Misconduct Committee.

Duke: No response.

George Mason: Plagiarism is a violation of our honor code, and if it were discovered, even after admission and attendance at the school, it could provide a basis for cancellation of an admissions offer or matriculation. We have access to programs that check for plagiarism should we choose to investigate a personal statement.

George Washington: I don't. We haven't done a good job of discovering it. One reason we don't is simply the volume we receive. We just don't have time to double check each and every one. The only time I became aware of it is if two personal statements I've read are the same, or if one of my colleagues at another school alerts me to watch out for essays on a particular subject. Occasionally, I'll come across something that doesn't ring true or that isn't reflected in the academic record I'm considering. But none of this is an exact science. We do, of course, have a very strict policy on plagiarism at our institution. A student does not have to plagiarize willfully to be found in violation; an inadvertent mistake would qualify as well.

Georgetown: Plagiarism is a recognized threat, but Georgetown doesn't use software to try to catch this. Each application contains the writing sample from the LSAT exam, so the admissions committee will be aware if the personal statement reads differently from the applicant's sample.

Northwestern: No. It's extremely likely that someone else is editing [an applicant's] statement. That's another reason that the interview [which Northwestern has as part of the application process] is much more effective.

UMichigan: We simply try to pay attention—whenever one of the readers thinks language or topics sound familiar, we compare notes; we will search through other applications and search for essays on the web and in various databases to which we have access. Every year we uncover a few plagiarists.

IF YOU HAD THE OPTION OF DOING AWAY WITH PERSONAL STATEMENTS ALTOGETHER, WOULD YOU?

Berkeley: No. We're interested in admitting human beings, not numbers. Our graduates have the opportunity to affect the lives of real people, the outcomes of public policy, and to become leaders of our society. We get a sense of this potential from the personal statement. I believe that it's irresponsible to use only two numbers to make admission decisions.

Duke: No. Given that we can't have face-to-face contact with every applicant, this is the best way for us to see what applicants are like beyond their academic records.

George Mason: No.

George Washington: No, I find it to be a helpful part of the admissions process—sometimes more useful than the LSAT or the writing sample. The personal statement together with the academic record and test scores are, for me, the best indicators of an applicant's potential for success at my school.

Georgetown: No—although during the height of our application season in mid-February, it is tempting! First, the personal statement gives me a sense of how well a person writes. And second, the essay often adds information about candidates that isn't reflected in other parts of their applications. The personal statement gives the applicant the opportunity to take the admissions committee members by the hand and guide them through his or her application, on the applicant's terms. It is the applicant's responsibility (and advantage) to highlight the strongest parts of the application to maximize his or her chances of admission. At the same time, the essay gives the applicant the opportunity to deal with the weaker parts of his or her application up front and shape the terms on which the committee members will evaluate the weak points.

Northwestern: No, although it may be nice to replace it with a series of required and specific questions.

UMichigan: Absolutely not. I think it's an incredibly important part of the application process. It provides a real window into the applicant's personality and character—sometimes intentionally, and sometimes unintentionally.

UPenn: Absolutely not! It is my favorite part of the application. And it is often the piece of the application that we use to distinguish strong applicants from one another. Personal statements bring our applicants to life. There is nothing more gratifying for me than skimming the personal statements of our incoming first year students right before orientation to get a sense of the class. I am always amazed at the broad diversity of our students' backgrounds, their rich experiences, and their accomplishments.

Do you prefer to receive applications online or in paper form?

Berkeley: We have a strong preference that applications be submitted electronically through the LSAC.

Duke: Applicants should use whatever format is most convenient for them. It is slightly easier for us to receive online applications because it saves us some data entry, but that should not be a consideration for the applicant.

George Mason: We receive application materials in both formats, even receiving hard copies of everything submitted electronically. I prefer to use the hard copies; however, most other reviewers seem to prefer electronic format.

George Washington: No preference either way.

Georgetown: Georgetown applicants must submit their applications electronically.

Northwestern: We now require online application submission. We were the first law school to do this. The reason is that law school and the field of law require proficiency with computers, so we're preparing our applicants for this reality.

UMichigan: No preference; we print out any materials submitted online.

UPenn: We receive all application materials in electronic submission.

Do you or your staff read every personal statement that comes to you?

Berkeley: Yes, every one.

Duke: Yes. Each application is reviewed in full by at least two people.

George Mason: Every personal statement is read by one or more members of the committee.

George Washington: Yes, I'm the first reader for every file. After reviewing the academic credentials and test scores I turn to the personal statement. I then read a sufficient amount of the statement to feel comfortable with the decision I will be making. In some instances, the statement may make you change your vote; but that does not happen often. In most instances, the statement reinforces an inclination to vote one way or the other.

Georgetown: Yes.

Northwestern: Yes.

UMichigan: Absolutely.

UPenn: Every application that we receive at Penn is read in its entirety by two members of the admissions committee and, in some cases, by three members of the committee. Some files are read by as many as three or four committee members.

How many personal statements do you and your personal staff receive? How much time do you spend reading each application? Each essay?

Berkeley: In 2010 we received more than 8,000 applications and had four people reading more or less full-time from the end of October through the end of March.

On average, [I spend] at least ten minutes on each application.

Duke: In 2005 we received 4,500 applications, and all personal statements and optional essays were read. They are read by at least two people, and each probably receives fifteen to twenty minutes of review per reader.

George Mason: Mason Law receives over 5,000 personal statements. The amount of time spent on each file varies greatly, depending on reviewer and complexities that arise in reaching a final decision on some applicants.

George Washington: We made decisions on more than 11,250 applications in 2005. As I indicated earlier, I am the first read on all and the final read on over three-quarters of the applications. This means I don't have free weekends from December to May. Some decisions are quick, and some you agonize over. On average, each application takes five to ten minutes.

Georgetown: For many years, Georgetown University Law Center has received a larger number of JD applications than any other school in the country. During the last admissions cycle, Georgetown received approximately 11,500 total applications. The amount of time spent reading depends on the application. Some applications are easy to get through; not all files are hard to evaluate. The average length of time spent with each application is forty-five minutes to one hour; however, some may take fifteen minutes and others three hours.

Northwestern: We get 5,000. We each probably read about half of the overall pool.

UMichigan: Every application has at least one personal statement, and I would estimate that about two-thirds contain one extra essay, and perhaps a tenth contain two essays. The time spent on reading the applications and essays can vary enormously—a minimum of about five minutes to digest information apart from the essays and a minimum of five minutes to read a personal statement. At least two people look at every application, and we spend more time with applications when we're inclined to make offers. Multiple readers will read those files multiple times.

UPenn: In 2009 we received 6,200 applications, all of which included a personal statement and many of which included an additional optional essay. The time that we spend reading each application varies widely. There are applications on which I might spend twenty minutes; some that I will read two, three, even four times; and there are others that I will be able to read in ten minutes.

What is the process that each application undergoes, from receipt to decision? How many hands does it pass through on the way?

George Mason: Most applications are received via LSAC. Once we receive notification of the application, we request hard copies. When hard copies are received they are placed in files folders and checked for completion. Emails are sent regarding missing items, and if none, then an application complete email is sent. The file is then distributed for review by multiple members of the committee.

George Washington: Our admission committee has two staff readers and three faculty members. All of the applications are ranked by a combination of GPA and LSAT into an index number. As chair of the committee, my vote is final on files with index numbers above a certain point and below a certain point, but only if I vote to admit those above and deny those below. All others (including those with index numbers between the likely admit point and the likely deny point) must be reviewed by other members of the committee in addition to me until we have a majority voting to admit, deny, or place on a waiting list.

Northwestern: Most applications get two reads; some get three. The first is done by the assistant director. If he or she votes waitlist, then the faculty gets to read them; then I or our Director of Admissions does.

What work experience do you require from the people reviewing applications? Are there any particular qualities that you look for in a reader?

Berkeley: My fellow admission officers are all associate directors at the School. Two of them have a JD and one has an MA.

Duke: We want people with open minds who will read carefully and closely. It helps to have people from a wide range of backgrounds, since each will bring different perspectives into the process.

George Mason: Decisions on who will review files are made by the Dean of the law school and the faculty committee for admissions.

George Washington: A willingness to read. Some love to do it; others would rather pass it off to someone else. In general, I keep the same committee from year to year. It speeds up the workflow. Training new members only slows down the process.

UMichigan: All of our readers either have JDs from Michigan or extensive admissions experience (roughly a decade each), or sometimes both.

UPenn: Our readers include admissions professionals, faculty, and our own students and alumni. They come from a broad range of backgrounds and are highly accomplished in a range of areas. Readers who are not faculty or students typically hold an advanced degree and have prior experience reviewing applications.

HOW MANY APPLICATIONS, GENERALLY SPEAKING, GO TO COMMITTEE EACH YEAR?

Berkeley: Depends on the year.

Duke: Relatively few applications are reviewed by our admissions committee. We seek their input in difficult cases (e.g., serious disciplinary issues in an otherwise strong application), but it takes a lot of file reading to have an appropriate understanding of the context of our applicant pool.

George Mason: Each file is reviewed by a sub-committee of at least two and as many as three people. A small percentage of files will go to a larger group.

George Washington: All decisions made are decisions of the admission committee.

No files are admitted or denied on the basis of the numbers alone.

Georgetown: Georgetown's full admissions committee reviews approximately 10 percent of our applications, and the rest are reviewed within the admissions office.

Northwestern: All of them.

IF AN ELEMENT OF THE APPLICATION IS MARKED "OPTIONAL," IS IT TRULY OPTIONAL? IF A CANDIDATE OPTS NOT TO COMPLETE THAT PART OF THE APPLICATION, IS HIS OR HER CANDIDACY WEAKENED?

Berkeley: Those items that are marked "optional" are optional.

Duke: We offer two topics for an optional additional essay: an academic essay or a diversity essay. This is truly optional. It does not hurt their candidacies [not to submit one], except to the extent that more information is often helpful, and (if they don't submit an optional essay) they may be missing an opportunity to tell us more about themselves. I do think that anyone we want to admit could write on one of those topics.

George Mason: If something is marked optional, it is optional, with little or no impact on the applicant other than the reviewers are left to either ignore the absence or infer the missing information from other parts of the application.

George Washington: We don't require letters of recommendation. That has to do with my own history, due to my own experience. I found it very burdensome to get academic recommendations because I had been away from school for several years. However, we do recommend submitting at least two. There is also an optional question about race on our application. Many applicants choose not to answer it, and it has never made a difference in the committee's decision.

Georgetown: No, an application is not weakened if the candidate chooses not to complete the optional statement.

UMichigan: If it says optional, it is definitely optional! This question arises most frequently in connection with our optional essays, and I can assure you that many people are admitted without submitting additional essays beyond the personal statement—but at the same time, we often find that they add extremely helpful depth and perspective, and many people make up for a weak personal statement with a strong optional essay.

UPenn: Penn Law School requires a supplemental essay in its application.

Do applicants send extra material to you? If so, which materials are helpful? How much is too much?

Berkeley: We put aside CDs, videos, senior theses. We don't have time to view them.

Duke: In general, we have asked for the material that we think will be necessary to make our decisions. Some applicants do send newspaper clippings, additional writing samples, and so on, but these are usually not helpful.

George Mason: Yes, some applicants do send additional materials, like additional letters of recommendation, senior theses, etc. Most of the time, these materials are not helpful.

George Washington: Yes they do; and no, it's not always helpful. I receive copies of dissertations, CDs, videos, all kinds of things. They're not as helpful as the standard personal statement.

Georgetown: Applicants are welcome to include extra material with their applications; if in doubt, send it. Usually these items are extra statements and letters of recommendation. However, I discourage applicants from sending a thesis or other bulky materials, as the more they send, the more they dilute the product. With respect to recommendations, in general three letters will provide enough information, though some have led complicated lives. For example, some forty year-olds are working two jobs, and in that case I don't mind a little extra.

Northwestern: Sometimes. If it's just a one-page addendum, we'll probably read it. If it's something they've made, we'll at least notice it. If it's a video or a senior thesis, we'll notice it, but we aren't going to read it or view it (in the case of the video).

UMichigan: We ask for a lot of information (many complain, too much!) and cover a lot of territory in the material requested. As a result, it is almost never helpful for people to send along additional material outside of what we have set forth in the application.

UPenn: Yes. Applicants who are placed on hold or on the waitlist often send additional letters of recommendation, additional essays, and/or writing samples. How much is too much? It depends. Applicants must, obviously, use some discretion. A good rule of thumb is one additional document, whether a letter, essay, or writing sample, for each communication from the law school. In other words, if a school waitlists you in March, send in an additional letter or essay shortly after receiving the waitlist decision. If the school later sends an update as to your waitlist status, for example, informing you in June that you are still on the waitlist and no final decision has been rendered, send a letter to the dean of admissions reiterating your interest in the law school and providing any updates to your record, such as a job promotion or graduation honors. If a school keeps you on the waitlist, that means the school is still interested in you. It may be that additional offers are never made because those admitted students who have deposited at the school remain committed. But often, some of those students decide to defer law school, decide not to enroll, or make plans to attend another law school. You never know if and when you may be admitted from the waitlist; but as long as you are on the waitlist, the possibility exists. Demonstrate your interest and commitment to the school without being intrusive and burdensome.

THE LOW LSAT SCORE EXPLANATION: WHEN IS THIS NECESSARY? UNNECESSARY? HOW OFTEN DOES THIS CHANGE YOUR MIND? (HAVE YOU EVER RECEIVED ANY RIDICULOUS EXPLANATIONS THAT YOU'D LIKE TO SHARE?)

Berkeley: If you have a low LSAT score and a history of poor standardized test scores, yet you have a very high college GPA, then you should talk about this in an addendum. Be sure to provide copies of previous standardized test scores. Many applicants claim they have a problem with standardized tests but don't provide proof. Documentation is required for us to believe the claim.

Duke: We're willing to consider an applicant's testing history—if the SAT/ACT seriously underpredicted his or her undergraduate performance, we will weigh that in our consideration of their LSAT. Applicants should provide documentation if at all possible. If the test was taken under difficult conditions—illness, family crisis, problems with the test site—an addendum is appropriate to let us know, but it's not often something we can do much about.

George Mason: If there is a legitimate explanation for a low LSAT, then we like to hear about it in a one-paragraph addendum to the application. It is not helpful for the applicant to go on for one or more pages about one or multiple low LSAT scores; it places too much emphasis on the weakness of the application.

George Washington: I'm trying to review thousands of files and make decisions that are fair to all the candidates under consideration. In my review, I am focusing on a few items that have equal weight in my decision—the academic record, LSAT scores, and everything else I know about the applicant from the personal statement, resumé, and letters of recommendation. With one-third of the weight of the decision on the academic work and one-third on test scores, it is in the applicant's interest to report whenever there is a good reason why these items do not honestly reflect a candidate's potential.

The most common explanations given for a low LSAT are "I was sick," "I had a family emergency," or "I was overwrought." Those explanations are fine if your second score improved. Another common explanation is to detail a history of poor performance on standardized tests. If you make this argument, you should have some evidence to back it up, such as your scores on the ACT or SAT. As far as ridiculous explanations go, I had one candidate write about a person chewing ice next to him and one who complained that she had her period during the exam. Some come up with explanations that make me wonder why they took the test instead of rescheduling it. It is a big mistake to present a score that does not represent your best effort. If you don't take it in October, take it in December or February. It is better to have one score that shows true ability rather than two conflicting scores.

Georgetown: This is my recommendation for the low LSAT score explanation: Some individuals have a history of poor standardized test scores, so include with the application a paragraph on your standardized test history written in a nondefensive way. It also is helpful if the applicant has a recommendation letter from a professor who can say: "This student has always had high grades but poor standard tests, so please disregard the tests." This type of information sometimes can make a difference.

Northwestern: A candidate should write an addendum about a low LSAT only when there's been a history of poor standardized test scores. Provide a copy of low SAT scores, so you can show that your low SAT score obviously wasn't predictive. Divulge details of getting sick before or during the test, though the rule of thumb is that you need LSAT or GPA at the median; when they're not, you're against the wall.

DO YOU USE AN ACADEMIC OR OTHER INDEX INITIALLY TO SORT APPLICANTIONS INTO "FOR SURE," "MAYBE," AND "LONG SHOT" PILES? IF NOT, HOW DO YOU DO YOUR INITIAL SORTING?

Berkeley: We do use an index, but it's not used to separate applications. We read them in the order that they become complete.

Duke: We have an index calculated, but don't make much use of it. Our sorting is largely chronological (by date received), with priority given to applications with strong academic records.

George Mason: Files are randomly assigned to committee members without sorting.

George Washington: We pull applications based on a completion date. All files completed are reviewed alphabetically. The index score is part of the review, and it is based on the GPA and LSAT score. In my review of a file, the first thing I look at is the LSDAS report, and from there, I can make an initial assessment. I read the rest of the file to see if my initial reaction was correct or if it should be changed. If the index number is above a certain point and I vote to admit, my vote will be final; likewise, if the index is below a certain point and I vote to deny. Those between the two points go on to a second committee member for their review together with candidates with high indices whom I did not admit and candidates with low indices whom I did not deny.

Georgetown: No, Georgetown doesn't use any type of index to sort applications; rather, because of Georgetown's rolling admissions policy, we read the applications in the order they are completed, so it's an advantage to apply earlier in the cycle.

Northwestern: We do not.

UMichigan: No. We assign first readers based on geography of undergraduate institution and have no other sorting mechanism apart from that. The director of the office (me) reads every application and makes every decision.

UPenn: We do not use an index to sort applications. We read applications in chronological order by date of completion.

DO YOU HAVE AN OVERALL MISSION STATEMENT THAT YOU FOLLOW WHEN LOOKING AT ADMISSIONS STATEMENTS AND APPLICATIONS?

Berkeley: Yes, we do. Included among the values articulated in this vision statement are the following: the "responsibility to educate lawyers who will serve the legal needs of all members of society;" the importance of drawing "a student body with a broad set of interests, backgrounds, life experiences, and perspectives;" and the commitment to selecting "students who will attain the highest standards of professional excellence and integrity." The mission statement can be found in its entirety at www.law.berkeley.edu/45.htm.

George Mason: No.

George Washington: Not really. GW is large, and there is room for all kinds of people with all kinds of goals. I think our campus is better served with a variety of backgrounds.

Georgetown: No.

Northwestern: For the department, it's to admit and enroll who we predict will do best in law school and in their future careers.

IF YOU HAVE AN APPLICANT WITH LOWER NUMBERS BUT A GREAT PERSONAL STATEMENT, WHAT DO YOU DO? IF A PERSONAL STATEMENT IS UNIMPRESSIVE BUT THE STUDENTS GRADES ARE GREAT, WHAT THEN? IS IT POSSIBLE FOR A PERSONAL STATEMENT TO CHANGE YOUR MIND ABOUT A CANDIDATE?

Berkeley: First and foremost, we look for strong academic potential, so you have to have competitive numbers, as well. All law schools are looking for high academic potential, but Berkeley especially values interesting people to comprise each entering class. Finding that combination of academics, aptitude, and diverse and interesting qualities is what our admissions process is all about. The way the law is taught requires that there be different voices throughout our classrooms, but all of the people in [each] classroom must also have the academic ability to grasp the concepts, nuances, and issues that are being discussed. The caliber of the resulting dialogue is a function of the depth and range of their respective voices.

Duke: In the first instance, we're likely to set the application aside until later in the process. We are able to take some people each year with modest academic records but otherwise interesting applications, but we need to make those decisions toward the end. An average personal statement won't hurt an otherwise strong application, but downright bad statements or showing minimal effort will give us pause regardless of the numbers. Essays, recommendations, and the resumé can definitely change our assessment—for better or for worse.

George Mason: What happens to an applicant based on a personal statement depends on the applicant's numbers, the applicant's recommendations, the time of year the application is being reviewed and how many offers of admission have been extended already. In general, a great statement alone is not going to get you in. On the other hand, you can be a great student (great numbers) and your personal statement can keep you out if it is poorly written or contains errors. A great personal statement holds sway in choosing one similarly situated candidate over another.

George Washington: Sometimes I become convinced that this person is worth it regardless of record, and it is a combination of the personal statement and recommendations that convinces me. But, when this happens, it is usually because of the life experiences of the candidate and not simply the submission of a well-written personal statement. If you discover when you read something that the candidate is a jerk, you certainly will not want him or her around for the next three years. Personal statements can become the deciding factor in decisions to admit or deny applicants. However, this is not normally the case. Those instances are the exception to the rule.

Georgetown: This is what I tell students: If you picture your goal of gaining admission as jumping over a bar, your GPA and LSAT will set the height of the bar. Depending on how high the bar is set, the other parts of the application, including the personal statement, have to be proportionally more or less strong to successfully get you over. Thus, the applicant with lower numbers must be especially strong in other areas to gain admission. Every applicant gets to jump, and, conversely, everyone has to jump, no matter how high their GPA and LSAT. A large percentage of law school applicants subscribe to the theory that admissions is strictly a numbers game and that most personal statements are never read. At Georgetown and, I assume, most law schools, this is simply not the case. Of course, the numbers are very important in any decision, but we read every personal statement. Applicants should write their statements with great care, as in many cases, they will be the determining factor.

Northwestern: The applicant won't win out if he or she has a low GPA and LSAT. He or she may win out if the GPA is low and the LSAT high or vice versa.

UMichigan: It is absolutely possible for a personal statement to make the difference; every element of the application carries weight. But there's no formula—it's all a balance, and the outcome will vary based on the relative strength of the various pieces.

UPenn: Unfortunately, there are more applicants who have lower numbers but a great personal statement than we can admit. Some will be admitted outright, but many will be referred to our faculty or student committee for additional input. Much of the decision, however, depends on what else the applicant has accomplished and will bring to the community (work experience, academic background, service, personal background, and so on). Conversely, a weak personal statement can kill an application, regardless of what the numbers are. Sometimes, we will hold or waitlist an applicant who has strong numbers but a weak personal statement to see whether the applicant will "redeem" himself or herself by submitting an additional essay or writing sample that is perhaps more revealing than the personal statement and knocks our socks off.

HOW IS YOUR DECISION AFFECTED BY A PERSPECTIVE OR OPINION (EXPRESSED BY AN APPLICANT IN HIS OR HER PERSONAL STATEMENT) WITH WHICH YOU CATEGORICALLY DISAGREE?

Berkeley: We don't take political views into account at all in the admissions process.

Duke: As long as it's well argued, it's fine. I'm not crazy about people who seem overly combative, but applicants who can make a productive contribution to a healthy exchange of ideas at the law school will be fine, regardless of my personal feelings about their ideas.

George Mason: I tend to think in terms of the diversity of opinion the applicant might add to our student body. However, it is risky to choose controversial topics as some reviewers may not share that sentiment.

George Washington: Well, I believe everyone is entitled to his or her own beliefs and that the entire student body is well served by being exposed to varying beliefs and experiences. I don't have to agree with someone's politics or beliefs to offer admission. I think there is a place for different views. However, if I feel that someone is a little beyond the pale or the candidate tells me that the CIA is monitoring their brainwaves, I would not offer admission.

Georgetown: Opinions expressed in a personal statement make no difference in my view of the candidate. Candidates aren't applying to be my friend or ideological soul mate, so it's of no consequence if I disagree with their views.

Northwestern: We don't let personal biases get in the way; that isn't [among] our criteria.

HOW DO YOU FEEL ABOUT OTHER ACADEMIC CREDENTIALS? DOES HAVING AN MPA, FOR EXAMPLE, BETTER A CANDIDATES CHANCES OF GAINING ACCEPTANCE, EVEN IF HE OR SHE HAS A LOW UNDERGRADUATE GPA OR LSAT SCORE?

Berkeley: A graduate degree is a definite plus factor.

Duke: Post-college graduate experience is helpful; we treat it more or less equivalent to work experience. Strong performance can help offset a weaker undergraduate record.

George Mason: A graduate record can help overcome a lower undergraduate GPA but it will have no impact on a low LSAT score. They are two different indicators of potential law school success.

George Washington: I'm very concerned with a candidate's academic record.

I think that a person can overcome a problem. For example, if someone started and flunked out, then joined the military and became a 4.0 student afterward—so the combined average is 2.9—those are two different candidates. If a candidate has had an outstanding career in the business world, I'm willing to look beyond the numbers. Likewise, graduate study can often compensate for a less-than stellar undergraduate record. It's much harder to compensate for a weak LSAT. The LSAT, for all of its faults, is the only record that all the candidates have in common. It gives us a sense of how someone measures up to everyone else, and it's harder for a candidate to compensate for a weak score.

Georgetown: Anything that is an accomplishment will add to an application, so having completed another graduate degree is helpful. Also, because trend in grades is important, having additional education lets me see whether the candidate's grades continued to rise as he or she progressed through school.

Northwestern: Generally, it doesn't make a difference.

DOES COMING FROM A SPECIFIC FIELD, UNDERREPRESENTED IN LAW SCHOOL (ENGINEERING, FOR EXAMPLE) HELP OR HURT SOMEONE?

Berkeley: I don't think it helps or hurts; it depends on the total package.

Duke: We are looking for people from a wide range of academic backgrounds, and the law school applicant pool has grown more diverse in that regard. It doesn't really help or hurt. I am wary of people from performing arts backgrounds when their curriculum is not supplemented with a solid array of liberal arts electives.

George Mason: It helps in terms of enrolling a class of diverse and unique individuals, which in turn makes the classroom dialogue more interesting. For some schools, underrepresented as used here may not apply. For instance, since we have an Intellectual Property specialization, we have a significant number of applicants from typically underrepresented fields.

George Washington: One's major alone is not the deciding factor in evaluating the quality of the academic record. We consider the transcript and take a close look at all the courses taken on a semester-by-semester basis. In most instances, the major dictates the program followed and, in some cases, can almost guarantee a rigorous course of study. However, it is the rigor of the overall program, not the major, that is the basis of the decision.

Georgetown: I don't believe any particular academic major provides better preparation for law school than another. I advise applicants not to choose their majors based on what they think law school admissions committees want to see, but to take whatever courses they want.

Northwestern: It can help if it's a tougher major, in which case, we [may] allow a slightly lower GPA. The same is true for graduates from military academies.

DO YOU HAVE A DESCENDING DEGREE OF IMPORTANCE THAT YOU ASSIGN THE DIFFERENT APPLICATION REQUIREMENTS? IS THE LSAT SCORE, FOR EXAMPLE, THE MOST IMPORTANT MEASURE OF ABILITY? WHERE DOES THE PERSONAL STATEMENT FALL?

Berkeley: The personal statement is on par with the academic record and LSAT.

Duke: I tend to think of three roughly equal pieces: undergraduate record (not just GPA, but also courses, institution, grade trends, [and so on]), LSAT, and personal/life experience (as reflected in resumé, essays, recommendations). The people who we admit tend to be above average in our pool in at least two of the three areas. There's a lot of flexibility to this, depending on the circumstances of each applicant, but it gives a general idea of how things shake out.

George Mason: LSAT and undergraduate record (including school, coursework, grades) are most important, but at the next level, personal statement can be just as important as recommendations or resumé, etc. We have a holistic approach to file review, and we do strongly consider all components of the application.

George Washington: There are three parts of the application. I give equal weight to these three: LSAT, academic record, and everything else I know about the applicant from the personal statement, resumé, and letters of recommendation.

Georgetown: As I mentioned earlier, Georgetown doesn't use any type of index or formula in evaluating applications, but if forced to give an explanation, I'd break the parts of the application into thirds: LSAT and other standardized tests generally are given a one-third weight in evaluating an application; undergraduate and graduate grades [make up] the second third; and the final third is made up of the subjective parts of the application, including personal statement, letters of recommendation, activities, and work experience.

Northwestern:

1. LSAT

2. GPA

3. Interview

4. Work experience

5. Extracurricular leadership

6. Personal statements

And at the bottom: recommendations.

UPenn: No, we do not assign particular degrees of importance to different application requirements. The LSAT score and academic record are, of course, significant components of each application. But the admissions committee takes the time to read every application holistically because every individual is different. People learn differently and mature at different times in their lives. People come from very different backgrounds. Different majors carry varying degrees of difficulty and complexity. Grade point averages from different undergraduate schools mean different things—a 3.6 average may put a student in the 50th percentile at one school, but in the 85th percentile at another school. Making admissions decisions is a bit numerical, a bit humane, and a bit intuitive; it requires the balancing of many factors. I like to think of myself more as a sculptor than a statistician.

OFFICIAL DISCLAIMER!

Our editors aren't asleep on the job.

The following personal statements and secondary essays appear exactly as they did for law school admissions officers. We only changed the layout so that the essays fit on the pages of this book. Because we have not edited the essays, you may find errors in spelling, punctuation, and grammar. We assure you that we found these errors as well, but we thought it would be most helpful for you to see what the admissions officers saw—not what they could (or should) have seen. We recommend that you carefully proofread your own personal statement, but should you miss an error, take comfort in the fact that others (accepted applicants, even!) sometimes did too.

The Applicants

We grouped applicants by the law schools that they have (or will have) attended. Each student profile is divided into several parts. You'll find the name of the student (unless he or she opted to publish the statement anonymously) and, in some cases, an accompanying photograph. We also offer a short paragraph that summarizes the major accomplishments and activities that each applicant highlighted on his or her application. You'll be able to read the student's statistical record (test scores and GPA) and demographic information (hometown, race, gender, and class year). Next is a list of the law schools to which the student applied as well as the ultimate results of those applications. Following that is the student's personal statement—with no corrections or excisions from the original document. In a few cases, we printed more than one essay by the same student. (Some schools require a Statement of Diversity, for example, in addition to the primary personal statement.)

You may wish to learn more about the law schools that offered (or perhaps denied) admission to the candidates whose essays are printed in this book. You can find such information on our website, **PrincetonReview.com**. Each online law school profile includes such data as average LSAT score of admitted students, number of applicants, and yield (the percentage of accepted students who ultimately enroll). These Stats, together with qualitative information about each candidate, provide a relatively comprehensive scope of the admissions profiles of successful applicants at each school.

We hope that you will read these essays not just for the purpose of identifying effective schemes and tropes (but by all means, take note of such things!), but also with the objective of putting into context the admissions profiles of applicants at your target schools. In this way, you'll learn what you can do to make yourself a more competitive candidate and ascertain the schools for which you may already be a good match.

We wish you the best of luck in crafting your personal statement and in taking this important step toward your future career as an attorney!

ANONYMOUS

Anonymous majored in English at Colorado State University. He did not receive many honors or participate in many extracurricular activities as an undergraduate, and he attributes his admissions success, at least in part, to his personal statement, which, he writes, distinguished him "from myriad other applicants."

Stats
LSAT score: 161
Undergraduate GPA: 3.3
College attended: Colorado State University
Year of college graduation: 2004
Hometown: Colorado Springs, CO
Gender: Male
Race: Caucasian

Admissions information
Law school attended: American University, Class of 2007
Accepted: American University, Catholic University, New England School of Law, Northeastern University, Temple University, University of Denver, Villanova University
Denied: University of Connecticut, Yeshiva University
Waitlisted: The George Washington University

Personal statement prompt

Anonymous notes that he sent this personal statement to "all of the law schools" to which he applied and that he only tailored the last sentence to each individual school.

She said she was going on a business trip. It wasn't until two weeks later when I noticed that the only thing remaining in the kitchen was half a bottle of ketchup that I figured she wouldn't be returning. I was right—and so I spent my seventeenth birthday, alone with my Heinz, petrified with incredulity.

I must include this terribly unfortunate incident in my life in order to illustrate the repercussions it has had on me. My mother abandoning me is not the defining factor in my life—but it served as the catalyst for the changes that have shaped me into who I am today and who I would like to be tomorrow.

Still ensconced in my daze, I left Colorado three weeks into my senior year of high school to live with my dad, who works for the American government in Germany. I may have lost my mother, my friends and my country, but I discovered something new— the world. It is too easy, sitting amid corporate coffee chains and grotesquely large super-stores, to assume that the world ends at the shores of the Atlantic and Pacific oceans, that life exists only north of the Rio Grande and south of Niagara Falls. Living abroad, like a character straight out of Hemingway, created untold adventures, tribulations, awakenings and lessons—it obliterated the cataracts of apathy that blocked my vision by introducing me to the virtues of humanity and empathy.

Although the Iron Curtain lifted from the Czech Republic over a decade ago, the country retains an aura of gloom—especially when it is a drizzly and bleak autumn day when the daytime becomes shorter and the clouds become more ominous. I was outside the town of Pilsen, covered in that exhausting combination of dirt and sweat. In stark contrast to the consuming grey of the weather was a fire-truck-red jungle gym, newly erected a few meters in front of a dilapidated school. The blisters on my hand moaned out to me constantly, but as the children began their recess on the new playground, I forgot my pain amidst a gushing feeling of hope and fulfillment.

At first I refused to go on that trip to build the playground—arriving in Germany only a month ago, I was still in a shell of disbelief. I was attending an American high school on a military base, though I had refrained from making friends since self-pity was the only companion I needed. Some other students persuaded me into going, though (perhaps I just needed a little nudge to push me past my perpetuating sullenness). The trip was incredibly beneficial to me; not only did I see firsthand the positive impact I could make in other people's lives, but I did so while crossing cultures and immersing myself into a challenging situation.

After this experience, my wall toppled over; I vowed that I would explore as much as I possibly could. When I helped others, the part of my soul that ached so painfully when my mother left began to heal—by making others' lives better, I was repairing mine as well. I volunteered on other trips like the original, but organizing a holiday event in Germany that introduced local, disadvantaged children to a traditional American Christmas proved to be my proudest achievement. Donned in that famous red-and-white suit and belting out my best "ho-ho-ho's," I delivered gifts to all the children — for many of them, I was the first American Santa Claus they ever saw. I might have been one of the most comically clumsy-looking Santas to ever put on the beard, but with the sheer exuberant glee of the children, I realized firsthand some of the magic old Saint Nick spreads every year.

While I loved being abroad with all my heart, my appreciation of America never waned—so my four undergraduate years were spent in Colorado. I was stateside only when classes were in session, though, which left four months a year to be in Europe. Since I first moved to Germany, four and a half years ago, I have been to nearly every country on the continent and am fluent in German. My French is improving—and after the summer of 2004, I should be even closer to my goal of spending substantial time in every European country—thanks to my ability to travel on a shoestring budget.

From the lush valleys of Ireland to the sun-bleached islands of Croatia, from the rolling hills of Tuscany to the jutting fjords of Sweden, I've experienced some of the most strikingly beautiful scenes the world has to offers. What has stayed etched into my being most though, are the people I have encountered. An octogenarian glass-blower in Bavaria. A teenage socialite in Brussels. A seven-year old Pakistani immigrant in London. The list goes on and on, but while the people I have met have spanned generations, ethnicities and classes, they all share a basic humanity that everybody in the world possesses, regardless of categories.

Each new person I met reminded me of that dismally gray day in the Czech Republic. When those kids started playing and laughing on that red, rain-glazed jungle gym, I realized the significance of language barriers, citizenship, and religion slowly melting away. Their beaming eyes and toothy smiles told me everything I needed to know: that I have the ability and the burning passion to help people around the world.

I could stand here today, still motherless and entrenched in self-pity, but instead I stand empowered with the lessons learned thousands of miles away from America. My love of people and cultures married to my ability to face hardships and tackle challenges ensures that I will succeed in law—and that I plan on making American University an integral part of that success.

MICHAEL LEAHY

Michael majored in political science at the University of St. Thomas. While an undergraduate, he worked full-time as a waiter and part-time for a test-prep company to pay for his education. Because he also maintained a heavy course load throughout college, he was able to graduate a semester early.

Stats
LSAT score: 168
Undergraduate GPA: 3.6
College attended: University of St. Thomas (MN)
Year of college graduation: 2003
Hometown: Chicopee, MA
Gender: Male
Race: Caucasian

Admissions information
Law school attended: Boston College, Class of 2007
Accepted: Boston College, Boston University, Brooklyn Law School, Case Western University, Cornell University, Northeastern University, Santa Clara University, St. John's University, University of Connecticut, University of Miami, University of Minnesota, University of St. Thomas (MN), Yeshiva University
Denied: Harvard University, University of Notre Dame
Waitlisted: University of Pennsylvania, Washington and Lee University

Personal statement prompt

Michael reports that he wrote this essay, which he submitted as part of his application to Boston University, in response to the following prompt: "What significant personal, social, or academic experiences have contributed to your decision to attend law school?" He notes, however, that he "submitted this essay, or a variation of it, to every school" to which he applied.

When I applied to college, football defined me to such an extent that I only considered schools where I thought I would be able to play. The sport was so important to me that I even used "Football is my life" as the theme of my college application essay. Little did I know that by the end of my freshman year, I would undergo a metamorphosis that would bring me from a teenager, who excelled at little other than football, to a man, who through logical and systematic planning would overcome considerable economic obstacles and achieve a series of seemingly unattainable goals.

I can still remember the day that my parents called to say that they were sorry, but due to my mom's long term unemployment, they would be unable to help with my tuition or expenses as we had planned. It was mid-November and the football season was coming to a close. I was eighteen years old, about a thousand miles from home, and faced with a seven thousand dollar tuition bill for my first semester, not to mention the bills awaiting me for future semesters. It was a bad situation, but I was determined to not be that kid who went off to college for six months only to return to the same block he grew up on. It was time to make some changes and start planning. The next day I began job hunting. I walked from restaurant to restaurant in subzero Minnesota cold, and I ultimately applied for about two-dozen positions. Although I secured interviews with more than half a dozen restaurants, I ended up being disappointed by every one of them, primarily because I was from out of state, and not seen as a good investment, since most employers thought I would leave at Christmas and for the summer.

I ultimately ended up securing a waitering job with the Olive Garden chain, where I had worked during high school in Massachusetts. I took the position despite the fact that there was no bus route available, I couldn't afford a car, and I therefore had to pay a $15 cab fare to get to work. I immediately began a regular schedule of three to four double shifts—40 to 50 hours of work each week—with the goal of making six hundred dollars a week to meet my budget.

As I settled into my backbreaking work schedule, I began to formulate both an academic and a career plan. With football out of the question, I was determined to use my limited study time to rise from an average to a high performing college student. I also planned to take summer courses at a relatively inexpensive community college and thus graduate early, which would allow me to save money on tuition. Finally, I thought that I might be interested in a JD degree, and contemplated that I needed to secure employment in a law firm, and, if possible, take coursework at a law school to ensure that my interest in law was well founded.

I guess it must have been hard to believe that I, Mr. "Football is my life," would be able to achieve even half of what he had planned, and so it is no wonder that, no sooner had I finalized my plans, when both my first year academic advisor and my father declared that I would be incapable of achieving my goals. The doubts of my father were especially hurtful and hard to dismiss, but I was confident in my abilities. I was convinced that, as I had succeeded in football through systematic planning and hard work in the weight room and on the field, so too would I succeed in academia, by logical planning, hard work in the library and active engagement in the classroom.

The combination of full time work and a rigorous focus on my studies was at times physically exhausting. During work at the restaurant, not taking a break—even to eat—became my trademark; I couldn't afford the loss of tables and tips. Meanwhile, I went many nights on less than three hours sleep, so that I could prepare for class. It was very difficult to wake up for 8:00 A.M. classes after working a double shift; so I developed the habit of waking at 6:00 A.M. and jogging to get my mind and body going.

Ultimately, it did not take long for me to confirm that the key to success inside the class is focused, systematic preparation outside of class. I put myself in the habit of not just doing the required readings, but also exploring relevant arguments presented in a range of publications that had not been assigned by my professors. Immediately, the results I achieved in the classroom soared, and I began to develop a deeper interest in academics. Soon the *New York Times* editorial page and the *New Yorker* would take the place of the *Boston Globe* sports page and *Sports Illustrated* in my life. In addition, my coursework at St. Thomas, ranging from economics to ethics to Zoroastrian and Indian philosophy, complemented my logical and systematic approach to life and challenged me to develop a worldview that was more rational and comprehensive.

While I do at times regret leaving my football career behind, there is no doubt that I am better for having done so. I have not only significantly lowered my financial burden, but I am also graduating with honors and as a member of multiple honor societies, and I am doing so in three and one-half years rather than four. In August, I completed an internship with a large law firm, where I performed research and did work on estate planning for individuals with disabilities. And, during the current fall semester, I became the first undergraduate student at my college to take a law class when I secured permission from the University of St. Thomas School of Law and my political science department to take a first year course in Civil Procedure.

My undergraduate plan has been executed flawlessly. Now it is time to launch my new plan at Boston University. I know that the systematic approach that enabled my success at St. Thomas, will ensure continued success at Boston University.

IRENA ZOLOTOVA

Irena worked full-time during her junior and senior years of college at Columbia, managing a Russian-American periodical-publishing business. After graduating, she founded a marketing company focused on serving media and new technology start-up firms. She continued to participate actively in the Russian American community and also volunteered as a pro-Israel advocate, a position for which she edited a weekly newsletter and organized events geared toward unifying Russian and American Jewish communities. During this period, Irena also started a family, entering law school while raising a nine-month-old baby girl who "enabled me to keep my priorities straight and never get trounced by the minor stresses of school."

Stats
LSAT scores: 164, 163
Undergraduate GPA: 3.65
College attended: Columbia University
Year of college graduation: 2001
Hometown: New York, NY
Gender: Female
Race: Caucasian

Admissions information
Law school attended: Boston University, Class of 2006
Accepted: Boston University, Boston College, Fordham University, Yeshiva University
Denied: Columbia University, Georgetown University, New York University
Waitlisted: None

Personal statement prompt

Irena reports that she did not write this essay in response to a particular prompt.

It was called shock therapy. The initial euphoria from the collapse of the oppressive Soviet state slipped into upheaval stemming from the flash introduction of privatization and the virtual dismantling of the state's well-famed social service net. And, just a few years earlier, the excitement of escape from the rampant anti-Semitism of that state turned progressively into a personal identity tangle. As my parents strove to "Americanize" me and bring me up to speed on the cultural heritage that I missed behind the Iron Curtain, they severed my contact with other "Russians" and enrolled me in a modern yeshiva high school. My story is one of overcoming the shocks of immigration and separation from the community, and working back through multiple identities to define a unique and prominent place in that community.

In high school, the language barrier yielded much easier than the social one. I shelved the dictionary after a month and learned English from reading and researching. By audiotaping and reviewing lectures, I brought my language skills to my classmates' level within two years. Yet, as the only refugee in my school, I remained extremely self-conscious of my lingering accent and fearful of speaking up, which relegated me to the role of a perpetual quiet observer. I then convinced myself, propelled by an early interest in history and politics, that I was forever destined to humbly study and analyze the actions of others. To develop the analytical skills necessary for this study, I participated in debate, often picking the side opposite to my personal inclinations. I became highly sensitive to multiple perspectives, bolstered naturally by my discrete position as an immigrant within the yeshiva school setting.

I tentatively set off to develop my own voice once I started working full-time at Lesti Publishing, which produced a start-up Russian-language daily "Vecherniy New York". This was not merely because my English skills instantly made me a spokesperson for the company. Rather, Lesti gave me the first real responsibility of working within a team environment. The realization that my performance affected the success of the common goal became a powerful drive for achievement.

I had no strictly assigned responsibilities. Lesti Publishing was a fairly small business (20 employees at the time) with a tight budget and gaping procedural holes, which I was meant to fill. The first such hole appeared in the absence of a subscription service. I took it upon myself to file for periodical rates, quickly getting stuck between USPS bureaucracy and the mediocre way the newspaper's distribution was tallied by hand on paper. The Postal Service required a detailed account of every newspaper printed for the filing issue, but such paperwork simply did not exist. Since I could not do much about the USPS, my only solution was to first computerize whatever records existed. In a few days, I compiled and organized the database, which not only solved the original problem, but also allowed us to efficiently analyze the distribution network. Once revealing that computerized data management saves time and money, I embarked on the next project of automating the sales department.

This entire experience, which took place in a span of two very short months, taught me that the smallest of responsibilities, setbacks and seemingly tedious formalities are simply disguised opportunities for moving the company forward and, coincidentally, for personal advancement. I learned to actively and confidently search for such responsibilities. Those first few months became a model for my future academic, professional and social achievement.

In retrospect, my work offered much more than a fertile ground for personal fulfillment. For several years prior to my start at Lesti, I had been playing catch up at school (coming in from behind and finishing at the top of my class) and at home (raising my baby sister, who has grown up too quickly, it seems, into a beautiful and quite independent 10-year old). I was too busy then to concern myself with such evasive issues as self-identification and the ultimate purpose of this chase. When Lesti put me back in touch with the Russian-speaking Jewish community of New York, my work compelled me to face those identity issues. It did not take long to appreciate that, despite a 6-year lapse in contact, I belonged to this community. Armed with this lasting impression and renewed energy, I dedicated the next 6 years of my life to involvement with my community and the development of the company, which made it all possible.

On the entrepreneurial side of my mission, I have successfully led the expansion of marketing and PR services to the Russian-American community under the Lesti banner. As before, I managed expansion projects by initially looking to solve concrete problems, learning through exercise, using the acquired expertise to advise and manage our internal team, and finally offering this expertise to our clients. For example, while looking for ways to institute a more effective feedback process between advertisers and our design department, I quickly learned major aspects of graphic design and mastered common design software. By becoming an authority in this area, I was able to implement better workflow organization in the department, using conserved resources to create collateral design projects at no additional expense. Ultimately, as a result of this and similar projects, I consolidated marketing services under the mark of Lesti Media LTD, revitalizing the original publishing company.

As I gained conviction in my ability to affect change and manage an often-complacent workforce, I led the restructuring of the publishing division. In a record 3 weeks we launched a weekly entertainment magazine and website "Russian TV Guide", which became a remarkable financial and societal success. As a uniquely apolitical publication in a tough market (comprised of over 70 newspapers, 50 magazines, 10 internet portals, 5 TV and 25 radio stations nationwide), in due course the "Russian TV Guide" unwrapped a wonderful opportunity to celebrate the achievements of the thousands of talented journalists and producers who inform, entertain, challenge and at the same time represent the Russian-speaking community of the U.S. A year later, the 1st Annual Russian-American Media Awards were born. As one of the chief organizers of the event, I was grateful for the ultimate opportunity to express my personal thanks to the cultural community.

Just as I was working to unite the community under a cultural banner, promoting the Media Awards, an explosive wave of terrorism and painful counter-terrorism measures engulfed Israel and highlighted the community's traditional political immobility. I should note here that of over 3 million Jews who left the former Soviet state, roughly a million came to America and another million to Israel, with the rest scattered throughout the world's other democracies. Now, a very personal dilemma faced every person I contacted — privately, one worried about the fate of relatives and friends in Israel and likewise worried about the prospects of peace in the Middle East. Publicly, one was faced with a general media trend to blame the militarily stronger party, with rigidly framed disclosure of information, which precluded the possibility of any open serious discussion of the conflict in the Middle East, and with lack of organized avenues for expressing concerns and opinions. As a result, most shied away from either humanitarian or political action.

In light of these developments and my own research and insights, I founded the "Common Home" Initiative Group — a grassroots organization, which aims to educate our community by providing a balanced discussion of the Arab-Israeli conflict, vigorously avoiding the common pitfalls of left (moral relativist) or right (intransigent) propaganda. "Common Home" promotes political action and humanitarian support by publicizing means of action in the media and creating a clearing/translation house for petitions and letters to government officials. I also work enthusiastically with Group members to weekly publish the "Common Home" newspaper insert, which has achieved public acclaim and readership of over 50,000. As the Executive Editor of this publication, I screen dozens of articles and letters and hundreds of news items weekly, and find myself relentlessly walking a very thin line between arrays of prejudices. Engaged daily in this intricate task, I have learned to question assumptions and define terms brought by each author into his writing. Having studied — in practice — the influence of media on common understanding, I realize all too well that no position can claim to be truly objective. Nonetheless, one can minimize distortions by defining terms and assumptions, and, most importantly, by constantly questioning and verifying one's own positions. Simply put, one must be true to oneself.

As the Chairperson of the Group, I am responsible for building relationships with American advocacy groups and the media, as well as fine-tuning policy recommendations to be both fair and representative of our entire community. In June 2002, as a direct result of my efforts, I became the only representative from the Russian-American Jewish community to the 34th World Zionist Congress in Jerusalem. I was also named Director General of Americans for Beiteinu, the American arm of an international movement that unites Russian-speaking Jews behind Israel. As I look forward to continuing my work of promoting intelligent discourse and political involvement in our community and beyond, I now undertake to acquire the legal skills necessary for becoming an active policy-shaping contributor to this discourse.

A strong liberal arts education afforded to me by Cornell and Columbia Universities has provided an effective background in all my endeavors. During my first two years in college, I used the program flexibility offered by Cornell University to expand my academic horizons, concentrating on classes in political science, philosophy, psychology and economics. When I transferred to Columbia, I benefited from the better-structured Core Curriculum and the interdisciplinary approach of the Economics-Political Science program, which engaged students in extensive research and writing, promoted independent innovative thinking and helped to refine analytic dexterity, all of which are necessary for the study of law.

Conversely, diverse experiences in publishing, management and political activism have continually enhanced my formal education. While I worked full-time during my undergraduate career, I was able to exercise and perfect organization skills, to bring an enriched perspective into the classroom and a creative dilemma-solving approach into my presentations and written work. I will bring these experiences to Boston University Law School, as I fully dedicate the next three years to the study of law.

Thank you for your consideration.

JASON AMSTER

Jason Amster was a copy chief with Network Computing and worked as a journalist for almost ten years before deciding to attend law school.

Stats
LSAT score: 171
Undergraduate GPA: 3.4
College attended: State University of New York—Stony Brook
Year of college graduation: 1992
Graduate school attended: Syracuse University
Year of graduate school graduation: 1993 (MS in Journalism)
Hometown: Long Island, NY
Gender: Male
Race: Caucasian
Admissions information
Law school attended: Columbia University, Class of 2005
Accepted: Columbia University, Fordham University
Denied: None
Waitlisted: New York University (withdrew application)

Personal statement prompt

Jason notes that he submitted this personal statement as part of his application to Columbia in response to the following prompt: "Candidates to Columbia Law School are required to submit a personal essay or statement supplementing required application material.

"Such a statement may provide the Admissions Committee with information regarding such matters as: personal, family, or educational background; experiences and talents of special interest; one's reasons for applying to law school as they may relate to personal goals and professional expectations; or any other factors that you think should inform the Committee's evaluation of your candidacy for admission.

"This statement should be printed on a supplementary sheet or two and should be returned to the Law School with other application materials."

About three years ago, a frightful brush with a libel suit rekindled my long-dormant desire to be a lawyer. As Sunday editor of a midsize daily newspaper, I copyedited a story and wrote an accompanying headline about a survivalist camp that was in a tax dispute with the town. The camp was training its members in the use of firearms, survival skills and military tactics on a local tract of land. Soon after the story ran, my managing editor called me into his office and told me this group was suing the newspaper over the story and had specifically cited the headline, which characterized the camp as "militant." He and the executive editor assured me the coverage and headline were fair. Even so, I began to fear for my job. Sensing my concern, the managing editor had me meet with the newspaper's lawyer, who shared my boss's confidence. The lawyer was reassuring and, as I realized later, inspiring, as he discussed libel laws and his daily role in defending the newspaper and other clients.

This experience taught me more than the importance of careful word choice. It reminded me how close I had come to following other career paths and of the lessons that would eventually guide me to law school.

About 10 years earlier, I chose to major in engineering as a college freshman. I did this not because I felt a calling but because engineering seemed like an impressive vocation. And that's what I believed was the point of a career: to impress people. Although I survived the rigors of first-year college engineering classes, impressing people turned out to be insufficient motivation to truly excel. But then came a turning point: an upper-level class in Shakespeare. Verbal analysis, writing, discussion? At last something felt natural. I abandoned engineering and followed my heart through academia: social sciences, literature, religion, studying abroad. I learned the fulfillment that comes in pursuing my interests.

Toward the end of my undergraduate studies, I found myself torn between careers in law and journalism. Both fields' emphasis on communication, public service and the truth were appealing. Although law exerted the stronger emotional pull, I chose journalism because I felt better prepared for it. But in fact, I wasn't entirely ready for journalism either. I had yet to learn the true value of hard work and focus.

In my first jobs after graduate school, I was distracted by the thought that advancement should be easier. Was I out of my league? Did I belong in this career? My concerns mounted until I tried a new tact: I would focus not on reward, but on the task at hand. Every sentence I wrote or edited would be as perfect as I could make it. With that new strategy, I achieved the success that had been eluding me: At Dow Jones Newswire, I was promoted from copy reader (junior reporter) to editor in only a year, a unique achievement. My self-confidence grew as I advanced to new responsibilities in new positions.

Indeed, the lawsuit was a rare dark moment in an otherwise joyful career. Fortunately, my anxiety over the suit was brief. The newspaper quickly prevailed, and I remained a valued editor, though I now saw myself as powerless. I was forced to watch from the sidelines while the lawyers waged the real battles. My passion for the law grew, but I hesitated from taking the leap. A final epiphany gave me the push I needed.

About a year after the libel suit, my son was born. It was a time of happiness and introspection. I wanted my son to benefit from the lessons I've learned, but what wisdom could I possibly impart? It now seemed simple: If you pursue your interests and work hard at them, confidence and success will follow. Don't be afraid to follow your heart.

If I can give this advice, I must take it as well.

MICHAEL BRUECK

Beyond serving as a presiding officer and board member on his university's student honor council, Michael held the positions of treasurer and newsletter editor of the College Republicans and was a member of several campus honor societies, including the pre-law society on campus. A finance and international business double major, he completed internships at a financial services firm and a retail bank during his undergraduate career. Upon graduation, he worked for one year as a client accountant with the law firm of Skadden, Arps, Slate, Meagher & Flom.

Stats
LSAT score: 172
Undergraduate GPA: 3.61
College attended: University of Maryland—College Park
Year of undergraduate graduation: 2001
Hometown: Harrington Park, NJ
Gender: Male
Race: Caucasian

Admissions information
Law school attended: Columbia University, Class of 2005
Accepted: Columbia University, Fordham University, Georgetown University, New York University, University of Chicago
Denied: Harvard University, Stanford University
Waitlisted: University of Pennsylvania
Other: Cornell University (withdrew application)

Personal statement prompt

Michael notes that he submitted this personal statement as part of his application to Columbia in response to the following prompt: "Candidates to Columbia Law School are required to submit a personal essay or statement supplementing required application materials.

"Such a statement may provide the Admissions Committee with information regarding such matters as: personal, family, or educational background; experiences and talents of special interest; one's reasons for applying to law school as they may relate to personal goals and professional expectations; or any other factors that you think should inform the Committee's evaluation of your candidacy for admission.

"This statement should be printed on a supplementary sheet or two and should be returned to the Law School with other application materials."

"You're ruining my life," the respondent whimpered, tears streaming down the cheeks of his distraught face as they had been for the last two hours. From across the room, his family looked on. "I have done nothing wrong, and now you're taking everything away from me."

I was used to dealing with emotionally fragile respondents during Student Honor Council hearings, but this person stood out. He was perhaps the most dejected and physically shaken I had encountered, requiring frequent adjournments to regain his composure. I felt empathy for him, as I had for all respondents during hearings. They all reacted in different ways: some with anger, some with fear, others expressing hopelessness. It was my job to ensure that, regardless of any emotional overtones, all sides of a case were fully heard. Doing my job right required disregarding my emotions, but that was often easier said than done.

At the University of Maryland, when an infraction of the Code of Academic Integrity is alleged, an honor hearing is convened to adjudicate the matter. The Presiding Officer leads and directs these hearings, which can involve as many as 20 participants, including professors, students, attorneys, and family members. The presiding officer is depended on to provide procedural authority and must have intimate knowledge of all relevant rules and their proper applications. In addition, he or she must initiate the questioning of respondents, lead deliberations with other board members, and draft written opinions after each hearing that must withstand the scrutiny of the appeals process and, in some cases, legal action.

When I first joined the Honor Council as a Board Member, my main intention was to build skills for a career in the law, and my experience has greatly improved my abilities in dispute resolution, mediation, leadership, and communication. I also joined for some of the same reasons for which I wish to pursue a life in the law: intellectual challenge in a demanding and meaningful atmosphere, and the opportunity to continuously grow as a critically thinking person. However, the more involved I became with the organization, the more my personal goals yielded to our mission of promoting academic integrity on campus. Inevitably, during the course of that mission, punishments were dealt. Peoples' lives were altered; their academic careers were sometimes ended. In the view of some respondents, we were ruining their lives.

Those of us on the Honor Council knew we were not perpetrators of an offense upon the respondents; we were only administering the rules. I never doubted that the cases our Board had worked on had been handled accurately and professionally. We made great efforts and spent many hours deliberating to explore every angle, assuage every doubt, and ensure that the evidence was fully supportive of our decisions. However, two years of deep involvement in such a group had begun to take an emotional toll.

Since starting my tenure on the Honor Council, I had felt misgivings about being in a position in which I was asked to judge my peers. My reservations had been manageable, but after that night's hearing, they had reached an unbearable crescendo. I felt my sense of duty clashing directly with my sense of compassion and felt torn between two essential principles. I no longer wanted to be in a position that controlled the fate of another, regardless of what the rules were. I kept envisioning that respondent's sobbing, pleading face, and even though I hadn't placed him in his position, I couldn't help but feel a sense of responsibility for his situation.

There was no definitive event that ushered me back into full acceptance of my duty. It was a gradual process of internal conflict, shaping and reshaping my ideology case by case until I once again knew in my heart what I had always known in my head:

that the administration of justice is not a burden but an honor, and that doing what is right does not always mean doing what is easy. Throughout this process, I reaffirmed that the enforcement of our academic standards and compassion for others are not mutually exclusive concepts. My determination was strengthened by elevating my standards of personal responsibility and respect for my community far beyond that which was required of me by rule, for only by exceeding those requirements could I feel more comfortable enforcing them. The knowledge that I was making a positive impact on campus overshadowed my previous sense of doubt. My outlook gave me the mental strength to make difficult decisions with confidence and to feel at peace with myself in doing so.

The law is a profession that demands the ability to make critical decisions that impact the lives of others. Throughout a career in the law, the lessons I have learned will surely be put to the test, and I am ready for that challenge. When asked what the most important thing I learned in college is, I proudly respond, "honor."

EMMA GREWAL

Emma held leadership positions for various international and student groups while in college. She graduated from the University of Florida with a degree in political science and economics. Emma interned with the State Department before starting law school in the fall of 2002.

Stats
LSAT score: 163
Undergraduate GPA: 3.85
College attended: University of Florida—Gainesville
Year of college graduation: 2002
Hometown: Plantation, FL
Gender: Female
Race: Asian
Admissions information
Law school attended: Cornell University, Class of 2005
Accepted: Cornell University
Denied: None
Waitlisted: None

Personal statement prompt

Emma reports that she did not write her personal statement in response to a specific prompt.

At the age of 66 days I was offered the first of many extraordinary opportunities—to travel and live abroad. When I went to India with my mother, I lived a culture and lifestyle different to the one that I am accustomed to now. This was the beginning of my love for international people, travel, and affairs. Over the years, I have traveled to many countries including Kenya, Argentina, the Dominican Republic, and France. Each country that I have visited has encouraged me to be a true global citizen—one that has a deep understanding of international people, cultures, practices, and laws. As the world becomes more intertwined and interdependent, my skills with diversity and my multicultural educational background will aid in a pursuit of a career in international law.

My interest in international affairs extends to the University of Florida activities with which I am currently involved. Volunteers for International Student Affairs (VISA) is the largest, most diverse student organization at the University of Florida with a mission to promote cultural awareness to the student body. As Vice President for International Affairs, I serve as a liaison to the International Center, Hispanic Student Association, Black Student Union, and Asian Student Union.

The most interesting aspect of working with VISA is not learning more about my culture, but rather learning about other traditions and viewpoints. For instance, through VISA I have learned that in Palestine, there is a significant population of Christians whose life experiences are significantly different from Palestinians of other religions. VISA allows me to gain experience working with international students and organizations to understand and resolve the unique situations arising from an international environment.

Coming from a family that is originally from India, I have a different set of life experiences than other people. My culture is an important part of who I am and helps me better relate to people of other cultures and backgrounds. Through my experience living in India, and my numerous trips since, I understand the issues and problems that exist in developing countries and that people of these countries face.

Even though I have a great interest in international affairs, I love being an American. Sometimes I feel as if I am not considered an American because of my skin color or heritage, but my heritage makes me appreciate America even more. I have lived in another country so I know how original and special America is. Although America is a blending of different cultures and ideas, which could be a cause for massive social unrest, America overcomes these differences to create a united society found nowhere else in the world.

Especially in light of the World Trade Center tragedies, I feel even more proud to be an American. I helped VISA sponsor a series of discussions with 'Islam on Campus' to promote unity among people of all faiths, as well as a fund-raiser for Afganistani refugees.

One of the reasons I would like to study international law is so that I can show my love for America. I want others to know of my deep pride for America and the principles that it stands for by working for an international organization. I hope to one day help write international laws and treaties that incorporate American ideals of fairness and justice. As the world's people become more mutually dependent and nations' borders are diminishing, the world will require a more cohesive system of law to ease the transition of globalization.

I will bring maturity, intelligence, and a determined interest in international affairs when I pursue my legal education. My diversity and extensive experience in multicultural issues will be an asset that will be a unique contribution to Cornell University School of Law.

CAROLINE H. RYAN

As the chair of the Williams College Student Activities Council, Carrie doubled its operating budget, tripled its events calendar, and spearheaded a project to renovate and run a student lodge/ pub. She was an elected officer on the College Council, was admitted into the Gargoyle Honor Society, was an alternate Ful- bright scholar, completed an honors thesis on the personal essay (the first of its kind), made the Dean's List, and was a member of various sports teams. After graduating from college, she worked first as the assistant technology director and then as a paralegal in a local law firm. She is a member of the Romance Writers of America, has completed two novels, and has designed and run a large romance-writer Web forum.

Stats
LSAT score: 168
Undergraduate GPA: 3.4
College attended: Williams College
Class: 2000
Hometown: Greenville, SC
Gender: Female
Race: Caucasian

Admissions information
Law school attended: Duke University, Class of 2005
Accepted: Duke University, College of William and Mary, Emory University, University of Richmond, University of South Carolina, University of Virginia, Wake Forest University
Denied: None
Waitlisted: None

Personal statement prompt

Carrie submitted this essay as part of her application to Duke in response to the following prompt: "Every applicant is required to submit a personal statement of no more than two pages. The statement is your opportunity to introduce yourself to the admissions decision maker and should include

- *What you think have been your significant personal experiences thus far beyond what may be reflected in your academic transcripts and on your resume, and*

- *Your personal and career ambitions.*

"From your personal statement, we should be able to understand why you want to go to law school and why you have decided to apply to Duke." Also included is Caroline's Statement of Diversity, which she submitted as part of her application to Duke.

Torts vs. Tarts

It was three o'clock on a Saturday morning, and I had just finished typing a paragraph when it hit me: this was the end. I tinkered with the spacing of the lines, calculating the page count (and subsequent word count) from various angles, each time falling within the editorial guidelines for a single-title romance novel of 90,000 – 110,000 words.

I shrugged, yawned. Waited for the choir of angels to sing, but nothing. And so I just went to bed. Even today, a year and another novel later, I'm not sure I truly appreciate the achievement of finishing my first manuscript. However, I do understand the accomplishment of dedicating myself and working hard to achieve a lofty goal. Furthermore, I recognize how this accomplishment can translate into other areas of my life, including law school.

Not many people would draw a comparison between writing a romance novel and practicing law, but there are similarities, not the least of which is a collection of misconceptions held by those outside the profession. Just as most non-romance readers claim that all romance novels are the same -trashy and formulaic - many laymen proclaim lawyers as an ambulance-chasing hoard.

It doesn't help that to the uninitiated writing a romance novel seems to be a simple task: take a guy and a girl, put them somewhere in time, give them a conflict, make them fall in love, rip them apart, reconcile them in the last four pages. But as a fellow writer once said, "Saying all romance plots are boilerplate is like saying there is only one land route from DC to San Francisco." Crafting a believable story is as difficult as crafting a case—there must be a logical flow to the events, there must be motivation and consequence, and when all is said and done every loose end must be satisfactorily tied.

Add to this mixture an extremely knowledgeable and dedicated demographic of readers, and, as in law, writing a novel begins to entail a tremendous amount of research. Romance readers know their history, and are for the most part unforgiving of those writers who do not know theirs. Hence, research becomes vital if one does not want to horrifically embarrass oneself.

Perhaps the most obvious similarity between writing a romance novel and practicing law is the actual writing itself. While the words employed in a romance novel are vastly different from those used by lawyers (excluding divorce settlements, of course) if the stacks of files on my desk at work are any measure, the amount of writing in both endeavors is commensurate. Indeed, the first lesson I ever learned as both a writer and a paralegal is that paper fuels each profession.

Finally there is the passion. Not the kind of passion that most people associate with romance novels, but the passion of pursuit. Law School is demanding, and hard work and dedication is necessary. But true dedication, the kind that can keep you awake working until 3:00am Saturday morning, must have a root in passion - a desire to learn and push forward. I feel that this will be my greatest contribution to Duke Law School: a passion for knowledge that extends beyond the classroom walls to my family, to my community, and to life itself.

Back to that early morning when I finally typed "The End." Was I proud? Undoubtedly so. Did I fully understand my accomplishment? Unfortunately no. It was never an option for me to NOT finish my first novel. Furthermore, the end was just another beginning. There were publishers and agents to query, not to mention over 400 pages of editing and re-editing and re-re-editing. In that regard, finishing my first manuscript seemed to be just one step in the course of many. But I do know that in the process of achieving this goal I have learned lessons that will serve me well through law school and beyond: how to dedicate myself and work hard; how to write and persevere. And finally, how to enjoy the process.

Statement of Diversity

"Diversity Essay (not to exceed two pages).

> *"Because we believe diversity enriches the educational experience of all our students, Duke Law School seeks to admit students from different academic, cultural, social, ethnic and economic backgrounds. If you choose to submit this essay, tell us how you think you would contribute to the intellectual and social life of the law school."*

Average

I should be considered average—I'm sure most people think of me as such. I'm a white woman from an upper middle class family, the youngest of three daughters with divorced parents. I attended a private Episcopalian high school where I was top of the class, but was still considered average.

From Williams I graduated with high marks. I occasionally took five classes—one more than was considered normal. I had the normal disappointing first semester during my freshman year that I then overcame in the spring. I ran a few college clubs and was active in campus politics, but every student made their mark in some way or another. After graduation I did what many college graduates do: worked for a boarding school for a year before choosing a profession. Average.

And yet, as much as I should be average I've never felt average. I have helped autopsy bodies from murder scenes that I helped investigate. I've walked on ancient Mayan palace floors that I uncovered with my hands. I've written two novels and walked five miles out of the Wind River Mountains with a split knee and a hip-to-toe leg brace made from a sleeping pad and two large sticks. But then again, everyone has his or her accomplishments—at least everyone in my world does.

Perhaps that is why I am able to feel extraordinary and yet be considered average—because I live in a world where accomplishment is the norm. I grew up in a family in which attending college was never a question and pursuing a career in law is whole-heartedly supported. In my world, achieving lofty goals is the expectation.

Technically I could be considered a minority—my grandparents being born in and my mother being raised on a banana plantation in South America. Technically I could call myself Latina. But I don't, because that is not how I choose to define my diversity. In my mind diversity can't be claimed of grandparents who I never knew nor of a lifestyle in which I was never raised.

Instead I claim diversity in the variety of my experiences; that I am a painter, a Vietnam War buff, and a southern debutante at the same time. ThatI know how to sail, how to knit, and how to shoot a rifle. ThatI am not only open to new ideas and experiences, but also one who seeks them out.

EMORY UNIVERSITY

SHARON ZINNS

Sharon graduated from Emory University with a major in interdisciplinary studies and a minor in violence studies. During college, she played lacrosse on the Emory club team, worked as a peer tutor in the writing center, and "took as many film classes as possible." She earned high honors at graduation for her thesis on campus violence and safety at Emory. In law school, she served on the student government for three years, the third year of which she was its president. She wrote a law review comment on trade in the Middle East for the Emory International Law Review, and she "loved being in the courtroom" for trial-skills classes. Although she "didn't discover it until the end of law school," Sharon's area of legal interest is intellectual property.

Stats
LSAT scores: 164, 165
Undergraduate GPA: Columbia University (first and second years): 3.608; Emory University (third and fourth years): 3.919
College attended: Emory University (transferred from Columbia University)
Year of college graduation: 2002
Hometown: Boca Raton, FL
Gender: Female
Race: Caucasian
Admissions information
Law school attended: Emory University, Class of 2005
Accepted: Emory University, The George Washington University, Tulane University, University of California—Los Angeles, University of Miami, University of San Diego, University of Southern California
Denied: None
Waitlisted: Georgetown University
Other: Stanford University (withdrew application from consideration before decision)

Personal statement prompt

Sharon submitted this essay as part of her application to Emory University, which, she notes, provided the following guidelines: "Emory law school requires the submission of a personal statement. The statement should describe any unusual aspects of your background that may provide an element of diversity in the law school. You also should describe any skills or traits that you have had an opportunity to develop to an unusual level. Discuss as well any significant activities or work experiences that may enrich your law study. You may choose to write about any topic(s) that you believe will be most helpful to the Admission Committee members as they review your application for admission."

Every Friday morning I walk into Public School 192 and climb two flights of stairs to classroom 307, homeroom of the fifth grade. As I stand in front of the rows of small desks, little bodies squirm in anticipation of the coming weekend. Their movements subside and their eyes and ears open as I start to tell my story.

"I'm a *Suul*: I'm extroverted. I like to stand close to people when I talk to them. I like to get personal. I like to give and get advice, and I am very adaptable. Running shoes or high heels, the mountains or the theater, all are just fine with me. In general, my people, the *Suuls*, get along well with everyone, but I have a hard time communicating with my neighbor. She's an *Icthalonian*. *Icthalonians* are introverts. They consider it rude to get too personal with people. To an *Icthalonian*, family life is private and should stay that way. "Why do you want to know how my mother is feeling?" she asks me in an irritated voice, backing away from my handshake. The look of horror on her face when I tried to give her a hug last week let me know exactly how she feels about me. To her, a polite little bow is the only greeting that is appropriate, and she is always very conservatively dressed. I can't stand the way she gawks at my bathrobe as we both pick up the Sunday morning newspaper. By nine o'clock on a Sunday morning, she's already in a dress with a full face of make-up. I struggle each time to overcome the desire to spill my cup of coffee all over her."

Telling this story is how I start explaining my favorite game, *Suuls and Icthalonians*, to my fifth grade class of Peace By PEACE students. Peace By PEACE, which stands for Peace by **P**layful **E**xplorations in **A**ctive **C**onflict-resolution **E**ducation, is an international program designed to teach elementary school students basic communication and non-violent conflict resolution skills. This particular game, *Suuls* and *Icthalonians*, forces students to interact with people of very different backgrounds in order to see how often people misinterpret different cultures and customs as rudeness or disrespect. By using the role-playing of *Suuls and Icthalonians*, students can maintain a relatively unbiased point of view. Once they have established a basic understanding of this concept, young students can make the transition more easily to understanding the differences between Black, White, Hispanic, Asian, Christian, Jewish, Muslim, etc. Peace By PEACE uses games of this nature to communicate its lesson of non-violence. These games engage students in active learning, encouraging them to learn through educational activities rather then listening to a teacher lecture. Accordingly, I never walk into a classroom with a speech to make or thinking I have all the answers. Rather, I am there to work through the problem of violence with my students.

Peace By PEACE has been one of the most important aspects of my college career. In my first two years of college at Columbia University, I was a classroom teacher for fifth grade students. As a transfer student at Emory University, I helped found a new chapter of Peace By PEACE, in which I took on the role of Educational Coordinator. In this capacity, I wrote our curriculum, trained over 30 volunteers, and planned a graduation festival for 200 students. Moreover, I garnered the support of the Emory administration, faculty, and local community leaders. The strong support of the Violence Studies faculty helped me to see the practical application of my school work. Thus, I was able to link my scholastic pursuits with my extracurricular activities to start a successful, educational, and exciting program.

One of the reasons that *Suuls and Icthalonians* is my favorite Peace By PEACE game is that I have many of the characteristics that I ascribe to the *Suuls*. I'm adaptable. I'm extroverted. I like to get personal, and I like to give and get advice. These aspects of my personality have heavily informed the shape of my college career.

I am adaptable. I transferred to Emory in my junior year because I was not satisfied at Columbia during my first two years of college. Almost immediately, I was able to thrive academically, socially, and extracurricularly. The change from a big city to suburbia was not a problem for me. I was excited about the opportunity to meet a new set of students, professors, and administrators. Although I missed some of my friends from New York, I was able to adapt to life at Emory with ease. Most importantly, I have found at Emory what I was looking for at Columbia — satisfaction, even excitement, about being in college.

I like to get personal. I am a survivor of sexual assault. Therefore, I joined Take Back the Night as soon as I arrived at Columbia. Take Back the Night is a campus organization dedicated to educating students about domestic violence and sexual assault. Our most important event each year is a solidarity march and protest around campus and the Morningside Heights area of New York City followed by an anonymous speak-out at which anyone can share their experiences with sexual assault. This powerful night is always the largest student program on campus each year. For me, the most important part of Take Back the Night was having a forum in which to talk about my experiences and to encourage others to do the same. Most survivors of sexual assault are told that they did something wrong, that it is embarrassing to talk about what happened to them. I, with Take Back the Night, worked to combat this code of silence.

Recognizing that the problem of sexual assault affects all college students, I transferred to Emory dedicated to continuing my efforts at breaking through the pervasive silence. I helped to restart a defunct organization called CARE, the Coalition Against Rape at Emory, and I was selected as a member of the new Women's Task Force. While CARE is dedicated solely to educating students about sexual assault, the Women's Task Force is charged with finding, studying, and changing any problematic issues relating to women's lives. Our main goals are to include sexual assault education in the Freshman Mentoring Program, to add the definition of stalking to the university's code of conduct, and to improve women's healthcare at Student Health Services. My involvement in CARE and the Women's Task Force allows me to continue the work I began at Columbia—helping to educate college women about their safety and well-being.

My commitment to the study and alleviation of violence heavily influences my scholastic goals. I have chosen to write a senior honors thesis about violence and safety on Emory's campus. I intend to survey Emory's students in order to determine how to make our campus feel safer to students and how to deter violence on campus. I plan to offer my thesis to the administration in the hope that they will implement any changes that will benefit the safety of their students.

I like to give and get advice. Working for the American Civil Liberties Union of Florida gave me the opportunity to do just that. Part of my position at the ACLU entailed answering questions posed by callers: What exactly is a civil liberty? Who can I turn to for help? By observing the ACLU staff and other interns, I was able to learn enough about the legal world of Florida to direct callers to further legal assistance. Moreover, I was able to make informed decisions about which cases involved real legal and Constitutional breaches and, thus, required the assistance of the ACLU. While my position at the ACLU was not the most glamorous, I firmly believe that it was an important part of my college career because I learned so much from the dedicated lawyers who directed the office and the enthusiastic law students who interned there. I was never able to vocalize such a succinct description of myself until I came upon *Suuls and Icthalonians*. I am continuously amazed that one word, *Suul*, can so accurately describe me. When I teach this game to my Peace By PEACE students, I feel as if I am revealing parts of myself: my dedication to the study and alleviation of violence, my energy and enthusiasm at being both a student and a teacher, and my passion for experiencing all things new and exciting.

MICHAEL DALLAL

After receiving a bachelor of science with honors in mechanical engineering from Hofstra University, Michael obtained a master's of engineering in mechanical engineering from The Cooper Union for the Advancement of Science and Art. His GPA earned him the Republic Aviation Assistance Award and led to his repeated appearance on the Dean's List. Concurrent with his graduate studies, Michael worked full-time as an acoustical and structural dynamics engineer and as an acoustical consultant to the New York City Department of Design and Construction. He has also remained active in his hometown of Great Neck, New York, where he helped found a synagogue that brings together those who share his Iraqi-Jewish heritage.

Stats

LSAT score: 163
Undergraduate GPA: 3.40
College attended: Hofstra University
Year of college graduation: 1999
Graduate school attended: The Cooper Union
Year of graduate school graduation: 2001 (master of engineering)
Hometown: Great Neck, NY
Gender: Male
Race: Jewish, Iraqi American

Admissions information
Law school attended: Fordham University, Class of 2005 **Accepted:** Fordham University, Brooklyn Law School **Denied:** Columbia University, New York University **Waitlisted:** Yeshiva University

Personal statement prompt

Michael reports that he did not write his personal statement in response to a specific prompt; he notes, however, that the length was "restricted to two (2) single-spaced pages."

While researching and writing my Master's thesis, I discovered how I could best utilize my knowledge and experience in engineering for the benefit of society. My thesis focuses on the effects, regulation and mitigation of construction noise. It is based upon a research project that I performed with the New York City Department of Design and Construction, and it was published and presented at national meetings of the Acoustical Society of America. By comparing noise regulations from around the world and measuring sound levels at construction sites in the New York area, I found that many current noise regulations in the United States are inadequate, vague and impractical. Residents neglect to ensure their own auditory safety while construction projects are in progress, and they focus only on filing complaints against the projects. Unfortunately, these complaints are rarely followed. In addition, construction managers and contractors consistently neglect community environmental and noise regulations, and environmental regulations are only specified in construction contracts covering long duration projects. I also found that environmental regulations and their enforcement fall far short in the United States in comparison to those of Asia and the European Union. As part of my research, I was charged with proposing specific, enforceable specifications and guidelines for construction bids that are currently in the process of being adopted for New York City street construction projects. Due to time and budget constraints, detailed environmental specifications cannot be written for all projects. Nevertheless, citizens must be protected from environmental damage at all times and not only during ongoing construction. Modern society needs to further its development of environmental law and community regulations in order to expand its increasingly demanding goals for protecting citizens from environmental hazards. It is imperative that regulations are practical, easily monitored and continually updated to consider new technologies that reduce the cost and increase the performance of environmentally friendly products. An attorney who knows both environmental law and developing technology is best qualified for this undertaking.

My academic journey to this point has been rather circuitous, spanning such diverse disciplines as medicine, theology, and acoustics, each of which has helped formulate my interest to use law and engineering to improve the environment. I spent my formative years in Tehran, Iran before moving to the United States. In my new country, I was struggling to master the English language while speaking both Farsi and Arabic at home, while other children were excelling in any number of academic areas. As I began to excel in school and to show a talent for mathematics and science, I was encouraged by everyone in my family to become a doctor. Therefore, I began my undergraduate education studying the sciences at Columbia University. Moreover, because my parents had always emphasized the importance of exploring our historical and cultural background, I simultaneously studied Jewish law and Hebrew text at the Jewish Theological Seminary. Although I enjoyed my introductory science courses and was successful in Judaic studies, it became clear to me that I was following an academic path that had been selected for me, and not one that I had selected. My growing discontent was exacerbated in the fall of 1994 by the death of my cousin, who was nothing less than a brother to me, in a senseless automobile accident. My spirit and my desire to learn were nearly destroyed. I transferred to Hofstra University in order to be as close as possible to my grieving family, as my focus was completely on loss, and academics were no longer important.

After a grueling year, I motivated myself to direct my energies back to my academic endeavors. In the spring of 1996, I selected engineering as a vocation and also became an active leader in the Hofstra community. I was tapped for Theta Tau Professional Engineering Fraternity and later became President of my chapter and National Outstanding Student Member. I organized outreach events including two engineering competitions for 70 high school students throughout Long Island. To help my peers, I coordinated a regional conference at Hofstra for 50 university students from the Atlantic seaboard and tutored others in a wide range of courses. My academic efforts were recognized by the Hofstra administration and generated my induction into the Kappa Mu Epsilon National Mathematics Honor Society. Concurrently, I remained and continue to remain involved with my Jewish heritage. My family and I helped to found our community's synagogue, where I later met and married my wife, Loretta.

Since receiving my bachelor's degree with honors, I have been working full time in the engineering field and will earn a Master of Engineering degree from The Cooper Union for the Advancement of Science and Art in December 2001. I also passed the National Council of Engineers for Engineering and Surveying examination to become a New York State certified intern engineer. My employment thus far has allowed me to analyze various structures from bridges to naval ships and submarines, as well as to utilize my knowledge of acoustics to design music studios and concert halls. I was most fortunate to have been given the opportunity to assess the safety and potential structural damage of buildings that may have been impacted by the destruction of the World Trade Center on September 11, 2001. I am currently strengthening my experience with international environmental regulations while working with Physicians for Social Responsibility by investigating the development of alternative energy production and consumption requirements according to United Nations policy. My experience has been exceptional and exciting, and it has drawn me towards the goal of using both legal and engineering knowledge to advance environmental regulation.

The fusion of engineering and law can be utilized to impact every facet of American society, and I plan to use my engineering knowledge and experience, coupled with the legal expertise I expect to gain at Fordham University Law School, first to help corporations to comply with existing environmental law effectively and efficiently; and then to develop advanced environmental regulations for local, regional and national agencies. Community regulations should be updated to consider those who must comply with regulations and those who must enforce the law. With a specialization in environmental law, I would be able to use my engineering skills to aid the legal field, investigating and developing environmental regulations for the demands of the new millennium. To that end, I am looking forward to working in environmental advocacy through the Fordham's Public Interest Resource Center. Applying my knowledge of environmental law while representing clients in actual cases will allow me experience and understanding that I could not gain anywhere else. The education that I would receive while helping others, as well as from the Fordham Law School faculty, would enable me to achieve all of my goals.

KATHERINE CHRISTINE HUGHES

Katherine worked during all four years of college to pay for her tuition, rent, and books. After graduation, she took a year off to travel the world, began working as an editor (a job she held for seven years), and ran her first marathon. Her travels inspired her to pursue a master's degree in race and ethnic relations, for which she deferred her law school enrollment for a year. She has done a great deal of volunteer work, including visiting the elderly, teaching English in New York City, and working for the Make-A-Wish Foundation in London.

Stats

LSAT score: 164
Undergraduate GPA: 3.72
College attended: Emerson College
Year of college graduation: 1997
Graduate school GPA: 1:1 ("First-Class, comparable to an A")
Graduate school attended: University of London
Year of graduate school graduation: 2005
Hometown: Gilmanton, NH
Gender: Female
Race: Caucasian

Admissions information

Law school attended: Fordham University, Class of 2008
Accepted: Fordham University, Northeastern University
Denied: None
Waitlisted: None
Other: Boston College (application put on hold)

Personal statement prompt

Katherine used this essay—which she "modified slightly for the applications to Northeastern and Boston College"—for her Fordham application. She notes that she responded to the following prompt: "Include a personal statement—two pages maximum—that demonstrates your ability to communicate effectively and concisely. While you have the widest possible latitude in choosing the substance of your personal statements, experience shows that the most successful personal statements are those which develop a sense of the person, his or her values, aspirations, and concerns. A discussion of the unique contributions you would likely make to the student body, the legal profession, and ultimately the larger society would also be well received."

My father was a biker, my mother an Irish immigrant and a high-school dropout. I've got half-brothers and sisters peppered across the state of New Hampshire. I grew up on a farm.

"Learn all ya can, kid." While I waited for the school bus on icy, black mornings, these are the words my father would holler from our front porch, his pale, thin legs poking out beneath an old robe. "Learn all ya can." This was the advice he shouted back to me as he sped off on his Harley Davidson, his leather jacket billowing, his beard twisting in the wind. Through my education, volunteer work, career, and travels, I have kept my father's words with me, relying on them to carve my path in life.

I excelled in high school. I joined every club, participated in athletics, and acted on stage. I edited the school paper and took advanced classes in English and history; I graduated in the top five of my class. While in college in Boston, I did well but grew frustrated with the generality of my communications classes; I felt I wasn't learning specific skills, and I wanted to be challenged. With my father's words in mind and my Irish grandfather's encouragement, I took a year off and travelled to Ireland, my mother's birthplace. While working as a barmaid and living with my cousin in a down-at-heels north Dublin community, I quickly realized that college was a choice, that I could exploit it to excel in life or that I could grumble about it unceasingly. I discovered the vision of achievement that my grandfather had in mind when he immigrated with his family to America in the 1950s. With a promise to my mother, who had never enjoyed the luxury of a college education, that I would graduate on time no matter how many summer courses I had to take, I returned home, transferred schools, and waitressed my way through a degree in writing and literature, determined to learn all I could. My coursework at Emerson College pushed me to develop critical reading skills, refined my writing abilities, and, above all, nurtured my editorial eye, all invaluable tools in my current career and my eventual practice of law.

It was after my graduation, when I moved to New York City, that I met Jocelyn and began to further examine the implications of immigration. Jocelyn was the near-silent Haitian woman who sat at the back of a class I taught for Literacy Partners. While the class was aimed at those whose native language was English but who had somehow been lost in the shuffle of public education, we rarely turned anyone away. Jocelyn must have been around 65 years old, and her first language was Creole. At first, I overlooked Jocelyn for some of the other more loquacious students who continually brought in passionately personal projects from home to develop their skills. I had one student, a man from the Bronx, who adored Neruda and set about writing a book of love poems. Another student, Sam, who had been in and out of prison his entire life, worked on reading his Alcoholics Anonymous Bible. Jocelyn's project was to find a job as a cleaning woman.

Her dogged determination moved me. I began to seek her out in class, and I accompanied her to the job-bank computers at Federal Plaza in order to assist her in reading help-wanted advertisements. It was then that I began to realize that there are stages of immigration. I looked at my own family and observed that on the maternal side, where I am the first American, I am also the first to graduate high school, let alone college. Although my father's roots are firmly Irish, in his family I am fourth-generation American. His father had been a New York State Supreme Court Justice, a Fordham graduate, and his brothers were accountants and lawyers. They had been given opportunities that my mother's brothers had never seen. The days of the disadvantaged immigrant are far from over, but it is now less likely to be the Irish than it is to be the Mexican, Haitian or Jamaican families who struggle to find work and make a better life for their children. Over time, I found myself thinking more about the diversity of the City and the implications of immigration over generations. It was Jocelyn who revealed to me the tribulations of immigrants in America firsthand.

After my year of tutoring, I began to consider a legal career. My family is full of lawyers and I knew I had a knack for words. I was seeking more satisfying work, but I wanted to make certain that this was the path I should follow. I took a job as an assistant in a ferocious one-woman family law practice. Because the firm was so small, I was able to explore New York's legal system up close. I got to know judge's clerks; I dealt with filing offices and sat in on trials. I typed affidavits and served papers and did research in the courts' archives. I did a lot of photocopying. Then, before my all-important next step toward law school, I was approached by my former boss, who asked me to take on the role of managing editor at my last office. It was an opportunity to learn managerial skills and to oversee the production of a daily magazine with a monthly circulation of 350,000. Once again, I took my father's advice to learn all I could and jumped at the chance.

Living in New York during those years, I was overwhelmed by the mixture of races and religions I encountered, surprised and often shocked by my feelings and fears about them. The daily barrage of cultures provoked near-racist thoughts in me on several occasions, despite the fact that I had been taught tolerance as a child. I dreamed of escaping the City, to see where all of these people had come from, to begin to understand this maelstrom of identities. I needed to garner a perspective of world cultures beyond my own Irish-Catholic one, and I could hear my father's voice pushing me to learn more. I decided to see the world for myself. In September 2001, with some trepidation at the events of that month, I left the comfort of my editorial office, where, for over two years, I had organized, scheduled and rewarded a staff of six editors, and embarked on a yearlong trip around the world.

I spent much time in Australia, Thailand, and India and travelled through New Zealand, Fiji, Turkey, Egypt and Europe. Time after time, I observed the remnants of colonial empires with their class boundaries. I looked on, troubled by the disintegration of indigenous Aboriginal culture, by the rampant alcoholism, and I was unable to avoid drawing obvious parallels with the US's own Native Americans. While in India, I heard many strange and terrible stories from Tibetan refugees, all desperate to immigrate to the US but lacking the exorbitant fees required to pay for dodgy passports. I spent the spring in the little Indian town of McLeod Ganj, while the world watched the conflict between Pakistan and India rear its ugly head once again. I cancelled my trip to Nepal after a wave of beheadings swept through that tiny nation. Throughout my journey, opinions on religion, women's roles, and Americans washed over me. I arrived in Europe, happy to have hot showers again, but reeling from all I had learned. Armed with a widened worldview and the ability to examine issues from multiple perspectives, I focused on how I could incorporate my experiences into an academic setting. This fall, I begin a post-graduate certificate course, the first year in a master's program, at the University of London, studying race and ethnic relations. There, my studies will include courses on immigration policy and its effects on society, as well as an examination of discrimination law, war, and migration. I look forward to blending this certificate into my legal education.

My father could never have known how literally I would take his words. Throughout my life, his advice has taunted me into choosing the more unusual route, the road less travelled. His throwaway line, tossed into the wind as an afterthought, continues to push me, to set me on new paths of discovery. I cannot imagine entering law school as the person I was when I graduated from college. It is only now that I can begin to understand the fine gradations of the law's interpretation, to realize that these interpretations aim to intersect with society and somehow change it. I seek to hone my experiences through further education, especially through the lens of law, in order to understand and help shape our world, in order to learn all I can.

THE GEORGE WASHINGTON UNIVERSITY

SOMA KEDIA

Soma applied to law school during her final year of college and enrolled the following fall. In college, she participated in a flute ensemble and a choir, coordinated the Schreyer Honors College First-Year Student Orientation Program for two years, and cofounded a student Shakespeare company. Soma held part-time jobs during college as a teaching assistant and as a student-programming assistant. She also worked as a writing tutor for three years, a job she continues to hold in law school. After law school, Soma plans to work in child welfare law or policy, with the ultimate aim of establishing a career in academia.

Stats

LSAT score: 165
Undergraduate GPA: 3.67
College attended: Penn State University (Schreyer Honors College)
Year of college graduation: 2002
Hometown: Allentown, PA
Gender: Female
Race: South Asian (East Indian)

Admissions information

Law school attended: The George Washington University, Class of 2006
Accepted: The George Washington University, American University
Denied: Georgetown University, University of Michigan
Waitlisted: Northwestern University, University of Pennsylvania (also summer Waitlisted)
Other: University of Chicago (admissions office requested additional materials, which Soma was unable to send from abroad)

Personal statement prompt

Soma notes that she wrote her essay in response to an open-ended prompt.

What George wanted more than anything else in the world was to be able to laugh. He was a shy, quiet boy with a reputation for being "sweet" and his voice was soft and monotone; you wouldn't have guessed he was more than twelve when you met him, though he was almost fifteen. He had a surprisingly developed sense of humor, but he couldn't express it. He wasn't deaf or mute; he had no physical disability that kept him from laughing. He even loved singing in his church choir, though his shyness prevented him from joining his school chorus. George was also a writer and loved reading—during free hour, we counselors could usually find him in his room poring over a fantasy novel. However, despite his quiet nature, this diverse bunch of "underprivileged" high school kids who were together for Penn State Upward Bound's Summer Program welcomed him. Many of the kids he was surrounded with had lived had their own problems, and yet, away from the pressures of popularity at their regular schools, they helped each other learn and grow. The kids tried everything they could; they told him the funniest jokes in their high school repertoire, they made silly faces, and they would send the girls in to tickle him. He would double up shaking sometimes, but not a sound came out of his mouth.

I noticed George during the first week of the program; he wasn't in my group, but his love of reading, writing, and music and his shyness reminded me of myself at his age. George was a communicator, just like me, but he needed help realizing that. I was distinctly nervous about talking to him, being a new counselor, and this was the first time I had consciously tried to be an influence in someone else's life. I wasn't sure how to approach him, but it turned out that my peer tutoring skills were the best preparation I could have had. In tutoring writing, I learned about rhetoric and composition, but I also learned how to create dialogue with a person, how to ask the right questions—in short, how to help the other person how to revise and work with their own writing. I tried to use the same technique with George: rather than giving him advice or just telling him he was a great person, I tried to help him realize this on his own by having him list his good qualities. I talked to him about my perception of the world from writer to writer, but encouraged him to be active in forming his own perceptions. At the same time, I was learning what it means to be part of a community; my nervousness at working with the kids faded as talking with George helped me realize that my performance wasn't the focal point of the world around me—the important thing was to collaborate with others to bring about a change. It didn't matter if I didn't have all the answers; George and I figured them out together.

As the summer progressed, I could see a change; George became more active around the other kids and began to approach others more often. He talked more, and learned to overcome the things he didn't like about himself and focus on the characteristics he did like. I don't know if I fully realized the transformation in George, though, until I saw him standing on stage at the end of summer talent show: he had chosen to sing a duet to an audience full of people. I could hardly believe that George, who barely opened his mouth at the beginning of the summer, was standing on stage singing in front of his friends. There were a lot of kids up there who sang, who did comedy routines, who were quite good at what they did, but it didn't—it couldn't have—taken as much courage as it did for George. I'll be honest, he wasn't very good—the musician in me cringed at his practically silent voice, slightly off key. But the music didn't matter; the amazing part was that he had finally learned to put himself on the line, to let himself be vulnerable. The other counselors and I had helped him learn how to communicate to people and how to be happy with himself. He got a standing ovation, not for learning to laugh, but for being who he was.

So was this the moment I decided to go to law school? Well, no. I've actually been anticipating law school since I was about ten years old and, believe it or not, already advocating for women's employment rights on the playground; I solidified my desire through my years on the debate team in high school and college. I've known intellectually that legal education was something that I could do and wanted to do for years. What George taught me that summer was how I wanted to use my education. I had been recently making the transition from volunteerism to more substantial efforts, and it was then I realized that I wanted to spend my career in public service, collaborating with others for social change.

Because of this, I have spent most of my college years learning how to connect with people one-on-one, through tutoring at the writing center and learning how to find solutions in problems within my community through my work with student programming and teaching. The activities and classes I've been in have helped me learn both how to succeed in law school and how I can use my legal education to serve others. Whether I eventually get involved in public policy, public interest law, or work with a non-profit organization, I want to improve education, help alleviate poverty, and work on other social issues. I'm not yet sure whether I want to work locally, nationally, or globally, nor do I have firm plans for focusing and achieving my goals, but I have learned enough to know that I can succeed at effecting change. I know I helped George change and grow; a legal education can help me do that for a larger community.

THE GEORGE WASHINGTON UNIVERSITY

ERIC L. KLEIN

In the five years between his college graduation and attending law school, Eric held down a variety of interesting jobs, which included being a Barnes & Noble coffee slinger, community newspaper reporter, and Medicare analyst. He spent the six months before he began law school teaching English and math to high school students in Dubai, United Arab Emirates.

Stats
LSAT score: 175
Undergraduate GPA: 3.87
College attended: The George Washington University
Year of college graduation: 2000
Graduate school attended: Medill School of Journalism, Northwestern University
Year of graduate school graduation: 2003 (MS in journalism)
Hometown: Overland Park, KS
Gender: Male
Race: Caucasian

Admissions information
Law school attended: The George Washington University, Class of 2008
Accepted: The George Washington University, Emory University, Georgetown University, University of Michigan, University of Virginia
Denied: None
Waitlisted: Yale University

Personal statement prompt

Eric reports that he did not write his personal statement in response to a particular prompt.

Oh, how I agonized over whether to buy that saw.

I wanted it. But it was so expensive. But I *needed* it. . . . No, I wouldn't get enough use out of it. But I wanted it so bad.

I slept on a mattress on the floor in those days—early summer 2003. My room consisted of four walls, a bare wooden floor, and that mattress tucked in the corner. The mattress was plenty comfortable, but when the late afternoon sunlight slatted through the blinds, the ghostly room fairly cried out for furniture, any furniture. But I had none. What I did have was a shiny new master's degree in journalism, a poorly paid reporter's job and a monthly love note from my girlfriend, Sallie Mae.

The answer, I felt, lay not in borrowing more money from Sallie, nor in cheap Swedish furniture. The answer lay in a *saw*—and a drill, a cheap sawhorse and some measuring tape. I would *build* myself a bed, on which I would sleep like a normal furnitured human being. A desk and a bookshelf would follow. If only I had a saw!

A man tires of sleeping on the floor, and one day I was no longer content to stand outside the Home Depot at Seven Corners with my longing face pushed up against the glass. The next Saturday found me out on the porch, standing among stacks of raw wood, holding my new tools, the reality dawning slowly that I had no idea how to use a saw or any other woodworking instrument. What do you do when you own a saw, a precious power saw at long last, but haven't the faintest clue what to do with it?

The answer: You fire it up and start cutting wood. It doesn't matter where or how. And that's what I was doing two hours later when my new roommate walked up.

"Looks great!" he said. I glanced up and the shriek of the blade cycled down into silence. Sweat poured off me, each bead leaving a little trail in the sawdust caked all over my exposed skin. My goggles steamed. Wood shavings fell out of my ears. The porch looked like a dusty wooden swamp, with ugly misshapen cuts of lumber spread about like old, half-submerged skeletons. Wood hung in the air like fog. No shadow of a bed was visible anywhere among these ruined boards. I figured I must have misheard him.

"Listen, let me know when you do your next project," he said. "I want to help out. But I'll need your close supervision, because I've never done anything like this before." And he went inside. I stood there, speechless. Dog walkers ambled by. My neighbor quietly mowed his yard. My assumptions about the world were softly sawed away, vanishing into the heat of the afternoon like the finest scattering of sawdust.

He thought I was a carpenter. He didn't see me for how I felt—a boy playing dress-up with daddy's tools. He didn't seem to notice that *I'd never done anything like this before either*. He looked at me and assumed I knew what I was doing. He asked for my supervision!

The more I pondered what happened that day, the more the world seemed to open. In the eyes of my roommate, I was a carpenter because I presented myself that way. And he never found out the truth, because before long his mistake *was* the truth. I learned how to use my tools, and I became a carpenter. Did anybody ever take on a new role any differently? Have careers ever been built on anything besides sheer nerve and great piles of wood cuttings? The greatest lesson I ever discovered for myself is this: The only difference between a carpenter and a boy in an empty room is the daring to pick up a saw.

The law degree is the saw, I came to understand. When I bought the saw, I sensed its possibilities only dimly, though its value to me has grown with each piece of furniture I've envisioned and then realized. My room is beautifully furnished, and I've built things I couldn't have imagined when I first picked up that blade. Now I want to build a career in government and politics, and though I see the details only indistinctly right now, at this point it's enough to know I need to buy—to earn—the right tools. My journalism degree and my reporting experience are extremely valuable to me, and I expect them to serve me well the rest of my life, but they aren't enough. My travels through the Middle East in 2005 will be exciting, but the toolbox isn't full yet. I need the law degree to open the doors through which I eventually hope to step into the arena of public debate.

The truth is, I've always had strong opinions, and I've always dreamed of making my arguments before the public. But I never dared pursue that goal, or even admit it. I never acquired the tools that would advance me in that direction. Instead, as with the saw, I agonized.

No more. When I dared imagine myself a carpenter, I became one. I finally understand that the world will see me exactly as I choose to see myself. I'm limited only by own confidence—willingness to sweat—and sense of possibility. All these I have. I need only pick up the saw.

SVETLA PETKOVA

Svetla, a native of Bulgaria, pursued legal studies with high distinction in France. In 1995, she transferred to school in the United States to join her family. Svetla received numerous academic awards while in college. For three years post-college, she worked as a legal assistant/global relocation specialist at Dechert Law Firm.

Stats
LSAT score: 156
Undergraduate GPA: 4.0
College attended: Drexel University
Hometown: Bulgaria
Gender: Female
Race: Caucasian
Admissions information
Law school attended: The George Washington University, Class of 2005
Accepted: The George Washington University
Denied: None
Waitlisted: None

Personal statement prompt

Svetla notes that she wrote this essay, which she submitted as part of her application for GW, in response to the following prompt: "All applicants are required to submit a personal statement, which should include any additional information you think may be of assistance to the Admissions Committee in considering your application. Examples of such information are significant extracurricular or community activities, the reasons why you want to study law, a discussion of your background, or an explanation of any unusual aspects of your academic record. This statement must be written on separate pages and must accompany this application."

"I will never give up my convictions." These were the last words of my great-grandfather, Ilia Stefanov, judge and candidate for the Bulgarian Parliament, before he was assassinated by the Communists in 1945. Heir of a long tradition of West European-educated lawyers and advocate for the plurality of political structures, he had refused to collaborate with the dictatorial regime. In the following 45 years under totalitarianism, members of my family were banned from practicing law. The story of this proud man, whose eyes looked at me inquisitively from an old black and white picture, fired my imagination into a burning desire to return to the tradition of legal practice in my family. What started as a romantic idea of youth became the beginning of a quest for knowledge and personal growth.

I grew up in Bulgaria in the last decades of the Iron Curtain, in a dictatorial system that did not allow ideas and opinions to diverge from the communist dogma. Early on I learned the meaning of the concept "forbidden": music, books, movies from the "West" or with dissident ideas, names of scientists and writers, as well as facts of world history and scientific discoveries, were forbidden. The hardest part for me was growing up with the fear that I belonged to a different family, a family that had lost several memberskilled or sent to camps by the communists. As a result, being a third generation of that family, many venues in life were closed forever for me. In retrospect, I feel blessed to have parents who showed me at that time the truth behind the mask of the regime.

I was attending the French High School in Sofia in 1989, when the winds of change brought events that turned the world I knew upside down. As Eastern Europe embraced dramatic political changes, I welcomed my first free vote with exultation. The passionate speeches I gave at political debates in school and the reading of then incomprehensible political documents were remarkable lessons in civic duties and political consciousness.

Following the debates surrounding the drafting of a new constitution, I learned that law was not just an abstract text, but a process that embodies various interests. I researched definitions of civil rights and mechanisms to protect them, realizing the limitations of a constitution that reflected the social tides of a particular era. As I witnessed the struggle of an entire nation to establish the democratic structures of its new society, my desire for a career in law grew steadily. In 1992, I was accepted with honors at the University of Sofia, having won the prestigious National Competition in Literature, and I successfully participated in my country's first competitive exams for admission to French universities. At that time my dream to study law within a long-established judicial system was stronger than ever, and I chose to pursue my studies in France.

When the train pulled into the station at Nancy, France, I knew I had started an extraordinary journey. During my three years studying law at the University of Nancy, I absorbed the fascinating history of the French legal system, the logic and precision of law and the influence of social perceptions and historical circumstances on legal principles. I continued to research and relate French laws to those developing in Bulgaria, thus broadening my interest in the comparison of legal systems and the search for unifying principles.

My experience in France was a rite of passage from adolescence to adulthood. Coming from a small and rather homogeneous nation, I discovered the meaning of being "the other" and being "different." To break cultural barriers, I hastened to learn about West European history, politics, economics and society. This motivation reflected also in my role as a co-founder of the first organization for business and cultural relations between Nancy and Bulgaria. In the process I rediscovered a sense of me that was stronger than I have ever known. Thrown into a new culture and away from my family, self-reliance became a way of being. I worked at night to support myself and was twice as proud to achieve honors in an educational system where only one-third of the students were promoted to a higher level each year and where I was the only student for whom French was not a native tongue. Eager to apply my knowledge, I persuaded an international company to utilize my legal skills and was thus introduced to the practical legal world. There I focused on the interpretation and use of legal principles in the functioning of a business unit of society - the corporation.

In 1995, while I was visiting my parents who were working in the United States at that time, the former communist party regained power in Bulgaria. I had to make a quick and radical decision about my life. "My country is the one where I feel Freedom," Benjamin Franklin had said. For me this country became America. I was fascinated that people from different races, religions and cultures live and work side by side. I realized that I was not "the other" here. Once again, I challenged myself to learn a new language on my own, and to adapt rapidly to a new educational, social and cultural system. At last, I could satisfy my longing for knowledge in areas, such as psychology, philosophy, anthropology, and foreign politics, which were banned by the communists. I wanted to understand the human psyche, the social forces and political circumstances to be an effective legal practitioner. Thus, I enrolled in the International Area Studies program at Drexel University to study the historical, political and cultural fabric of American society, and to relate it to foreign politics, economics, and cultures. My studies in this rigorous program, which focused on research and writing, alternated with full-time cooperative work as a Paralegal, and I soon excelled in both.

After graduating *summa cum laude*, I immediately landed a position as legal assistant at Dechert Immigration Group, one of the leading immigration law practices in the U.S. Mastering the vocabulary and intricacies of immigration law was a challenging task that has provided me with a unique perspective on the application of law to the individual. I have researched legal precedents, analyzed complex case issues, communicated opinions and written persuasive documents to advocate the merit of outstanding researchers, investors, and people with exceptional abilities who further the United States' economic, medical, scientific, and artistic progress. Recognizing the value of my creative and independent work, the attorneys have promoted me to the position of Global Relocation Specialist. Responsible for more than two hundred corporate and individual clients, I have learned the discipline, precision and minute attention to detail that are critical for the study of law.

In making my choices in life, I have constantly sought challenge and growth. I have overcome economic, cultural and social obstacles while proving to myself that there are no heights that cannot be reached. Through my academic training and "real life" experiences, I have learned firsthand how law applies to all layers of the social structure. Today, my thirst for knowledge in the sphere of international legal affairs is ever growing. This is an area where my diverse background and abilities will find the best realization. Combining an U.S. law degree with my European law expertise will enable me in many ways to contribute to a better global understanding and cooperation. I am convinced that the universality of many legal principles creates bridges between nations. I would like to walk such bridges with a deeper sense of fulfillment, having given all my efforts to promote the freedom of creativity and to eliminate the borders of prejudice and discrimination. I want to look at that picture of my great-grandfather with pride, knowing that I too will practice the noble profession of law, in freedom, in the country, which is my home.

THE GEORGE WASHINGTON UNIVERSITY

ANONYMOUS

Anonymous was a double major in government and politics as well as sociology. He was active on campus and received several awards for outstanding leadership in campus organizations. He paid for 100 percent of his college expenses by founding an Internet publishing company and received national media attention for his sites. Professionally, he interned in the U.S. Senate and published several papers on African American policy issues while interning at one of the nation's premier minority think tanks.

Stats
LSAT scores: 151, 158
Undergraduate GPA: 3.48
College attended: University of Maryland—College Park
Year of college graduation: 2001
Hometown: Pittsburgh, PA
Gender: Male
Race: Caucasian

Admissions information
Law school attended: The George Washington University, Class of 2005
Accepted: The George Washington University, University of Maryland
Denied: Georgetown University
Waitlisted: None

Personal statement prompt

According to Anonymous, "For GW the directions were as follows: 'All applicants are required to submit a personal statement which should include any additional information you think might be of assistance to the Admissions Committee in considering your application. Examples of such information are significant extracurricular or community activities, the reasons why you want to study law, a discussion of your background, or an explanation of any unusual aspects of your academic record. This statement must be

written on separate pages and must accompany this application.' Mary-
land's and Georgetown's [prompts] were quite similar."

As applications from hopeful law school applicants roll into admissions offices this season, it is clear that admission decisions will be as competitive as ever. Those applicants who are able to define themselves as disciplined, focused, serious, and excited about their future legal education will likely find success. I believe that I am one such candidate, and I believe that my unique background, academic and professional experiences, and personal drive define me as a candidate that will be a strong addition to The George Washington Law School.

My decision to apply to law schools followed a different route than most. After attending a wealthier high school that was racially and socially homogenous in the suburbs of Pittsburgh, Pennsylvania, I felt that I was missing out on the "real world." It was difficult for me to shake the feeling that I wasn't truly experiencing the diversity of the nation and the peoples and cultures within it. I decided to move to and attend school near Washington, DC, where I felt I could further my interest in different cultures as well as get hands on opportunities in government and politics and social issues, my major choices of study.

In hindsight, I believe that my decision to move to the area was the right one, and my undergraduate years were times of further discovery personally, academically, and professionally. Money was often a problem for my family, and while both of my divorced parents made every effort to help me financially, more often than not, it was up to me. I fully supported myself throughout my undergraduate years, primarily through the founding of my own Internet publishing business. While I was fortunate to have been able to work in such a flexible way, the work was not easy. There was a high level of complexity and volatility in the infant industry at the time. I was forced to learn the ever-changing laws and regulations "on the fly," and my dealings with contract, tax, copyright, and intellectual property law helped me to begin to realize the extraordinary value of a formal legal education.

The fact that I needed to support myself was never one that I took lightly. I am completely financially independent, and there were always tough decisions to be made, especially when others around me had no such restrictions. The income from the business fluctuated greatly, and I was constantly faced with tough questions. Can I afford to take the LSAT test-prep course? How much rent can I afford per month? How will this financial choice affect my future ability to pay for school? There were many difficult decisions to make, but living with such restrictions, financial and otherwise, allowed me to gain a personal discipline that served me well in other aspects of my life.

My strong preparation for a formal legal education is further demonstrated in my ideologically diversified work experience. I worked at one of the most liberal think tanks in America studying African American political issues, and I also worked in the Senate office of one of the most conservative Senators on the Hill, Pat Roberts of Kansas. I served as a "tester" for a major civil rights firm by entering places of business to compare how I was treated as a customer compared to how clients of the firm reported that they were treated. I have also published two articles regarding minority political participation, one of which was presented to the NAACP in Baltimore, Maryland. All of these experiences helped me to realize that taking an approach that respects and appreciates different points of view is imperative. This is a realization that I constantly keep in mind in my day-to-day dealings, and one that I feel will serve me well as I further my education.

While at George Washington University Law School, I plan to continue to follow my interests in public service and social issues. I am especially excited about the institution's Public Interest Law Scholars Program. I believe that applying the knowledge that an individual has attained in a leadership setting is one of the most gratifying and valuable acts in which one can partake. I have aspirations of becoming a public figure or elected official in the areas of civil rights and constitutional law, and I believe the well-rounded legal education that The George Washington University Law School would provide me would be integral in my efforts to achieve these goals.

Certainly, there are many motivated and qualified candidates applying to law schools this year. However, I believe that the most successful students will be those who have clearly considered their life path, have practical experience, and are focused on their future legal education. I believe that my unique personal experiences, diverse professional background, strong academic record, and many leadership roles will give me an edge in a challenging educational environment. For these reasons, I believe that I should be carefully considered for admission to The George Washington University Law School.

BRIAN FRYE

After graduating from the University of California—Berkeley with a major in film studies, Brian worked for several years as a journalist, film curator, and artist. He has written feature articles and reviews for magazines, including The New Republic, Film Comment, University Business, Civilization, *and* Independent Film *and* Video Monthly. *In addition to co-curating The Robert Beck Memorial Cinema (New York City's only weekly experimental film series) for four years, he has served as curator of film programs at institutions including the Museum of Modern Art, the Whitney Museum of American Art, Pacific Film Archive, PS1, and Anthology Film Archives. Brian was one of 140 artists featured in the 2002 Whitney Biennial, and his films are shown frequently by museums and festivals around the world.*

Stats
LSAT score: 174
Undergraduate GPA: 3.6
College attended: University of California—Berkeley
Year of college graduation: 1995
Hometown: San Francisco, CA
Gender: Male
Race: Caucasian

Admissions information
Law school attended: Georgetown University, Class of 2005
Accepted: Georgetown University, Boston College, Tulane University, University of Wisconsin—Madison, Washington and Lee University
Denied: Harvard University, University of California—Berkeley
Waitlisted: Columbia University, Cornell University, University of Virginia

Personal statement prompt

In Brian's words, his statement "was not written in response to any particular question."

Some time ago, I encountered a charming—though quite possibly apocryphal—anecdote concerning the lawyer and poet Wallace Stevens. Supposedly, Stevens composed his poems in the morning while walking to his office, where he dictated them to his secretary for transcription. As the law cleaves to the Socratic method, his poetry apparently found its nourishment in the Peripatetics.

In Stevens's seamless integration of art and the law, I found a poetically ironic model for myself. Though Stevens's vocation and his avocation were quite distinct, they nonetheless complemented one another, metaphorically and otherwise. For almost ten years, I have devoted myself to the study and practice of film as a fine art. I do not intend to abandon it. I can only hope to strike a balance between art and the law so effortless and natural.

Fortunately, there is every reason to believe it possible. The law has long maintained a closer affinity to the arts than many might admit. Oliver Wendell Holmes—possibly the greatest Chief Justice of the Supreme Court—was a friend of literature, and even wrote sonnets as a young soldier. When he took up the study of law, it was with some trepidation, tempered by a deep belief in the richness of its dusty verities. As he put it, "law is human - it is a part of man, and of one world with all the rest."

My longstanding interest in studying law crystallized while reading Holmes. I found myself both broadly in agreement with his description of the law, and deeply sympathetic to his conception of the proper role of its practitioners. Holmes held that a man's highest duty lay in the assiduous performance of his professional responsibilities, the perquisite to "strive for the superlative."

An oft-wounded veteran of the Civil War, Holmes knew of the passions excited by convictions strongly held, and mistrusted their claim to truth. He brought to the law a rare, pragmatic humility and deference to historical experience, an understanding that the soul of our Constitution rests in the ability of its core principles to respond to history of their own accord, with a minimum of coercion.

In his dissent to Abrams v. United States, Justice Holmes described our Constitution as, "an experiment, as all life is an experiment." Consequently, he advocated a broader, more permissive reading of the amendment than previously known, in the expectation that the freest market in ideas should likely furnish the soundest ones. Significantly, Holmes argued not for an abstract and immutable freedom to say whatever one likes, but rather a staying of the still-reserved power to suppress that proven seditious.

I believe that lawyers are something like the laboratory scientists of the public sphere. While legislators create the law, the legal system shapes and makes sense of it. Lawyers address themselves to the law as it stands, rather than asking how it might otherwise be. Just as one doesn't fashion grand new theories in the laboratory, one doesn't write law in the courtroom. It is in the crucible of the laboratory, however, that the failings of an apparently plausible theory become apparent. I want very much to become one of those experimenters in the courtroom.

Until recently, it had become merely fashionable to proclaim the novelty of today's world. Suddenly, that claim has acquired a gravity none expected, and we must shoulder grave responsibilities none imagined. I believe that the demands placed by both commerce and justice on the law will, of necessity, reflect our changed world. But the problems and questions posed will not be solved by fiat. Rather, it will be by that familiar, slow process of accretion and inflection that the law will find expression. I hope to do whatever I am able to assist that process.

Edmund Wilson wrote of Holmes's "conviction that the United States has a special meaning and mission to devote one's life to, which was a sufficient dedication for the highest gifts." I can only agree. And if the great experiment that is our Constitution sufficed for one so great as Holmes, it is all the more ample for those of more modest gifts, such as myself.

EMILY WOODWARD

Emily was an English major at the College of William and Mary, from which she graduated summa cum laude. During her junior and senior years, she worked as an off-site communications intern for NASA's Stennis Space Center. After graduation, she worked as an online reporter for Defense News and as a weekend producer for www.WashingtonPost.com. She continued her work at both positions while attending the evening program at Georgetown University Law Center.

Stats

LSAT score: 165
Undergraduate GPA: 3.86
College attended: College of William and Mary
Year of college graduation: 2000
Hometown: Alexandria, VA
Gender: Female
Race: Caucasian

Admissions information

Law school attended: Georgetown University, Class of 2006
Accepted: Georgetown University (evening program), Chicago-Kent College of Law, George Mason University
Denied: None
Waitlisted: None

Personal statement prompt

Emily notes that she wrote this statement of purpose as part of her application to Georgetown in response to the following prompt: "Last year [2002], Georgetown received over 11,000 applications for the 450 full-time and 125 part-time first-year places. Most of these applicants are capable of successfully completing a Georgetown legal education. Because we cannot accept all qualified applicants, we have found statements to be valuable in the selection process. You may write your personal statement on any subject of importance to you that you feel will assist us in our decision."

My desire to apply to law school is not rooted in a childhood fantasy of arguing a case before a packed courtroom. I have never seen myself as trial attorney ala Perry Mason or Nora Lewin on *Law & Order*. However, I have come to recognize a legal education would enable me to advance in my career as a writer and analyst specializing in national security and global trade issues.

I first set my sights on becoming a writer around the time I learned my letters. Of course, mastering the ABC's may have been a long way from winning the Pulitzer. This minor detail did not prevent me, however, from completing three "novels" and my own version of Genesis before the age of seven. Throughout elementary and junior high school, I annoyed my teachers by writing 10-page themes whenever they asked for a few sentences. Later, as a high school and college student, I continued writing, though my attention was increasingly turned toward other subjects.

While attending Thomas Jefferson High School for Science and Technology in Alexandria, Virginia, I immersed myself in biology, chemistry, and physics. Although I dreamed of being a professional author or journalist, I had grown convinced that I needed a science background to succeed in an increasingly high-tech world. This belief stayed with me after I headed south to Williamsburg, Virginia, to attend the College of William and Mary. Only after spending my freshman and sophomore years as Chemistry major—pouring over red-band spectral signatures and inhaling sulfurous concoctions in lab—did I finally accept the fact that I was no Marie Curie. Indeed, I realized I would have to spend all my waking hours just to make it as a mediocre chemist. Still, I wasn't comfortable switching to the Humanities (perhaps as a result of my laborious study of inertia in Physics 102). My wariness ebbed, however, in the wake of an even greater change in my college plans.

In the summer of 1998, I underwent surgery, which precluded my return to William and Mary in the Fall. Fortunately, I was able to take classes as an Extended Studies student at George Mason University, while wrapping up my period of convalescence at my home in Alexandria. The change of scenery inspired me to pursue new fields of study. I started taking courses in Shakespeare, modern American Drama, Public Policy and Middle Eastern History. At the same time, I continued studying chemistry and biology, though I no longer wished to concentrate in the hard sciences.

Ultimately, one of my George Mason professors directed me on a path that would combine my background in science and technology background with my love of writing and my new interests in government and policymaking. With her help, I secured an internship with an Annandale, Virginia-based government contractor. I spent the spring and summer of 1999 writing copy for Web sites the company managed for NASA and the Department of Energy, while taking additional classes at George Mason and George Washington University.

I returned to William in Mary in the autumn of 1999 and completed my degree in English. I then went back to work briefly as a copywriter for the Annandale contracting firm. In February 2000, I accepted a job as a researcher at *Defense News,* a publication in suburban Washington, DC, where I am now an assistant editor.

My current job entails researching and reporting on defense appropriations bills and export legislation, as well as writing daily summaries of major contracts awarded by the Department of Defense and other defense ministries worldwide. It is with enthusiasm, but some degree of trepidation, that I attempt to decode pages of legal jargon for an educated lay readership, many of which I suspect know more than I about such policies. Too often, I find I lack the legal knowledge to fully grasp bills that control how U.S. companies do business overseas, the limits to which federal agencies can go to collect covert intelligence, or the amount of funding an agency can receive in a given length of time.

On one hand, these limitations have done little to impair me in my current position, in which I am called to turn out several short stories each day on a variety of topics without going into significant detail. However, I would like to advance to more difficult reporting assignments one day. I fear I will be unable to do so without acquiring more expertise than I can obtain within the confines of my deadline-driven job. I also would like to It is a belief shared by several of my colleagues, as well as many of the senior writers and editors at my company who hold advanced degrees in law, business and related disciplines. I feel that a law degree would put me in a better position to join their ranks, particularly if I could attend school while continuing to work as a journalist.

Given my circumstances and interests, Georgetown University Law Center, with its top-ranked programs in intellectual property and international law, is my ideal choice. I have a colleague that is currently enrolled in the Georgetown evening law program. His generous feedback has helped convince me that this program also would fit my needs, in light of its flexible schedule and its emphasis on legal writing.

CAROLINE JEAN BREDESON

Caroline volunteered at Hennepin County Drug Court working with low-risk offenders, participated in mock trial throughout high school and freshman year of college, and worked at the Center for 4-H and Community Youth Development from sophomore to senior years of college.

Stats
LSAT score(s): 175
Undergraduate GPA: 3.69
College attended: University of Minnesota—Twin Cities
Year of college graduation: 2007
Hometown: West Des Moines, Iowa
Gender: Female
Race: Caucasian

Admissions information
Law school attended: Harvard College, Class of 2010
Accepted: University of Chicago, Columbia University, New York University, Boston University, Vanderbilt University, University of Minnesota, Northwestern College, Harvard College, University of Southern California
Denied: Stanford University
Waitlisted: University of Pennsylvania

Personal statement

I stepped through the metal detector and buttoned my sport coat, mentally preparing myself for the opening and closing statements. Holding the gold-plated railing as I walked up the three flights of marble stairs, I was impressed, as always, by the intensely detailed paintings on the ceiling of the court house. It was during the four years I spent representing juveniles in volunteer peer court that I learned my first lessons about the practical application of law and criminal justice, and during those four years this stately building became very familiar to me.

My experience in the courtroom began as part of a high school project in which students were expected to spend a semester exploring career options. I responded to a newspaper article advertising the need for youth to help represent their fellow peers in juvenile court. Soon after, I was accepted into the program, and with great enthusiasm, started attending Polk County Peer Court every Monday night.

I began volunteering by sitting on the jury with other students and listening to the defendants' stories as they were questioned by student "attorneys" and a real juvenile judge. All of the youth in peer court had pled guilty to lesser crimes such as shoplifting, possession of alcohol or drugs, or minor assault charges. As a part of the jury, I would help decide which sentence the teenager should receive. Our options for punishment included community service hours, writing letters of apology, anger management, curfew, avoiding certain people, and sitting on the jury to listen to future proceedings.

Soon after I began, I was given the opportunity to act as attorney to represent my peers. Before each trial, I eagerly awaited the packet of information about the defendant and would pore over it as soon as it came in the mail. I would arrive at the court house an hour before the trial to meet with the terrified defendant for the first time. I reviewed the process with the teenager and family members, and then informed the defendant what punishment I would suggest to the jury. I was amazed at the way parents would put complete trust in me and believed that the punishment suggested must be the most fair. Parents would come up to me months after their child's trial and tell me what a wonderful job I had done or congratulating me on helping to change their child's life. Though I was a volunteer, I understood how important my contributions were and what an impact I was having on a family.

Through my experience in peer court, I learned about the formalities of a trial and gained a sense of familiarity with the court room. Legal terms became part of my vocabulary, and I became more skilled at asking questions of the defendant in order to draw out specific answers. I learned which punishments to ask for in order to best fit the crime and help the individual truly learn from the situation. I discovered which tactics to use in order to persuade the jury to award the fairest punishment. I also became much better at communicating after years of standing in front of the watchful eyes of my peers and a judge to deliver opening and closing statements.

Most importantly, I learned about how the criminal justice field works and can influence people's lives. No book or lecture could explain the nervousness of a teenager about to appear before a jury of his peers. These were real crimes and real trials that I had to carefully prepare for in order to have a positive impact. Unlike my involvement with debate or mock trial, my performance in peer court directly affected another person's life.

The insights I gained from my volunteer experience with peer court directed my decision to pursue a career in law. Seeing how effective this program was made me realize how much I could positively influence others. I did not just learn about the law, I learned that I wanted to know more about the law. I knew I would enjoy taking law classes and becoming more involved with the court system during my help in defending juveniles through peer court. As a lawyer I will have the incredible gift of making a difference in people's lives and I hope to continue representing juveniles in order to create a positive change.

JAMIE ALAN AYCOCK

Jamie double-majored in government and economics at Cornell. As a Cornell Presidential Research Scholar, he conducted research with professors in the social sciences during all four years of college. His research culminated in an honors thesis, for which he received a departmental award; he graduated summa cum laude. He was President of the Cornell InterVarsity Christian Fellowship, Manager of the co-op in which he lived, and President of the Cornell Class of 2001 Alumni Officers. He also lived in the Spanish Language house during his freshman year.

Stats
LSAT score: 171
Undergraduate GPA: 3.79
College attended: Cornell University
Year of college graduation: 2001
Hometown: Fresno, CA
Gender: Male
Race: Caucasian

Admissions information
Law school attended: Harvard University, Class of 2005
Accepted: Harvard University, Columbia University, New York University, University of California—Berkeley, University of Chicago, Yale University
Denied: None
Waitlisted: Stanford University

Personal statement prompt

Jamie notes that all of the schools to which he applied "asked only for a generic personal statement."

For as long as I can remember, I have always taken for granted that my only real limits were self-imposed. I guess you could call me a sucker for the American dream. As I look back at my life, structural determinism just does not describe one of my stronger qualities.

My parents married young, had me soon after, and divorced only two years later. Before long, my father disappeared as his world came to revolve around drug addiction. At the same time, my mother became a welfare mom who spent her time partying, sleeping around, and dealing drugs on the side.

Then, about fifteen years ago, my mother's world and my world nearly fell apart. Although I had only finished first grade, I knew enough to know that the words of love my mom was trying to express to me were intended to be her last. Later that day, my grandmother helped me pack up my things and move them to my aunt's house where I lived for the next year without any contact with either of my parents. Fortunately, my mother's attempt to overdose on sleeping pills was unsuccessful, and eventually both of my parents overcame their addictions and began to live more normal lives. Although my parents have made great strides over the years, serious damage was done to my relationship with them, and the lasting psychological impact they had on me is probably greater than I realize.

With this kind of background, it may seem odd for me to believe so adamantly that the reins of life are in our own hands. It should be obvious to me that social and economic forces beyond an individual's control constrain both choices and opportunities. While this is an important point, it seems to me that circumstances can only confine those people who allow themselves to be trapped. By this, I don't mean to say that social programs should not offer a helping hand to the disadvantaged because they should. But especially in America, where numerous educational opportunities exist and hard work is generally rewarded, I believe personal initiative and persistence can overcome adverse circumstances.

Somehow it was infused in me as a child that I could do anything, that the sky was the limit. So I made up my mind that I was going to be different from my parents, that I was going to escape the life of drugs, crime, poverty, and welfare dependency. This has been one of the most significant driving forces in my life. Because I wanted so desperately to escape the kind of lifestyle I grew up with, I threw myself into what I saw as my clearest means to success: schoolwork. This started as far back as first grade. Whenever my mom was strung out on drugs or hung over from drinking, which was often, she just did not take me to school. On one of those days, I decided that school was too important to miss, and I was going despite what my mom said. I made the nearly four-mile trek by myself, even though I had never walked it before.

My point is not that I am an incredible person because I have somehow transcended family circumstances. What I am trying to say is that, despite their circumstances, people are not predestined to lives full of misery and failure. I only wish my words could convey how passionate I am about working to transform society's attitude from one of cynicism to one of hope.

Bottom line, what can I offer a law school? Though my life experience is not incredibly uncommon, the way it has shaped my perspective would allow me to be a distinctive voice in the crowd of an elite law school consisting mostly of upper-middle class, suburban prep school kids who have grown up in homogenous circumstances. Like the typical law student, I am persistent and driven, but what should stand out is my keen sense of hope. I endeavor to achieve, not out of a frenzied state of panic and competition, but because I see endless possibilities for my life and for the world around me.

MICHAEL GIORDANO

Michael majored in PPE (philosophy, politics, and economics) at Pomona College and served for four years on the college's Judiciary Council. He spent the fall of his junior year abroad at University College, Oxford. Pomona awarded him distinction on his senior thesis, a revised version of which was subsequently published in the UCLA Entertainment Law Review. *After graduating* cum laude, *Michael deferred his Harvard Law School admission for a year to work at the William Morris Agency—the world's oldest and largest talent and literary agency—for a vice president who also happened to be a lawyer.*

Stats
LSAT scores: 165, 166
Undergraduate GPA: 3.76
College attended: Pomona College
Year of college graduation: 2001
Hometown: Walnut Creek, CA
Gender: Male
Race: Caucasian (Italian American)

Admissions information
Law school attended: Harvard University, Class of 2005
Accepted: Harvard University, Duke University (with large scholarship), University of California—Los Angeles, University of Michigan
Denied: Stanford University, Yale University
Waitlisted: Columbia University, New York University, University of California—Berkeley, University of Chicago. (Michael withdrew his application from each of these schools before any of them provided him with a final admission decision.)

Personal statement prompt

Michael reports that he wrote this personal statement as part of his application to Harvard in response to the following prompt: "Applicants present themselves, their backgrounds, experiences, and ideas to the Admissions Committee in a personal statement. Because people and their experiences are diverse, you are the best person to determine the content of your own statement. It is for you to decide what information you would like to convey, and the best way for you to convey it. Whatever you write about, readers will be seeking to get a sense of you as a person and as a potential student and graduate of Harvard Law School. In this context, it is generally more helpful to write what you think readers should know to have a better sense of who you are rather than writing what you think the readers want to read.

> *"The personal statement can be an opportunity to illuminate your intellectual background and interests, or to provide information about yourself and your achievements that may not be fully evident through other information provided in the application. In many ways, you are preparing a case. As in most legal cases, it is important to be persuasive, clear, succinct, and timely. There are few substitutes for careful forethought and planning in this process.*

> *"We understand that it can be difficult to discuss oneself on paper, but our experience is that written statements are valuable in the selection process. Candid, forthright and thoughtful statements are always the most helpful."*

Ninety-nine-point-nine percent.

"That's what they told me," "Sebastian" mumbled, unsure of himself. A black man who looked too young to get into a bar and sounded too naive to try, Sebastian came off as simple and innocent. But this father of four was nowhere near as young as he appeared. And according to the police, he was nowhere near as innocent either.

Sebastian was charged with first-degree murder, and he faced the possibility of a life sentence with no parole. Though inadmissible in court, his polygraph results were disheartening. They indicated that the chances were 999 in 1000 that he had not told the whole truth. I began to wonder whether I had been misguided when I boarded a plane for Washington, DC—with no place to stay and not enough money to afford the few places I would find—hoping to pursue justice.

A few months earlier, in the wake of an inspiring social and political philosophy class that had challenged me to redefine and then defend my conception of justice, I found myself swamped with applications for summer internships. Hoping to challenge myself while exploring the relationship between justice and fairness, I submitted an application to the Criminal Law Internship Program at the Public Defender Service for the District of Columbia. I felt fortunate to be offered a position as an intern investigator and case assistant.

After two weeks of intensive training, I was assigned to Rudy *****, the PDS Training Director who handled only first-degree felonies. Rudy's cases became my life, Sebastian my primary concern. Most days I would arrive at Rudy's office before he did, a bit worn out by my long commute from an economically depressed Maryland suburb, but interested in reviewing what I had done the previous day. In the midst of investigating other cases, it took me a week to locate Sebastian and another few days to complete an interview with him. Unfortunately, the friends whose names Sebastian had given me refused to answer my questions because the police had told them not to communicate with me.

Frustrated by the way in which the police had apparently tried to obstruct justice, I visited the crime scene in an attempt to determine the accuracy of their incident report. I noticed immediately that the eyewitness' window, obscured by large trees, would not have allowed him to view the entire altercation. Furthermore, the great distance between the window and the crime scene, coupled with the broken streetlight nearby, implied that a positive facial identification in the middle of the night would have been virtually impossible. How could the police have missed this crucial information?

The police probably did not miss anything, as they sought only corroborating evidence. I realized at this point that the scales of justice weighed heavily against Sebastian even before his trial began. While the well-funded U.S. Attorney's Office had an entire police force working toward Sebastian's conviction, PDS could hardly pay its hardworking lawyers a living wage, let alone hire enough trained investigators to counterbalance the police. Despite this realization, I continued to investigate the case, hoping to bolster Rudy's arguments demonstrating Sebastian's innocence.

Before the court set a trial date, summer drew to a close. I was disappointed that I would not be able to testify on Sebastian's behalf. My work led me to conclude that, while Sebastian may not have been entirely guiltless, he definitely was not guilty of first-degree murder. The eyewitness had mistakenly identified Sebastian as the perpetrator.

Shortly after I had returned to California, I received a call from Rudy. "We won the case—Sebastian's free!" Justice had prevailed. Frankly, I was surprised, albeit pleasantly, to hear that a seemingly unfair justice system had produced a just outcome. Then it hit me. Working within a system that gave the prosecution a head start, Rudy came from behind to win freedom for Sebastian. Justice prevailed only because of Rudy's efforts to overcome the disadvantages with which the system had saddled Sebastian.

Rudy's handling of Sebastian's case taught me that the conception of justice I had come to defend in my philosophy class is attainable even when the system seems to favor the prosecution. But it requires that a dedicated and well-trained defense attorney make up the lost ground. Because I believe in defending my conception of justice beyond the confines of a classroom, I want to attend law school so that I may follow in Rudy's footsteps. I only hope that I will be able to make up as much ground for my clients as Rudy did for Sebastian.

The last time I communicated with Rudy, I explained that working with him had marked a turning point in my life. Armed with a clearer sense of my goals, I returned to my studies more motivated and interested than I had ever been, and I received the best grades of my life last fall at Oxford and last spring at Pomona. After hearing this, Rudy asked what the chances were that I would be attending law school.

"Honestly? About ninety-nine-point-nine percent."

NEIL HWANG

Neil graduated from Weber State University, where he majored in mathematics, quantitative economics, and political science. During his undergraduate career, he was involved in Model United Nations, Mock Trial, and student government. After graduation, he was deployed with the U.S. Army to Iraq, where he served for thirteen months. Since his return, he has been pursuing an MBA from M.I.T. and a joint MPP/JD from Harvard.

Stats
LSAT score: 174
Undergraduate GPA: 3.88
College attended: Weber State University, and one year at Harvard University
Year of college graduation: 2003
Graduate school attended: Massachusetts Institute of Technology Sloan School of Management and Harvard University Kennedy School of Government
Year of graduate school graduation: 2006 (for MBA)
Hometown: Los Angeles, CA
Gender: Male
Race: Asian

Personal statement prompt

Neil submitted this essay as part of his application to Columbia. He notes that he responded to the following prompt: "Candidates to Columbia Law School are required to submit a personal essay or statement supplementing required application materials. Such a statement may provide the Admissions Committee with information regarding such matters as: personal, family, or educational background; experience and talents of special interest; one's reasons for applying to law school as they may relate to personal goals and professional expectations; or any other factors that you think should inform the Committee's evaluation of your candidacy for admission."

My Recent Deployment to Iraq as an American Soldier

One observation about the world (and one that particularly stands out among many from my recent deployment to Iraq) that initially encouraged me to think about a career international law is the conspicuous disparity in living standards across national borders, and subsequently my hopes to do something about it. On several occasions during my 13-month deployment in Iraq, I traveled through various towns and cities, including downtown Baghdad, only to witness the worst possible depiction of living poverty in action. In towns, women were seen washing their children and clothes in a pond of stagnant water, the same water other townspeople were using for drinking and cooking, among other things. What concerned me the most about the observations was the fact that this abject poverty could very well exemplify living conditions in a plethora of other underdeveloped nations.

With this in mind, I wondered whether international policy organizations such as the Organization for Economic Cooperation and Development (OECD) and the UNDP were taking any actions (and if they were, what type of actions) to resolve such blatant human calamities. And it was this curiosity in inception and my growing interest in related law and policy issues that gradually solidified my resolve to pursue a career in international law and development policy.

Curious about the international policymakers' response to this seemingly pressing need for action, I began reading articles and published reports dealing with economic development and public finance issues of less-developed nations. One article that caught my attention was a publication of the OECD, entitled "Harmful Tax Practices: An Emerging Global Issue" (the "Report"). The Report identified as a problem the over-aggressiveness with which some less-developed countries, known as the "tax-haven countries", were implementing harmful tax policies involving such measures as unfairly low capital-gains taxes and high level of bank secrecy afforded to foreign investors, which were geared toward attracting the largest possible foreign investment in order to stimulate economic growth. This was noted in the Report as a profound problem due to the fact that it directly led to the considerable erosion of tax base in other countries, especially other underdeveloped nations. In proposing a solution, the OECD recommended the tax-haven countries to: increase the transparency of activities of their financial institutions; require foreign firms to show proof of ongoing substantial business activities within the tax-haven jurisdictions; and allow the access to relevant financial data to taxation authorities of investors' home countries upon request.

What was amazing appeared in the follow-up report in 2000 labeled, "Towards Global Tax Cooperation." It showed that the recommendations put out by the OECD were taken by a number of the "tax haven" countries, and that as a direct result of the implementation of OECD policy recommendations, the fiscal dilemma of revenue erosion in the affected economies significantly improved as the tax erosion slowed and the all-important tax revenue in low-income countries began rising.

Reading the aforementioned OECD reports, among a number of other publications and articles on global public policy, facilitated my acceptance of the fact that problems of a global scale can be approached and resolved in the international policy arena. The 1998 OECD article on harmful tax practices and its follow-up report in 2000 showed just that. A number of other policy publications I have encountered to date attested to numerous success cases. Although the issue of poverty in many nations obviously stays unresolved, being aware of policy successes with other pressing issues and seeing that there remains much work to be done in public policy (income disparity and poverty) collectively serve as a significant encouragement and motivation for me to get involved with public policy with high hopes and unwavering idealism.

In addition to witnessing first-hand the human calamities due to regional poverty and reading about efforts of our international community in tackling such problems and subsequent successes in many cases, exposure to public policy and international relations in my undergraduate studies has also been a strong influence on my decision to pursue joint studies in law and public policy. As an undergraduate, I studied economics, political science, and mathematics as academic majors. Among the many courses I had taken, I especially enjoyed those dealing with international law and development policy.

I combined the theoretical training with studies in mathematics in a hope to develop a quantitative aptitude necessary to analyze policy issues in international law and legal development framework. During my senior year, I conducted a number of independent empirical and technical research projects combining what I learned in each of my major disciplines to critically assess a variety of global legal and policy issues and propose workable solutions. What I have realized through my cross-disciplinary studies is that I undoubtedly enjoy applying principles from social and natural sciences to the real-world problems. Rather than pursuing an advanced study in pure and abstract theories in a given field, I derive substantially more fulfillment and satisfaction formulating pragmatic policies and seeing them being implemented in response to real legal and policy issues.

My career ambition in law and public policy involves working with the international policy organizations, such as the International Labor Organization, the World Bank, the UNDP, and the OECD to help set the agenda for legal and social development of underdeveloped nations and contribute to crafting effective development policy solutions. It is my sincere desire to embark on the law school part of my graduate MPP/JD joint-degree educational career at Columbia, the place where I will be able to gain a thorough understanding of legal principles and develop a critical mindset to deal with a variety of practical issues that arise in international law and development.

Columbia Law School clearly presents itself as the most ideal place for me to study law and public policy owing to its unrivaled academic reputation and that of the university community, ideal geographical location in which to observe and even participate in high-impact legal policymaking, and the unique curriculum philosophy that allows for a flexible approach to pursuing a joint degree with public policy at the Kennedy School at Harvard. The legal education at Columbia would undoubtedly further my professional growth in becoming a competent lawyer and a policymaker.

DAVID KING KESSLER

David graduated summa cum laude *from Harvard and was a member of Phi Beta Kappa. He was also President of the International Relations Council (which had 300-plus members and a $350,000 budget), Cambridge Office Director for the Small Claims Advisory Service, President of the Harvard College Economist, and a recipient of the Detur Book Prize (awarded to the top 10 percent of the freshman class). He deferred enrollment to Harvard Law School for two years to work for McKinsey & Company.*

Stats

LSAT score: 173
Undergradate GPA: 3.89
College attended: Harvard University
Year of college graduation: 2004
Hometown: Douglaston, NY
Gender: Male
Race: Caucasian

Admissions information

Law school attended: Harvard University, Class of 2009
Accepted: Harvard University, Columbia University, New York University, Yale University
Denied: None
Waitlisted: None

Personal statement prompt

David submitted this essay as part of his application to Yale. The prompt requested "an essay of not more than 250 words about a subject of [the applicant's] choice." The prompt also included the following guidelines: "Faculty readers look to the required short essay . . . to evaluate an applicant's writing, thinking, and editing skills, as well as to learn more about the applicant's intellectual concerns or passions, sense of humor, and ability to think across disciplines. The subject is not limited; the choice of topic itself may be informative to the readers."

"Taught self to cook" doesn't show up anywhere on my resume, but it's still an accomplishment of which I'm proud. Through patience and practice, I turned an addiction to the Food Network into a broad repertoire of dishes, ranging from simple Tuscan bruschetta to a complex, multi-day chicken tikka masala that required nine different spices, some of which I'd never seen before (fenugrek, anyone?). While good cooking certainly leads to delicious food, I have found the process even more interesting than the product: the act of cooking appeals to both the scientist and artist in me. As a cook, I am scientist, carefully chopping vegetables into identical cubes for a *mis-en-place* (a term for the array of ingredients prepared prior to cooking), heating and mixing at just the right temperatures, and even using literal chemical reactions to caramelize onions and reduce sauces. As a cook I'm also an artist, tinkering with flavoring and texture, garnish and presentation; there are no rules or rote technique, only sense and feel. So much chopped parsley, dashingly applied to the rim of a plate, can make all the difference. I also believe that there are parallels between cooking and law that reach beyond expense-account lunches. A lawyer must methodically and exhaustively gather a *mis-en-place* of facts, evidence, and precedent, and then combine them into a palatable, compelling, and creative argument, just as a chef prepares his dishes. At law school, I hope cooking will continue to be a relaxing hobby, allowing me to study tortes after a day of studying torts.

RYAN SPEAR

Ryan majored in literature at the University of Washington. As an undergraduate, Ryan served as a research assistant, tutor, and mentor. He later edited a literary journal and a newspaper for immigrants, refugees, and low-income individuals. He also holds a master's degree in literature from Portland State University.

Stats
LSAT score: 170
Undergraduate GPA: 3.85
College attended: University of Washington
Year of college graduation: 1997
Graduate school GPA: 4.0
Graduate school attended: Portland State University
Year of graduate school graduation: 2000 (MA)
Hometown: Vancouver, WA
Gender: Male
Race: Caucasian
Admissions information
Law school attended: Harvard University, Class of 2006
Accepted: Harvard University, Stanford University
Denied: None
Waitlisted: None

Personal statement prompt

Ryan notes that he submitted this personal statement to both Harvard and Stanford, whose prompts were as follows:

Harvard: "Please present yourself, your background and experiences, and your ideas as you wish in a brief personal statement.

"To provide a context for writing your statement, we offer the following observations. The personal statement can be an opportunity to illuminate your intellectual background and interests. You

might do this by writing about a course, academic project, book, artistic or cultural experience that has been important to you. The personal statement can also be an opportunity to clarify or elaborate on other information that you have provided in the application and to provide information about yourself and your achievements that may not be evident to the readers of your application. Because people and their experiences are diverse, you are the best person to determine the content of your own statement. It is for you to decide what information you would like to convey and the best way for you to convey it. Whatever you write about, readers of your statement will be seeking to get a sense of you as a person and as a potential student and graduate of Harvard Law School."

Stanford: "Enclose a statement of about two pages describing important or unusual aspects of yourself not otherwise apparent in your application.

"While admission to Stanford Law School is based primarily upon superior academic achievement and potential to contribute to the legal profession, the Admissions Committee also regards the diversity of an entering class as important to the school's educational mission. If you would like the committee to consider how factors such as your background, life and work experiences, advanced studies, extracurricular or community activities, culture, class, race, or ethnicity would contribute to the diversity of the entering class and hence to your classmates' law school experience, please describe these factors and their relevance."

My first rushes of intellectual excitement were not literary or scientific; they were inspired by principles and procedure. I distinctly remember my mind awakening to itself on two occasions: while writing bills at Boys State and, later, while drafting examinations for our high school mock trial team. Neither of these experiences were revelatory. I was not, that young, inflamed with the idea that law school was my One True Destiny. But immature as I was, I could already sense that there was something recognizably right about this type of work.

No surprise, then, that as an undergraduate I spent much of my time at the intersection of people and rules. As a resident adviser, orientation coordinator and instructor,

I found that I was good at helping people relate to and navigate institutions. In my academic life, meanwhile, I was discovering a love of variety. I found that the sharper my facility with words and ideas became, the more sophisticatedly I could think about arguments occurring in other fields: ecology, physiology, physics. By the time I left the University of Washington, I understood that I was at my best and happiest wrestling with problems (environmental law, for example, or educational policy) that required a multi-disciplinary perspective and diplomatic bent.

Looking to mobilize that insight against more life-and-death sorts of problems, I gave a year of service to AmeriCorps. As a volunteer coordinator, I gained valuable experience in negotiation and community building. Perhaps more valuably, I ran up against many of the sobering realities of professional activism—partisanship, bureaucracy, the limits of my own patience—before I was able to over-romanticize that role.

Graduate school confirmed that purely aesthetic work couldn't satisfy me. I loved editing the *Portland Review*, but I did not love the feeling of irrelevance that often crept in while editing copy or selling a revision. Meanwhile, in the classroom, I was becoming a far more able critic of bad thinking. A voice at my shoulder (Stanley Fish, I now think) encouraged me to connect that ability to more practical issues.

Thus my editorship of *The Voice*, King County's newspaper for immigrants, refugees and low-income people. At *The Voice*, I've been able to disentangle the intricacies of HOPE VI redevelopment, publicize the human costs of welfare reform and ferret out anti-Muslim backlash after Sept11. This is a great job: fascinating and instructive. But it is also fundamentally observational and eccentric, and if I've learned anything about my mind, it is its preference for direct contact. I just wasn't meant to be a reporter, quite frankly.

So why sprint through all this? My story lacks an essay-ready burning bush moment, and its (admittedly inelegant) variety resists sweeping themes. But my intellectual and professional progress is relevant because it has been an education in the root sense of the word: a wide-ranging "leading out" from vague yearnings for an intellectually challenging, problem-oriented career to a mature understanding of why I want to attend law school. This is not to over-idealize the profession or my decision; I don't expect the law to harmonize the legislator, the academic, the activist and the editor in me. After all, to harmonize those impulses might be to neutralize them, and I intend to deploy them all at [school].

No, I'm not excited about a legal education because it promises some sort of intellectual nirvana, but because all my research suggests it demands and rewards much of what I've gained over the years: intellectual rigor, imagination and a love of learning (to name a few). More importantly, I believe a legal career will allow me to apply what I've learned—powerfully and directly—to a vast constellation of current and still unimaginable problems. Simply put, in [school] I see an education that marries my need to think with my need to do; a career that satisfies my desire to get at the guts of complicated problems; not an apocalyptic fulfillment of but the next chapter in my search for the best, most meaningful work.

SHANE SHELLEY

Shane received both his BA and MA from Stanford University, in English literature and sociology, respectively. He has traveled throughout Europe, and he spent a single academic term at Oxford University. During college, Shane supported himself with various jobs, including waiting tables, working in publishing, and conducting sociological research. During law school, he tutored and taught part-time.

Stats
LSAT score: 175
Undergraduate GPA: 3.72
College attended: Stanford University
Year of college graduation: 2001
Graduate school attended: Stanford University
Hometown: San Diego, CA
Gender: Male
Race: Caucasian
Admissions information
Law school attended: Harvard University, Class of 2005
Accepted: Harvard University, Columbia University, Duke University, Georgetown University, New York University, University of California—Berkeley, University of Michigan, University of San Diego, University of Virginia
Denied: Stanford University, Yale University
Waitlisted: None

Personal statement prompt

In Shane's words, "The question that prompted my statement, namely the one from Harvard, generally just asked for a couple-page statement about anything you would like to discuss."

In personal statements, we often struggle to convey exalted intentions, as though that could reveal our virtuous nature, or any nature really, in these several pages. A German philosopher wrote that because we have only one life, we can never know whether we have made the best decisions on our path. No one can honestly say what he should or should not do, nor what he should or should not have done; he can only say, and even then with little assurance, what he will or will not do. With this knowledge, according to the philosopher, I could not, in good faith, express an intention in this statement, having no knowledge of the outcome of any decision. This past summer I composed the following passage, based on an earlier experience in the Moroccan wilderness. Reading over the passage, I have found the excerpt aptly applies to a discussion of intention within this context:

"He kneeled at the side of the river and stared at his reflection; a bearded man stared back. As he dipped his hands into the brown waters his arms disappeared beneath the surface. He shook his arms in the water, cleaning them, and then gathered some in his hands and splashed his face. He looked again and now the reflection rippled, fragmented by the movement of the brown water. He could not see into the depths of the river and only saw the strange and fragmented face of the bearded man; he wondered if he knew himself at all.

The face of a large steer appeared before him in the reflection. The steer shook its head in the heat and he could feel its breath on his back. The steer seemed alone. He turned around and saw a small boy at the side of the steer hauling a cart of potatoes. The small boy led the steer to the riverside with a long reed switch. The sun was behind them, above the canyon edge and the waterfall, and cast the boy and steer in dark shadows; he could not see the face of the small boy, but he heard his shouted commands in the Berber language."

The assumption of intention presupposes that in some dark corner of our souls a causal force, free from the determinism of an indifferent world, forms the ground of an intentional act. Such a force runs as a dense and clouded river through the heart, much as the river described above. The river reflects everything of my being—appearance, demeanor, ideology, decisions made—and yet, when I plunge my arms into its murky depths, even they disappear in the obscurity. The river of an intentional soul remains concealed from its very possessor.

The waters of the river, however, are seasonal, and become clear in the fall. With winter comes death; I must wait, then, until the eve of my demise for the illumination of that dark corner. But out of desperate impatience I thrash with my arms the murky waters, shaking them into a momentary clarity. Cupping the clear waters on the surface into my hands, I raise the lucid pool from the brown river. The actual intention, the outward manifestation of a conscious decision, forms in the moment before the moment, the reflection disturbed to reveal another much the same but later in the day and changed, and a man forges himself and his intentions anew, thrashing almost indiscriminately, as best he can. Perhaps he has taken the proper course; perhaps no proper course exists; nevertheless he must try and disturb the waters, in an attempt to clear them for a moment and create new courses and new reasons for his being.

The short passage, written some time ago without any specific purpose, a naked and unsettled metaphor, becomes relevant through interpretation, an intention and meaning distilled from the murky waters of an obscure art and an opaque soul. This personal statement and the passage come to reflect the formless deluge of an intentional heart taking shape as outward intentions under the damming and distillation of my mind and its decisions. The thrashing about of an arm in the murky water becomes the decision to attend law school; and with the thrashing comes a new clarity in the river.

The study of law, from a humanist perspective taking law as a reflection of social development, could be viewed as the study of a gradual, groping realization of human potential, a potential inherent in every individual. Man realizes his human nature through an application of this vague potential—rather than a revelation of something already there—toward the creation of a human, social world, in this case a world founded on the formation of law. The philosopher may dismiss the presentation of intention as an impossible fiction, and at some level I might agree. But to the extent that something such as law creates a human truth for the world and our nature, I would like to do the same with myself, and create a personal truth through action and forged intentions, such as the action and intention of attending law school. That small boy was so young he could hardly understand why he drove the cart to and from the river, and yet he commanded a much larger steer with his reed switch. In my most honest moments, I see myself as that boy, trying, with everything he can stubbornly muster, to move a great world he only understands as important, wonderful, and somehow meaningful.

MEGAN WANG

Megan graduated from UCLA with a major in psychology and communication studies. She plays the piano and the flute, has published poems (while attending UCLA), and is an avid Beatles and Mozart fan.

Stats

LSAT score: 176
Undergraduate GPA: 3.9
College attended: University of California—Los Angeles
Year of college graduation: 2002
Hometown: Los Angeles, CA
Gender: Female
Race: Chinese

Admissions information

Law school attended: Harvard University, Class of 2006
Accepted: Harvard University, Columbia University, Cornell University, Georgetown University, New York University, Northwestern University, University of California—Berkeley, University of California—Hastings, University of California—Los Angeles, University of Pennsylvania, University of Southern California, University of Virginia
Denied: Stanford University, Yale University
Waitlisted: None

Personal statement prompt

Megan writes that the Harvard admissions committee advised the follow-
ing: "You may write a personal statement on any subject of importance to
you that you feel will assist in the admission decision."

I grew up smelling books.

My childhood room in China was also the family library, where I literally breathed books everyday for the first twelve years of my life.

Lacking an enticing toy collection, I spent most of my childhood thumbing through that collection of ancient epics, classic sonnets, philosophical treatises and historical chronicles. I discovered my favorite book when I was nine—*Dream of the Red Chamber*, a 120-chapter 18th-Century epic. Unable to put it down for two months, I even enacted some scenes with my Barbie dolls. It is still my most beloved book, one I read at least twice every year. Those dusty old books captivated me because I could become anyone—a princess, a hero, a narrator—with the turn of a page. No toy or cartoon could match that magic. Thus began my lifelong love affair with the written word and my ongoing quest for intellectual challenges.

My elementary school classroom, like the family library, witnessed many of my personal historic moments: my first taste of lipstick, first comic book, first public, first "F", first meeting with foreigners. Unlike these treasured memories, my elementary school education was rather bittersweet. With unrelenting teachers force-feeding me high school vocabularies and formulas as early as the fourth grade, learning became oppressive and dull. On the other hand, the demanding workload and the teachers' emphasis on self-discipline made me a focused listener, diligent learner, and quiet thinker. So while the test-oriented, grade-fixated Chinese education system stifled my early intellectual curiosity, it helped me develop study skills that have proved to be invaluable. From note-taking to time management, most of my study habits and work ethics were formed in those six early years. They are still with me today.

I immigrated to America when I was twelve, at the precarious dawn of adolescence, with a self-identity greener than the spring grass. My first day at school was a nightmare. I was lost and late, mute and deaf in the face of English, and stunned by the touchable presence of non-Chinese human beings. A Martian landing unexpectedly on earth, I faced both lifestyle maladjustment and an identity crisis. Here I was expected to talk and participate in classes, an act entirely foreign to someone educated to listen only. Group projects, class participation, individual presentations, these conventional exercises seemed like unconquerable challenges to me. A faltering novice in English, I felt inferior to my energetic and outspoken American classmates. I became a timid speaker, even when English was no longer a barrier. Unable to fully participate in and outside of school, I was an outsider lodging in America.

Determined to cure my fear of public speaking, I took an acting class the summer before college. Like Paul McCartney sings in "I Saw Her Standing There," "my heart went boom, when I crossed the room" filled with twenty strangers. I had to repress my impulse to flee when Charlie (my teacher) gave the first assignment – self-introduction. Had I not swallowed my fears and stayed that day, I would not be who I am now. While standing on that little stage, reciting lines and improvising characters, a voice stirred in me. Until that moment I had not realized that I could be so spontaneous, expressive, and vocal. I never knew I could articulate my thoughts with the same candor and ease as my American classmates did. It was no easy sailing after that first day, but my anxiety was eclipsed by the thrill of rising to the challenge I had set for myself. By the end of the course, public speaking and group participation were no longer my darkest fears. The only trait I retain from my silent days is a tendency to blush when I speak.

Now, I had two personas: one a circumspect Chinese, the other an opinionated American. Though others with similar background often choose one or the other, I wanted to keep both. Since parting with either persona would make me incomplete, I decided to fuse the reserved thinker and the assertive speaker into one—me. UCLA turned out to be an ideal environment for this task. The Chinese me found an academic curriculum that not only stimulated my intellectual appetite, but also fine-tuned my study skills. The American me discovered a social environment (especially in my counseling work) that further cultivated my communication abilities, both oral and written. No longer a Chinese lodging in America, I became a Chinese living in America.

I am an amphibian, born in the East but now living in the West. Finding a niche in this cultural intersection has not been easy; creating an identity that embraces both worlds is even harder. After two decades of observation, adaptation and introspection, I now enjoy the sweet reward of my efforts. Reading Chinese epics, writing English poems, making dumplings by hand, grilling hotdogs in the backyard, I feel privileged to be able to cross the cultural boundaries and explore the two worlds to my heart's content.

ANONYMOUS

*Anonymous double-majored in math and psychology at
Wellesley. She was deeply involved in college government,
especially during her junior year, when she managed the student
activity fees and oversaw the funding and accounts of all student
organizations on campus. She was a member of several significant committees on campus, including the cabinet of college
government and the budget advisory committee of the college;
and she supervised the work of three student employees. She
also had a show on the campus radio station and worked with a
group whose mission was to free the campus bookstore of sweat-
shop-produced goods. She spent two summers interning in the
marketing department of a large Boston law firm and worked as
a teaching assistant, grader, and tutor in the math department at
Wellesley during the fall of her senior year.*

Stats
LSAT score: 167
Undergraduate GPA: 3.85
College attended: Wellesley College
Year of college graduation: 2002
Hometown: Whitman, MA
Gender: Female
Race: Caucasian

Admissions information
Law school attended: Harvard University, Class of 2005
Accepted: Harvard University, Boston College, Boston University, Cornell University, Georgetown University, New York University
Denied: None
Waitlisted: None
Other: Columbia University (placed on reserve; Anonymous withdrew her application)

Personal statement prompt

Anonymous reports that she did not write her personal statement in response to a particular question.

It's two in the morning, and I'm taking a break from working on my Analysis problem set. Theorems have been swimming around my head, bumping into each other, and sometimes (thankfully) connecting, for the past four hours. Although I have a hard time admitting it to myself (can I really be that much of a math dork?), I'm in my element. It's times like this that make me feel like I have some sort of deeper understanding of the world around me. Like the blue print of existence, math is everywhere, and it is consistent. Propositions, functions, dimensions and limits —all of math, really—fit together like the most elegantly constructed puzzle imaginable. When you're in the middle of it, it's almost intoxicating in it's beauty.

Logic is the glue that holds the pieces of the mathematical puzzle together, and it is the reason that the puzzle pieces fit together so well. Similarly, logic is at the heart of legal reasoning. But the law has something more to it than that—the law is fundamentally human. While math exists outside the realm of the mind, law comes from the heart of the human soul. It is the set of rules that we, as a species, have created so that we can maximize our interactions with one another and improve our experiences on this earth. Consequently, I view the law as the common ground of math and psychology, and although I may get strange looks when I tell people that I'm a math and psych double major headed to law school, it all makes perfect sense to me.

The relationship between math, psychology, and law isn't the only reason I want to make my life in the law. Ideally, law improves the lives of those it encompasses, and it is noble in that respect. Maybe it's youthful optimism, but I'd like to think that when I die, the world will be a better place for having had me in it. In high school, I volunteered for a non-profit organization that focused on educating and supporting teenaged mothers. I've always remembered the night that I overheard Jill, one of the mothers whom I'd gotten to know quite well, crying on the phone to her daughter's father. Their baby was sick with a bad cold, and Jill didn't have enough money to buy her medicine, I was struck by how unfair it was that although Jill and I were the same age, and lived within a few miles of each other, our lives were worlds apart. I knew then that I couldn't single-handedly tackle all of the inequalities in American society, but that night I promised myself that whatever career I chose, I would work to level the playing field as much as I could.

Evil lawyer jokes aside, the law is perhaps the most powerful mechanism for both large and small-scale social improvements, and that is the real reason why I have chosen to enter the field. As much as I love math, I know that contemplating the magic of Fourier series isn't going to make the world a better place. You can't feed a hungry child with ternary expansion, or provide housing to low-income elderly with Lebesgue integration. Psychology does have the potential to improve human life, but it lacks the logical foundation shared by math and law. Thus while math and psychology aren't without merit, I don't want to spend my life with either subject.

I'm not sure where I'll be in ten years. I've already spent two summers working for a large, corporate law firm. The experience was valuable because it taught me a lot about the law in general, but I know that sort of practice isn't for me. Maybe I'll work for a non-profit like the one I used to volunteer for. Maybe I'll be involved in government, helping to make public policy decisions. Maybe I'll be on my way to becoming a judge on the Federal circuit. The possibilities are endless, and I don't really have a master plan. I do know, though, that law is a natural choice for me. Whatever I do with it, because of the promise I made to myself years ago, I'll fall asleep each night knowing that someone out there is better off because of the work I did that day.

ANONYMOUS

Anonymous graduated magna cum laude *from the University of Notre Dame with a major in government and a minor in international peace studies. She was the recipient of a Lilly Foundation Community Scholarship, a four-year, full-tuition award. Anonymous was on the Dean's List for eight semesters and is a four-time University Scholar. She was inducted into Pi Sigma Alpha, a government honor society, and interned for Phil Hope, MP in the British House of Commons, in 2000. Anonymous is a 2001 Truman Scholar for the state of Indiana. She worked for five summers at the Allen County Public Defender's Office as an investigator and court liaison.*

Stats
LSAT score: Did not report
Undergraduate GPA: 3.75
College attended: University of Notre Dame
Year of college graduation: 2002
Hometown: Fort Wayne, IN
Gender: Female
Race: Anonymous wished not to disclose her race.

Admissions information
Law school attended: Harvard University, Class of 2005
Accepted: Harvard University, Chicago-Kent Law School, College of William and Mary, Indiana University, Loyola University of Chicago, Northwestern University, University of Pennsylvania
Denied: Yale University
Waitlisted: University of Virginia

Personal statement prompt

Anonymous reports that she did not write her personal statement in response to a particular prompt.

I prefer the blues to Pavarotti. I'd take Shakespeare over Dickens any day. I hate red nail polish and I love to vacuum. I've played the clarinet for 15 years. I've played the saxophone for 10. I watch cartoons on Saturday mornings. *The Catcher in the Rye* is my favorite novel. I seem to have a propensity for the challenging. And I like it.

***

My mom and I lived in a rented house on the South side of town. I was often left alone in the early years of my life—left to cook for myself, to watch late night t.v. and left to answer the door when strange people knocked just after midnight. My maternal grandparents did what they could and picked me up once a week to give me a bath, often my only for the week, and to take me out to dinner. Other times, they sent over plates of food and packets of vitamins for me. My mom ate the food and tried to sell the vitamins for drugs.

Meanwhile, as I waited for my grandparents to pick me up on our front porch, I was so hungry I ate the peeling paint.

I saw my first gun Christmas Eve, 1989. Mom was afraid Big Bird was chasing her. When this happened, my grandparents looked at each other with worried eyes and said the drugs were talking again.

I don't remember what I got for Christmas that year.

My grandparents have had custody of me since I was 4 and they legally adopted me when I was 11, just after my mother's suicide. For the past 18 years, my grandparents have raised me, and run their household, on social security. But they never let me think of myself as poor or underprivileged—as a result I capitalized on the opportunities made available to me. Now that I am a university student, my grandparents have cashed in their retirement savings to continue to raise and have given their livelihood to shape mine.

I spent the last summer trying to preserve my grandmother's.

Every day this past summer I had a standing date at seven in the morning and night with my grandma to help her take her pills because she couldn't remember how. In the mornings before work I would spend an additional 20 minutes practicing picking up the phone with her and reminding her how to speak into it so she could talk to me when I called.

By mid-September that morning and evening date had turned into a date at the nursing home every weekend.

Instead of learning how the phone worked, she had me feel her face to make sure it was still there.

Thanksgiving day 2001 started out like any other and after dinner at a neighbor's house my grandfather and I went to visit grandma. I remember that her eyes were bluer than I'd ever seen and her breath like that of a fish out of water. And for the next 45 minutes my grandmother communicated to me through her eyes what her mouth could not—how our souls were connected and how she'd loved me before I was born.

At that Thanksgiving day, with her lungs full of water and her heart too tired to beat, my grandma passed from this world to the next.

***

I spend 10 minutes a day making my bed. I love horror movies and am in a continual quest to find the scariest movie. I enjoy reading Habermasian discourse of communicative action. I always, without fail, microwave my lunch too long. I listened to my first Ella Fitzgerald CD a week before she died. I haven't stopped listening since. I like delis. I appreciate my professors.

***

It's dominated my life for the past four and a half years. Because of it, my collection of suits has exponentially increased. It inexplicably pops up in a majority of my conversations.

My work at the Public Defender's Office has seen me do everything from prepare for daily arraignments, spend afternoons in the county jail advising our clients, liaison with various local, state and national agencies, interview witnesses for murder cases and substantiate defense alibis for use at trial. As an investigator and court liaison for the PD's office since I was 18, I have been able to interact with a colorful cross-section of the Ft. Wayne community—interactions that have helped me realize that there is more to our clients than just their reason for being incarcerated. After four summers, I can say with pride that I spent my summers "in and out of jail". And, four summers later, I'm addressed as 'public-defender girl' or 'Miss ——' and stopped by former clients on the street so they can tell me how their probation is going or how their son started in his first Little League game the afternoon before. Through the Public Defender's office, I've found something I know I will be quite comfortable doing for the rest of my life.

At 22 now, I've come into my own...as a student of Notre Dame, of political theory, as a student of society and, as a Truman scholar, I've been given license and affirmation to do what I love best and become a public defender myself. That's why, instead of fleeing to an ivory tower, I am choosing to work in what some may call the trenches.

To me, it rings of a somewhat comfortable familiarity—I am but little removed from those I wish to help.

ONIKA WILLIAMS

After graduating as salutatorian of her high school class, Onika attended Florida International University (FIU) on a full academic scholarship. At FIU, she was a student in the Honors College and the International Business Honors Program. A member of Delta Sigma Theta Sorority, Inc., Onika was also admitted to several honor societies including the Golden Key International Honour Society, Order of Omega, the National Residential Hall Honorary, and the National Society of Collegiate Scholars. In 2005, she participated in an Alternative Spring Break in Bangkok, Thailand, where she volunteered at a shelter for battered, HIV-infected women. She received the Sorority Woman of the Year Award in 2003 and the FIU Honors College Award in 2005. For all four years of her college experiences, Onika was a member of Peer Educators Advocating Cultural Enrichment (P.E.A.C.E.), a volunteer group that conducts workshops on sensitive topics such as race and gender issues. After graduation, Onika interned with the Congressional Research Service at the Library of Congress and worked as an Assistant Language Teacher in the Japan Exchange and Teaching (JET) Programme.

Stats
LSAT score: 150
Undergraduate GPA: 3.59
College attended: Florida International University
Year of college graduation: 2005
Hometown: Homestead, FL
Gender: Female
Race: African-American
Admissions information
Law school attended: Indiana University—Bloomington, Class of 2010
Accepted: Wake Forest University, University of Florida, University of Houston, University of Pittsburgh
Denied: University of Michigan, Yale University, University of Texas
Waitlisted: University of North Carolina

Personal Statement Prompt

Onika submitted a version of this essay with all of her applications in response to an open-ended essay prompt.

"Onika-Sensei, how many headzu do you habu inside you?!"

The excited first-year, Japanese high school student allowed these words to roll off her lips and into my ears. My mind drew a blank. I nervously whispered to the teacher, "I don't know how to answer this question…" Ando-Sensei, the primary teacher for the English course, informatively whispered back, "Japanese women believe that a woman is perfectly proportionate if she is eight times the height of her head." Taking control of my confusion, it was Ando-Sensei's turn to be nervous. "May I measure you?" He asked. I hesitantly responded, "Sure..." The male teacher proceeded to use a piece of paper that was about the size of my head and counted along my body. Uncontrollable giggles filled the room and perspiration began to ease its way down his face. After the measurements had been taken, Ando-Sensei stood up and announced, "You are about 7 and 1/2 heads." The students were in awe. As I continued to answer their challenging questions, I realized that I had officially achieved one of my life dreams: living in Japan.

Coming to Japan has been a self-defining journey for me and the most rewarding experience of my life. Being the only African-American Japan Exchange and Teaching Programme participant living in Tottori City, the capital of Japan's least populated prefecture, I have experienced a cultural awakening. After receiving countless stares that vary from amazement to disgust and being pointed at by children and adults alike, I am interested in knowing more about the differences among cultures. Being a walking anomaly in Japan has awakened my interest in comparative international law. What fascinates me most about this type of law is how a country's legal foundation seems to be influenced by the culture of that country. By comparatively learning about other legal systems, we can further our understanding of how our own legal system operates. I believe it is important to understand how our laws will work in today's age of globalization. By comparatively studying about our legal system, we can learn how to competitively perfect our existing laws. Participation in Indiana University—Bloomington's study abroad programs would allow me to find ways to improve our legal system by evaluating it through the eyes of other cultures. I am especially interested in participating in Indiana's semester long exchange program with the University of Hong Kong.

My time abroad has allowed me to realize how imperative it is to shatter ignorance about cultural differences and barriers. My motivation for accepting the JET Programme's offer to stay for a second year is to continue influencing the experiences of my students, my co-workers, and myself. I have provided them with a different perspective of foreigners and distant cultures by guiding their outlook on women, westerners, and African-Americans. In turn, they have motivated me to breakdown my own stereotypes of Japan.

Overall, I hope to use the knowledge that I have gained about myself, through my experiences in Japan, to influence my studies at Indiana University School of Law – Bloomington. I predict my time at Indiana Law will be the next rewarding experience of my life.

LESLIE M. FENTON

While in college, Leslie took a quarter-long leave of absence to work for the democratic campaign in the 2000 election season. She was a gender studies major and worked on extracurricular activities that pertained to her field of study.

Stats
LSAT score: 170
Undergraduate GPA: 3.7
College attended: University of Chicago
Year of college graduation: 2002
Hometown: Highland Park, IL
Gender: Female
Race: Caucasian
Admissions information
Law school attended: New York University, Class of 2005
Accepted: New York University, Columbia University, Northwestern University, University of Michigan, Washington University
Denied: Harvard University, University of California— Berkeley, Yale University
Waitlisted: None

Personal statement prompt

In Leslie's words, "I sent the same personal statement to each school as a general explanation of 'why I want to study the law.'"

My decision to dedicate my life to civil rights activism as a lawyer has been a years-long process. As a gender studies major and sometime activist, I have studied and participated in many forms of action directed at changing society. While observing various modes of civil rights activism, I came to realize that the most effective and permanent means of transforming social consciousness is through the law.

When I worked as a field coordinator for the Washington Coordinated Democratic Campaign, a group of anarchists staged an anti-Gore protest in our office.

While the initial group of protestors was small and focused, the protest soon became unruly and scattered. In the end, our office suffered significant damage and neither the press nor community members understood the protestors' goals. At first,

I understood their right to protest, but I soon realized that their methods had done nothing to deliver their message. They stormed our office hoping to change Gore's policies on oil companies, but when they left, the only thing changed was the newly spray-painted exterior of our building.

I began to sympathize with the initial goal of those protestors, however, when I helped stage a protest of my own at the University of Chicago last year. A student organization, with the help of our tuition money, invited an infamously racist speaker to visit our campus. As soon as I heard about the event, I posted fliers and emails to try to unite student and community groups against the talk. Unfortunately, I found that uniting groups in one cause for one event is a tricky, dangerous process. Each group wanted control of the organizing process, and they fought amongst each other as to the methods and motivations of the protest itself. I spent hours writing emails and talking on the phone just trying to convince representatives from one socialist group that a rival socialist group would not try to dominate the protest.

When the protest finally happened, it was in many ways successful. Almost 300 people showed up to oppose the speaker, while less than 100 came to support him. Many newspapers covered the event, each with unsurprisingly mixed reactions. For a moment, people in the community and on campus became more aware of issues pertaining to race and that particular student group. Beyond this, however, I have yet to notice any sort of permanent shift in social consciousness on campus. My goal in organizing the protest was to raise awareness among my fellow students. Very few African-American students actually attend our school, and yet the student group felt comfortable inviting a speaker that lashes out at African-Americans. Almost a year later, sadly, there is no increased discussion of diversity issues on campus, no unease about the lack of tolerance shown by certain student groups. We made people at our school think about race for a day, but these thoughts were only temporary.

I understand that societal change, initiated legally or otherwise, is slow to occur.

One has to look generations beyond the actual law to realize that change has happened. I think the example that best speaks to my point is the landmark 1954 Supreme Court decision *Brown vs. the Board of Education*. While there are still people who agree with segregation, our society as a whole recognizes that black students have fundamental civil rights under the Constitution that would be violated by segregated schools. *Brown vs. the Board of Education's* greatest gift, then, was not desegregation itself, but the societal understanding that came about as a result of the decision.

This process of changing social thought through law, in my mind, has many possibilities for the future of civil rights. For example, I would like to push for a federal hate crimes law, which might instill an absolute and distinct abhorrence of crimes based on race, gender, or sexuality. I also hope to help initiate legislation that would allow gays and lesbians to marry; decades after that happens, people may wonder why anyone ever opposed such laws. I truly believe that the path to universal civil rights begins in the law, the basis of those rights.

As a socially conscious person, I must choose between changing a moment and changing the world. Individual protests may cause a few individuals or a community to think about a given issue for a few more minutes than usual, but legal change subtly influences the *way* in which this society thinks. Perceptions and morals, over time, are shaped by the way this country legislates civil rights. This theory can work in a negative way; the sodomy laws that still exist in a few states help people to rationalize homophobia. I believe, however, that societal values translated from law can function in a positive fashion, and it is this phenomenon that I hope to use in my work as an attorney.

AMANDA MOTSINGER

Amanda graduated from Duke with a major in economics. She was a member of Delta Gamma sorority during all four years of college. She held offices and volunteered for its national philanthropy program, Service for Sight. In addition, Amanda served as a campus legislator and events programmer for the two largest quadrangles on Duke's campus and swam on Duke's club swim team. Amanda worked as a teaching assistant for a computer science course for five semesters. After graduation, she was employed for a year as a paralegal at a Wall Street law firm, where she worked predominantly on corporate liability law.

Stats
LSAT score: 174
Undergraduate GPA: 3.29
College attended: Duke University
Year of college graduation: 2001
Hometown: Winston-Salem, NC
Gender: Female
Race: Caucasian

Admissions information
Law school attended: New York University, Class of 2005
Accepted: New York University, Boston College, Emory University, Fordham University, The George Washington University, Georgetown University, University of North Carolina at Chapel Hill, Yeshiva University
Denied: None
Waitlisted: Columbia University, University of Pennsylvania, University of Virginia

Personal statement prompt

Amanda submitted this personal statement as part of her application to NYU in response to the following prompt: "The Committee on Admissions encourages you to provide any information that may be helpful to us in reaching a thoughtful decision on your application. While the choice as to whether or what information to submit to the Committee is entirely yours, any information you provide will be used to give you full credit for your accomplishments, to help the Committee reach an informed decision on your application, and to aid the Committee in selecting a diverse student body.

"Examples of information that have been useful in the past include descriptions or documentation of disabilities, an explicit history of standardized test results, unusual circumstances that may have affected academic performance, or personal/family history of educational or socioeconomic disadvantage. While this list is not all-inclusive, we offer it to you to think about as you consider whether such information may be relevant in your case and to assure you that including it is quite appropriate."

The first time that I recall giving thought to the profession of law was during high school Latin class. I studied Latin during all four years of high school because it seemed more interesting than other languages as Latin involves not only the study of literature but also of history and mythology. I remember learning my freshman year that the second king of Rome, Numa Pompilius, was notable for giving the city its vaunted laws, thereby instituting order and civility in the area. Having lived in a law-abiding society all my life, I was very interested and a bit confused by this fact. How was it that a city existed without laws, and how does one bestow laws on a society? I had never given any thought to these questions, simply believing the laws of American society to be universal and unchangeable, but throughout the next four years of high school Latin, I learned as much as I could about the malleability of the laws of ancient Rome and the different processes by which the legal system operated under the monarchy, the republic, and the Empire. Latin class also taught me that the American legal system has many similarities with that of ancient Rome. While I enjoyed the literature and the mythology that dominated Latin class, the influence of ancient Romans on the modern legal system interested me the most.

In college, however, I majored in the eminently more practical field of economics, finding to my pleasure that economics was integrally tied to the legal system in ways that I found even more interesting. I focused on economics courses dealing with government and its influences, both positive and negative, on business, in America and internationally. In these classes, I learned how the actions of Microsoft were considered by some as anti-competitive and why airline mergers were blocked because of antitrust concerns, and I was excited to be able to explain these complexities to my family and friends. These courses helped me to refine my area of interest to the intersection between economics and law.

This interest has grown during my recent employment with D'Amato & Lynch, a Wall Street firm that handles securities cases for the world's largest insurers of directors, officers, and corporate liability. Through my paralegal work, I have learned a great deal about how concepts that I studied in my economics courses are rooted in the legal world. This position has cemented my desire to pursue a career in law.

Thus, at New York University School of Law, I hope to focus on business law. My primary interests at this point are antitrust and intellectual property, both of which I have studied briefly and hope to learn in more depth. I find these areas of law intriguing for their intricacies and ever-changing natures in the current economy, and I want to be a part of the legal system as it evolves to deal with new issues in antitrust and intellectual property. No longer the high school Latin student intent on learning about ancient Rome, I want to study legal questions that are changing the future of business in the city that is now the center of the world, New York.

M. ANGELA BUENAVENTURA

Angela transferred from Grinnell College to Oglethorpe University during her junior year. She majored in economics and was a member of the Beta Omicron Sigma Business Honorary Society. She served as both format manager for her college radio station and copy editor for the college music publication. Angela was also a member of Amnesty International. At the time she submitted this essay, she planned to work at a nonprofit organization for a year before attending Northwestern University.

Stats
LSAT score: 165
Undergraduate GPA: 3.83
College attended: Oglethorpe University (transferred from Grinnell College)
Year of college graduation: 2002
Hometown: Atlanta, GA
Gender: Female
Race: Latina

Admissions information
Law school attended: Northwestern University, Class of 2006
Accepted: Northwestern University, Boston College, Emory University, Georgetown University, University of Georgia, University of Michigan
Denied: None
Waitlisted: None

Personal statement prompt

According to Angela, all of the prompts for which she wrote her personal statement "were something to this effect: 'Please present yourself, your background and experiences, and your ideas as you wish in a brief personal statement.'"

I was sitting on my bed studying for a chemistry test one night when my sister knocked on my bedroom door. She said that she and my parents needed to talk to me about something. A chill went down my spine, and I thought someone must have died. I would have never guessed that I'd be having the conversation that followed.

As it turns out, my family immigrated here illegally. I have lived in the United States since I was two years old and had never questioned my citizenship status, but my parents informed me that immigration restrictions would soon be tightened and that I should undergo immigrations proceedings before these stricter laws came into place. The next day, I skipped my chemistry test and went to the Immigration and Naturalization Service office downtown to turn myself in as an undocumented alien. I was fingerprinted, interviewed, and photographed. When I left INS building that day, I was scared out my sixteen-year-old mind.

Over the next several months, I spent endless hours in overcrowded INS waiting rooms. I also spent countless hours on the Internet, reading about immigration history and law and trying to interpret what would happen to my sister and me. During my senior year of high school, I was awarded conditional residency. My lawyer told me that I would eventually be awarded permanent residency, but there was no telling when. Finally, during my freshman year of college, I was awarded permanent resident status.

Somewhere in this dizzying stream of events, something clicked. I wanted to learn more about the laws that shaped my life as an immigrant. I signed up for an immigration history class during my sophomore year of college, and although my favorite classes had previously been math-and-science based, this immigration history class fascinated me. The next semester, I designed an independent study project that focused on modern immigration law from 1965 to the present. I have always enjoyed the sciences because they allow me to better understand everyday phenomena, and immigration history provides yet another lens through which to see the world around me. A quotation printed at the top of my immigration history syllabus still sticks with me today. "Once I thought to write a history of the immigrants in America. Then I discovered that the immigrants were American history" (Oscar

Handlin, Introduction to *The Uprooted*, 1951). I want to study law for intellectual satisfaction. I want to practice law to help provide others with the opportunities I have enjoyed in the U.S.

SCOTT SANDERSON

Scott was a mathematics major at the College of the Holy Cross. During his undergraduate career, he worked part-time and was captain of the club water polo team. He worked as an engineer for three years before beginning law school.

Stats
LSAT score: 169
Undergraduate GPA: 3.20
College attended: College of the Holy Cross
Year of college graduation: 2000
Hometown: Hollywood, FL
Gender: Male
Race: Caucasian

Admissions information
Law school attended: Northwestern University, Class of 2006
Accepted: Northwestern University, Boston College, Boston University, Fordham University
Denied: Columbia University, Harvard University, New York University, University of Chicago
Waitlisted: Cornell University

Personal statement prompt

Scott notes that he wrote one general essay that he submitted "to every law school."

My decision to apply to law school is a result of the insights I have gained from my liberal arts education and from my experience as a professional in the workforce. I chose to commit to full-time employment upon graduation from college. I did so partly for practical reasons, but also because I wanted to focus my goals and to determine which of my skills and interests would best serve as the basis for a career. At the time my most meaningful employment was a work-study job at the Calculus Workshop at Holy Cross. The Workshop is a program run by the department of Mathematics that consisted of Math majors assisting students with their calculus problem sets. I found that I derived a great amount of satisfaction from helping the students. I was especially good at adapting my teaching style to suit a group, whether it was two students working together or half of a 40-student section. I was regularly rated as the best tutor at the workshop, and I knew I wanted a career that made use of my ability to advise people on complex problems. Pursuing a legal education seemed like a strong candidate at the time, but I decided the benefits of entering the workforce were worth my time and effort.

After graduation and a relatively short term as an engineer at Eclipsys Corp., a Boston software firm, I began my employment at ATI Research. ATI is one of only two principal suppliers of 3-D graphics cards used in desktop computers as well as workstations and game consoles, and is one of the premier hardware manufacturers in the country. Computer Science was not an area I had been specifically interested in during college, but I was attracted to the challenge of learning an engineering discipline.

ATI was preparing to release a new chip when I started my employment in the Spring of 2001. Although I was somewhat under-qualified for the position, I was given the opportunity to join the driver team because of the impending chip release. My position as the build manager required numerous processes and methods that utilized the Perl programming language, and I began a self-taught crash course in it as soon as I arrived. My programming skills were limited, as I had only studied it briefly in a formal setting. Still, I had the advantage of a superior team of engineers as an available resource, and I was able to acquire a high level of proficiency by the day the new chip was released.

One of the greatest assets of ATI is the rather unstructured atmosphere. I am encouraged to do independent work on most any topic or problem I am interested in. When I reached the one-year mark at ATI, I made an initiative to expand the responsibilities of my department. I identified an area of development that had many requirements in common with ours, but was lacking the proper resources to maintain an efficient build and release process. Because I knew this was an opportunity to assume a leadership role in my department, I approached the lead engineer of the group and proposed my ideas of adapting parts of our framework to meet their needs. After several months of refining our existing tools and creating new ones, I was able to substantially decrease the overhead for their build and release process. Since the two processes now share much in common, they both frequently benefit from features and improvements originally intended for just one. Around the same time, I embarked on a rigorous program to improve my C programming skills with great result. Due in large part to these accomplishments, today I perform many of the same duties as co-workers who hold both undergraduate and graduate degrees in Computer Science.

My experience at ATI has been exceptionally challenging, rewarding, and enlightening. I have been challenged to learn an engineering discipline in a competitive environment, and have succeeded in gaining more responsibility than some of my co-workers who have over twenty years experience in the industry. Furthermore, ATI's greatest influence on my career is its contribution to my decision to study patent law. Given ATI's position as a pioneer of the graphics industry, I have seen firsthand the importance and the effects of claiming intellectual property on an idea. It is an area of vital importance to our business and one that I am keenly interested in. The resolution of an intellectual property dispute has impacted every part of our development; from our delivery speed to the marketplace, to the course of future research. A legal education is the preparation I need to become an active participant in the field of patent law; a field that is both a crucial component of our economy and a key element of future technological advancement.

The legal profession combines aspects of my work at ATI such as problem solving, independent work, and the accumulation of knowledge with the speaking, writing, and critical thinking skills I developed during my liberal arts undergraduate education. I have spent the past seven years developing skills in what I believe is a solid and broad foundation for the study of law. In addition, I feel an obligation to join a profession whose members show a commitment to participate in the political and social debate toward which my fellow engineers tend to show ambivalence. I am motivated to engage in a law career because it combines an intellectual challenge, academic rigor, vast opportunities for professional achievement, and the tools to effect positive change.

NORTHWESTERN UNIVERSITY

SANDRA

Sandra graduated summa cum laude *from Cornell University with a degree in English literature. She won several essay prizes for her work on British drama, including recognition for the best senior thesis in English, and was involved in the performance of both choral and instrumental music. Her experience volunteering as a conversation partner for Cornell's ESL program led her to South Korea, where she spent a year teaching conversational English through the Fulbright program.*

Stats
LSAT scores: 166, 171
Undergraduate GPA: 3.86
College attended: Cornell University
Year of college graduation: 2001
Hometown: Philadelphia, PA
Gender: Female
Race: Caucasian
Admissions information
Law school attended: Northwestern University, Class of 2005
Accepted: Northwestern University, Harvard University, Stanford University, University of South Carolina, University of Virginia
Denied: None
Waitlisted: University of Chicago, University of Michigan

Personal statement prompt

According to Sandra, "I used my statement for all the law schools I applied to; I recall that all of them had the general 'tell us about yourself' personal statement instead of a specific question."

"Korea? Why are you in Korea?" my friend's voice echoed down the line. I was a month into my year as a Fulbright English Teaching Assistant, and though I readily recited the answer on my grant application—the desire to gain perspective on my own culture and education by experiencing the "other side" of a classroom—my friend remained unconvinced. "You want to be a lawyer," she continued. "What's teaching in Korea got to do with that?" Her challenge silenced me; I had no easy answer for that question at the time. However, I now realize that although my legal career might end up having nothing to do with Korea, teaching here has affirmed my ambition to be a lawyer by transforming my views of the uses of language and consequently of the law.

My passion for language, and thus for literature, has long been a shaping force in my life. As a child, I constantly had bruised knees—the result of maximizing my book time by reading while walking. My bookish ways continued throughout middle and high school, and I was stereotyped as "the reader," "the writer," and naturally, "the English major." I rebelled against these assumptions in my first years of college, sampling anthropology, cognitive psychology, and computer science as potential majors. Yet my rebellion was a failure; I realize now that even these seemingly diverse fields are also abstract ways of thinking about language. However, I prefer the particular, and eventually I ended up majoring in English literature as predicted. My studies sharpened and deepened my liking for words as I tracked shifting narrative tone, searched for puns, and burrowed through layers of meaning, and I became interested in law because I saw it as an opportunity to continue working with words and using the intellectual skills I learned as an English major.

Consequently, when I came to Korea I fondly viewed language as an aesthetic object, and thought the enjoyment of my job would come from coaxing the same view out of my students. But as I quickly learned in my classroom, English can be a slippery and treacherous thing. My students have only studied the language for two years, and to them, English seems like a massive maze deliberately constructed to frustrate them. Why, they ask, can "must" only be used in the present tense? Why are "bread" and "chalk" uncountable nouns? Too often, I can only answer "Because," and my view of language becomes a little bit more like that of my students' each time. On my best days as a teacher, I feel that I have guided my students successfully through the maze, and that English is a tool that I am helping my students to use rather than an object for my intellectual contemplation. As an English major, I ferreted out the complexities of language, but now I seek its simplicities.

In the same way, my view of law has shifted. My intellectual curiosity and pleasure in words still draw me to the subject, but the lawyer's roles as guide and protector also attract me now. Before I began teaching, I rarely gave credit to practical applications, but I now see language and law as tools to be used as well as studied.

Similarly, teaching has shown me that using my understanding to assist other people increases that comprehension in ways I could not have anticipated. My friend's questions may once have puzzled me, but I now know that even though I came to Korea without thought to my future career, my time teaching here has given me a direction and purpose in the law.

JONATHAN CHRISTOPHER PENTZIEN

Jonathan spent four years on active duty as a United States Naval Officer. He volunteered as a mentor and tutor for high school students and coached a local basketball team. He attributes at least part of his admissions success to his technical background as a civil engineering major at Notre Dame because "engineers are not quite as common at most law schools."

Stats
LSAT score: 164
Undergraduate GPA: 3.46
College attended: University of Notre Dame
Year of college graduation: 2001
Hometown: Bremerton, WA
Gender: Male
Race: Caucasian

Admissions information
Law school attended: Rutgers University—Camden, Class of 2007
Accepted: Rutgers University—Camden, American University, University of Pittsburgh
Denied: George Mason University
Waitlisted: College of William and Mary, University of Notre Dame, University of Virginia

Personal statement prompt

Jonathan reports that the essay prompt to which he responded was open-ended.

Since graduating from the University of Notre Dame, I have had the privilege to serve as a commissioned officer in the United States Navy. Over the last three years, I have lived in four cities, traveled the West and East Coasts, and completed three Navy training schools before settling into my first job in Washington D.C. This constant moving has always been a part of my life, as my father was a career Naval officer in the Medical Corps. Despite the disruption that accompanies such a life "on the move," I value deeply what I have learned from this experience and believe that it has provided me with a foundation to succeed at law school, and ultimately, as an attorney.

My motivation for joining the Navy stems from a childhood experience involving my father's time in the service. In 1990, when I was twelve years old, my father was preparing to go to Antarctica for six weeks on a medical field expedition. Two days before his scheduled departure, he was told to assume command of the *USNS Comfort*, one of the Navy's two hospital ships that would be sent to the Persian Gulf for the possible start of war with Iraq. This was a disconcerting piece of news for our whole family. With the trip to Antarctica, we at least knew when to expect him home. With the new potential for war, this trip was indefinite. One week later, my father left for the Persian Gulf, and our family was forced to deal with the difficulty of the unknown. Following four weeks of hoping for the threat of war to subside, our worst fears were realized, and the Gulf War began. Usually, our only means of information came from the news media and the family support groups established by the Navy. Even when we were fortunate enough to receive a phone call from my father, it was brief due to security concerns and the high costs of satellite calls aboard ship.

Nine difficult months later, the war was over and we were standing by the pier in Norfolk, VA awaiting the *USNS Comfort* to dock. When the ship finally pulled in, there was an endless stream of men and women in dress white uniforms disembarking. As I saw my father cross the brow of the ship, my heart swelled; all I could think of was how proud I was to have a dad serving in the United States Navy.

Talking with my father after the war, I began to understand the values associated with being a Naval officer. For twenty-three years, he was committed to an ideal greater than himself, serving his country. He was devoted to ensuring the safety of the troops he led and the patients he cared for, so that they would all be able to return home to their families. His sense of duty and honor to his country awed and inspired me, and several years later, I joined the Navy by accepting a Reserve Officer Training Corps (ROTC) scholarship to the University of Notre Dame. Through this program, I learned the basics of being a Naval officer, while at the same time, I gained an excellent academic education and collegiate experience.

These principles and ideals embodied by my father can best be described by the Navy Core Values, which I have made every effort to internalize as an officer: "Honor, Courage, and Commitment." I will briefly outline how these values I strive to embody will translate to my potential as a lawyer. Another word for honor is integrity. As an officer of the court and as an executor of laws, whether civilian or military, integrity must be the foundation of one's character. If I cannot be trusted by my clients, superiors, or peers I will, and should be, questioned on my ability to practice law. There is also a great sense of honor that comes from being an ethical lawyer in all situations. Courage can often be misinterpreted in a military sense, as the willingness to give one's life for another person or for their country. However, the true definition of courage lies in the strength to take on challenges. This includes legal cases that may be difficult, posing considerable moral dilemmas, but recognizing that all have a right to a fair trial. Finally, commitment is embodied by the discipline required of law students and lawyers in advancing their understanding of the law. Ultimately, the greatest responsibility of a practicing or aspiring lawyer is the commitment to a higher ideal, which is upholding the freedoms granted under the Constitution.

Currently, I am working as an environmental engineer in the Navy's Civil Engineer Corps and am pursuing a program that would allow me to attend law school funded by the Navy. My commitment to serving others and my courage to accept challenges have greatly influenced my desire to study and practice the law, and I aspire to become a member of the Navy's Judge Advocate General (JAG) Corps. I believe that continuing to serve my country by embodying the Core Values and supporting our nation's frontline troops in a legal capacity would be very gratifying. However, regardless of whether I am accepted into the Navy's program to fund law school, I am very interested in serving as an attorney, either by entering the JAG Corps after law school or by pursuing legal work in the civilian sector. I feel confident that whether I am working as a JAG or civilian attorney, the values I have learned from military service, as well as my academic accomplishments, will enhance my ability to excel in the legal profession.

ERIN SHEEHAN

Erin racked up a long list of activities and honors during her undergraduate years at the University of Miami that demonstrated her progression from aspiring meteorologist to aspiring law student interested in entertainment and media law. Most significantly, she was involved in the Atmospheric Sciences Club and Media Convergence Conference of 2007 and interned for CBS Radio Philadelphia in the summer of 2008. Additionally, Erin received the Department of Media Management Outstanding Senior of 2008 award from her department faculty. Erin also showed dedication to community service by working at UM's Service and Leadership Center and volunteering for National Gandhi Day of Service, Hug the Lake, and United Way Orange Bowl Collection, among other service events.

Stats

LSAT score: 159
Undergraduate GPA: 3.43
College attended: University of Miami
Year of college graduation: 2004
Hometown: Wenonah, NJ
Gender: Female
Race: Caucasian

Admissions information

Law school attended: Rutgers University of New Jersey—Camden, Class of 2011
Accepted: University of Miami, Rutgers University of New Jersey—Camden, University of South Carolina, University of San Diego
Denied: Fordham University, Temple University, University of Maryland, Washington and Lee University
Waitlisted: Santa Clara University, University of San Francisco

Personal Statement Prompt

Erin submitted this essay as part of her application to the University of Rochester. She responded to the following prompt: Tell the Admissions Committee about yourself, your motivation for attending law school, and how you plan to use your legal education. Information about how your background and personal experiences bear on your professional goals is more useful to the Committee than general statements of principle.

I wish I could tell you that I have been dreaming of Law School since I was young, or that I come from a family of lawyers and it's in my blood, but I can't. That's not the way this decision to apply to Law School went for me. This decision came following a long process of self-discovery.

Since I was two, I have had an interest in performing. Whether it was through ballet classes, piano lessons, school plays, or pageants, I was always striving for a life in entertainment. I learned at a young age that enjoying being in front of a crowd doesn't necessarily translate into the natural artistic talent needed to pursue a career in the living arts. I simply didn't have it. Around the time of middle school, I found my solution when I decided that I was going to be a weathergirl. I have always excelled in math and science classes and had a natural curiosity about the weather, so it seemed logical to use those skills to get on television. I even did the daily weather television broadcasts during my high school's morning announcements, and followed that dream to the University of Miami where I enrolled as a double major in broadcast journalism and meteorology.

Issues arose during the fall semester of my sophomore year when I advanced past general core classes. I questioned continuing with meteorology while finding a greater interest in a class dedicated to discussing the first amendment and its applications to the media. I knew I needed a change of pace. Subsequently, I studied abroad in London during the spring of that year, which gave me the opportunity to step away and think about my future. It was there that I first came into contact with the study of law as I lived with two law students who were motivated and passionate about their studies.

Returning to the University of Miami for my junior year, I realized I had a decision to make. I began to explore my options not only for new majors, but also for career paths. It took meetings with four different advisors to decide on two new majors, media management and economics, to exploit both my interest in entertainment and background in applied math. Next, I moved onto figuring out my career options.

It had been suggested by teachers and my parents over the years that I should consider practicing law due to my diligence and penchant for the logical; however, it didn't click until I heard it from a third party. After changing my communications major, I was required to meet with a media management advisor. At first he just rattled off the different careers that media management majors tend to go into. However, after looking at my academic records he suggested that I consider law and MBA programs. As soon as I began researching the connections between the media and the law, I became fascinated by how everything from copyrighting to contract law, labor law, entertainment law, Internet law, and more come into play when dealing with the media.

This summer I interned for CBS Radio Philadelphia where I worked with the directors of business, sales, marketing, and programming at three of the stations within the Network. I was able to see first hand how important communication is between the departments, and the positive feedback I got for my work confirmed that the business end of the entertainment industry is where I want to be. The prospect of studying and practicing law in the entertainment industry has given me a new motivation to work hard to achieve my goal.

Over a year after beginning my new majors, I know I made the right decision. While my workload has increased, I am enjoying my education at the University of Miami. This shows in my academic performance, as I have made the Dean's List both semesters since the change. I look forward to continuing my education in the area of law, and gaining the knowledge and skills needed to succeed in entertainment law.

SOUTH TEXAS COLLEGE OF LAW

DIANE RENAE KLIEM

Diane has had a lot of business experience through her career as an accountant and CPA. She has held the positions of Assistant Controller, Controller, Human Resources Manager, and Credit Manager. Her experience spans many areas, especially in finance including credit, collections, employment law, lien law, acquisitions, financial decision making models, audits, financial statement analysis, and team building. Additionally, with her husband she has built a successful small business in the last five years. She has demonstrated active community and career involvement as a member of Texas Society of CPAs (Victoria Chapter), President-Elect and President of Victoria County Aggie Mother's Club, Treasurer of the Football Booster Club (Memorial High School), and member of NACM (National Association of Credit Managers).

Stats
LSAT score(s): 149 and 153
College attended: University of Houston—Victoria
Year of college graduation: 1992
Hometown: Victoria, Texas
Gender: Female
Race: Caucasian

Admissions information
Law school attended: South Texas College of Law, Class of 2009 (December)
Accepted: South Texas College of Law
Denied: None
Waitlisted: None

Why would a first generation college student and licensed CPA feel compelled to return to school to study law? In this personal essay, I will answer that question and also explain why South Texas College of Law (STCL) should grant me admission for Spring 2007. I believe that I have the qualities and experience that STCL is looking for in a successful law student, and that I can add value to the STCL organization as a student committed to excellence who would add diversity to the student population.

I completed my education in a very non-traditional way. I completed my bachelor's degree as a working married student with two very young children. The last three years of my education was completed under these circumstances and as my transcripts will show, I earned a very good GPA during that time. In fact, during that period my GPA was higher than my cumulative GPA; this, in my opinion, is indicative of my academic abilities that will help me to meet and exceed STCL's very high standards. As the foregoing demonstrates, I do not let obstacles stand in the way of achieving important goals and results. I overcome the obstacles. Consequently, I have achieved high results in any job I have undertaken as any of my co-workers or supervisors would attest.

In my professional life, I have had many opportunities and experiences that will make positive contributions in a law school environment. I have a range of experiences in accounting, human resources, and the legal aspects of business that will provide a foundation of practical knowledge and encourage discussion and thought in the classroom. I have experience with business reorganizations and evaluations of acquisitions. My husband and I also own a successful small business. We have grown this business in the last four years from a start up to a volume in sales that is over ten times what it was the first year. We have negotiated contracts, revised billing processes, built a team of contractors, and turned around problem areas for our major customer. We have reached a degree of customer satisfaction that is the best within the entire state per our major customer's surveys. These experiences make me uniquely qualified to add diversity of experience and value as a student at STCL.

The above experiences and achievements have led me to the study of law. I also want to study law because I enjoy dealing with contracts. I look for details that could swing advantage to one side or the other and try to mitigate those advantages to obtain fairness for both sides. My fairness, ability to negotiate and objectivity are traits that I believe are advantageous to an attorney. Attention to detail in a contract, being timely on a lien notice or letter, and rating people objectively as a supervisor are examples of things that I have experienced as a CPA, Human Resource Manager, and Controller. These have led me to the study of law and a desire to learn more. My strong ethics training as a CPA has also led me to study law. Ethics is of utmost importance as a CPA and as an attorney. I have had experiences in my career when my ethical principles were tested and I had to make a decision that was very unpopular but was the right thing to do. I have no problem making the tough decisions if they are the right and ethical decisions.

Many of my personal traits and habits will help me to be a successful attorney. Without exception, all my co-workers have told me that going into law would fit me well. The traits they see that I believe will help me to be successful are determination, planning skills, time management skills, follow-through, organization skills, knowledge retention, thoroughness, good research skills, flexibility and the ability to multi-task, and good team interaction skills. These traits should be evidenced by my GPA, the obstacles that I overcame in being a working first generation college graduate with a family, my CPA certification, my work experiences and promotion within my company, and my success in running a small business that my husband and I own. My abilities and strong skills in these areas are the reason that STCL should see me as a strong candidate for admission.

As a further basis for admitting me as a student and as an indicator of my character, I should reiterate that I am a CPA. The CPA exam is a very difficult "final" exam which is taken after completing an accounting degree. The bar exam is also a difficult exam that is taken after completing law school. I believe that having taken such a difficult exam and having passed all four parts on the second try is a good indicator that I will diligently study for and pass the bar exam to become a successful STCL alumnus and attorney.

Another thing that makes me want to take on the challenges of law school, despite its difficulty, is the reverence, desire and appreciation that I have for further education. I am currently the first and only college graduate on both sides of my family. I was the major influence in convincing both of my siblings who were in their thirties to return to school to complete their studies as a Licensed Vocational Nurse and Fire-fighter/Paramedic. I was the major influence on my daughter who is a student at Texas A&M to become the first one on both sides of our family to attend a major university. My involvement with community activities has also focused on education via funds for scholarships and support for school programs. I appreciate the accessibility to legal education that is stressed by STCL in its mission statement and other written materials. I believe that this appreciation and dedication to further education should serve as evidence of my strong commitment to achieve excellence at STCL.

I have been involved with and held leadership positions in several organizations within my community as my resume indicates. I believe in serving the community and profession that one chooses. I felt that STCL was the right fit for me when I saw the mission statement and its reference to students committed to serving their communities and the legal profession. After graduating from law school and passing the bar, I will become involved in organizations within my Victoria community such as the Legal Association and will continue to be active in the organizations that I select while at STCL. I have interest in several on the list of twenty six active organizations at STCL, including Board of Advocates and Student Bar Association. I want to be a positive mentor and example of how success can be achieved at different points in one's life. Traditional education works for some people but one should never count himself or herself out of a further education if it is desired. My dedication to school, community and professional involvement is further evidence that I would be a good candidate for admission to STCL.

In closing, my academic and professional background makes me uniquely qualified as a potential STCL student who would add diversity to the school through my multitude of experiences and ability to overcome obstacles. I would add value as a STCL alumnus and to the legal profession due to my commitment to achievement and desire to give back to my profession and community. My abilities, past achievements, and personal traits demonstrate that, if selected as a student, I will maintain STCL's commitment to excellence. I would ask that STCL admit me into the program for Spring 2007, and by so doing, give me the opportunity to succeed as a student and future attorney. Thank you very much for your consideration.

ADAM KENT ISRAEL

When Adam applied to law school he had numerous leadership positions and academic honors on his resume. However, he doesn't really think that helped him get into law school because admissions committees see resumes like his on a daily basis. He believes that it was the experience that he gained while working for a judge during his senior year of college, his community service involvement (about which he wrote his essay), and the recommendations attesting to his work ethic that his professors submitted on his behalf that contributed most to his law school acceptance.

Stats

LSAT score(s): 159
Undergraduate GPA: 3.83/4.0
College attended: Birmingham-Southern College
Year of college graduation: 2006
Gender: Male
Race: White

```
Admissions information
```
Law school attended: University of Alabama, Class of 2009
Accepted: University of Alabama, Wake Forest University
Denied: University of Virginia, Vanderbilt University, University of Texas, Boston College

Personal Statement Prompt:

Provide a personal statement that includes any information which you wish the Admissions Committee to consider when evaluating your application.

Haleyville, Alabama is a place from the movies. It is the quintessential Small-town, America. People gather daily at the locally owned sandwich shop to exchange pleasantries and catch up on each others lives. Attendance at the Friday night high school football games is essential for an active social life. The middle class citizens of Haleyville are always congenial and concerned for the well being of each other. However, racial, socioeconomic, religious, and intellectual homogeneity have made my hometown a stagnant ideological vacuum. For example, although my family stressed charitable values from the time I was a child, it was understood that we were to aid the poor by addressing their immediate needs. My beliefs did not call me, however, to advocate social justice, but simply to involve myself in charitable endeavors.

In fact, the idea of social justice was a foreign concept – foreign not only to me, but also to my community. No one seemed to ask why extreme poverty existed in some places because the answer was clear in our minds – poor people were lazy and didn't want to work. We were charitable, yet we hated the idea of America as a welfare state.

As long as I remained isolated in the microcosm which reared me, my views remained unchallenged. They were not my beliefs because I had formed them through reason and experience but rather, I adhered to them because they were spoon fed to me. I, like my peers, unquestioningly accepted them. The work I did in Woodlawn, an inner city community in Birmingham, Alabama, during my first Interim term at Birmingham-Southern College thrust me into a world which caused me to question my ideological views of poverty. When I served meals to homeless men and women I listened to their stories hoping to understand their situations. One man had been laid off of his job and was left without health insurance. Without an immediate source of income, his mounting medical bills buried him in debt and he found himself living on the streets. Another woman had gotten pregnant in high school and was forced to drop out and find a job. Her struggling family was unable to provide any support, and her minimum wage job left many bills unpaid. I could no longer simply tell myself that laziness was what kept homeless men and single mothers in poverty. Instead I saw defeated people who were being held prisoner by poverty. They could not find full-time employment because they could not afford necessities like reliable transportation and childcare. Paradoxically, due to the cyclical nature of poverty they could not afford these necessities because they could not find full-time employment.

The month in which I lived in Woodlawn left me with a belief system which I could no longer justify. I still recognize the importance of charity. Systemic change comes slowly and hunger waits for no one. However, I now understand that addressing the causes of destitution through social justice is far more important for the long term well being of others. The pit of poverty is deep and difficult from which to emerge. Working class oppression is not only unjust and costly to society; it is, in my opinion, morally reprehensible. We as a society must recognize that our lives are inextricably intertwined with the lives of others. When a child suffers from malnutrition or an adult is unable to afford adequate housing, it is not only they who suffer but societal progress also suffers.

I make no claim that institutional oppression is solely responsible for poverty. Such an assertion would be ignorant and counterfactual. However, the assertion that individuals choose poverty and have no desire to support themselves or their families – an assertion which I made many times before I began my college education – is equally as ignorant. My experience in Woodlawn taught me that the solution to poverty is complex. However, to produce any substantive change we as a society must address the root causes of poverty rather than continue to expect private citizens' charitable donations to effectively alleviate its symptoms.

Personal Statement #2

The practice of law is a noble endeavour; its actors continually working within an amazing system of laws and rules of procedure. It is, by no means, a perfect system. However, the American legal system is a work in progress. Its laws and rules of procedure are continually being fine tuned so as to most effectively serve equal justice for all. The complex system of laws and rules governing admissibility of evidence and discovery are what keeps Americans free. However, this complex system is not sexy. It can't be packaged into little hour long blocks of air time without losing the essence of its greatness. The American public doesn't want a real murder trial or products liability case, they want great oration. While many outstanding attorneys are unbelievable orators, the practice of law is so much deeper than oratorical skills.

I found over this January as I worked alongside Jefferson County's Presiding Judge that while I am, just like every other American, enthralled by the sensationalized version of the practice of law; I am, however, equally as fascinated by the routine filing of motions and pleadings. For me, no single component in the process from complaint to the disposition of a case is more interesting than the others. Rather, it is the complex dance of the litigious process about which I am passionate. While the reality of the American legal system may bore many, the professional path on which I wish to embark excites me. Frederick Buechner, a contemporary American author and theologian, once said, "Vocation is where your deep gladness meets the world's needs." For me, that intersection is the practice of law.

For me, the pursuit of equality is the bedrock of my system of morality. It is also the most basic tenant in the practice of law. All people, regardless of race, color, religion, ethnicity, or creed are given the same opportunities to present a case in a court of law or equity. This idea of equality, in my opinion, is the glue that binds our democracy together. Without the equality for all provided by the Constitution our democracy would cease to exist. We, as a people, could hold elections and enact legislation based on the will of the majority, but without equal protection for minority rights our government would be little more than the tyranny of the masses. This idea of equality protects us from ourselves and ensures the perpetuation of our democracy. The chief responsibility of the American legal system is to ensure this equality for all Americans.

It seems that in the increasingly competitive world in which we live evenhandedness is difficult to find. More and more Americans living on the margins are being left behind economically. Even in this age of political correctness, large classes of citizens are being denied fundamental civil rights. Martin Luther King, Jr. pointed out in his "Letter from the Birmingham Jail" that there is no greater threat to the rights of all citizens when he said, "Injustice anywhere is a threat to justice everywhere." For those Americans on the margin the Constitution is the great equalizer. I can think of no greater service to the American people than to fight for those for whom no one will fight. I truly believe that my calling in life is to advocacy through the justice system. I am passionate about the law not because of its sexiness, but because of its equalizing power. There is, in my opinion, no more dignifying vocation than one whose task is to ensure that equal justice is served for all.

KATY GRACE BURROUGHS

Katy believes there were many contributing factors to her admissions decisions. She did not have the best college GPA, but she went to a difficult private school and double majored. She also completed a senior thesis (writing a full-length play) which combined both majors. In addition to academics she did a lot during her four years. Katy wrote, acted in, and directed numerous plays while serving on the all-student board for the campus theatre organization. She helped found her sorority chapter and was on both the chapter and Panhellenic's executive board. She worked in the admissions office for four years and in the theatre for two. She also was named a member of Senior 25, Greek Person of the Year, and acted as class speaker at graduation. She is a good student, but she also used all the opportunities open to her like law students often have to do.

Stats	
LSAT score(s): 166	
Undergraduate GPA: 3.5	
College attended: Lake Forest College (Lake Forest, Illinois)	
Year of college graduation: 2003	
Hometown: Tuscaloosa, Alabama	
Gender: Female	
Race: Caucasian	
Admissions information	
Law school attended: University of Alabama, Class of 2010	
Accepted: University of Alabama, DePaul University	
Denied: University of Texas	
Waitlisted: none	

Personal Statement

I remember the first moment I realized that I was different from every girl I knew. I was seven years old. I was sitting at a table in my first grade reading class. Some ridiculous person asked the question, "Would you rather be really, really pretty or really, really smart?" I was at a table of eight girls and I was the only one who chose "really, really smart." But I did not stop there. When all of my friends immediately informed me that no boy would ever want to marry me if I was not really, really pretty especially if I was smarter than him, I retaliated.

I enlightened them by letting them know that if I was smart I could get a good job, make lots of money, and use it to make myself really, really pretty. They quickly told me that after all that, I would be too old for anyone to marry me. That pretty much ended the conversation since I had never considered that no one would want to marry a really, really smart girl who had a lot of money which she used to make herself really, really pretty just because she was too old. I have changed a bit since my time as a first grader, and I now realize that the above conversation was completely silly. However, I think it does say a few things about me as a person and about the way I interact with other people and their ideas.

I am an individual. I have never been afraid to disagree with the norm or to voice my own opinion on a topic. I enjoy doing my own thing and making my own path. I believe that this trait is the single most important factor which helped determine my development. It is why I left my hometown with its thriving university atmosphere for a tiny school in Illinois, in a suburb just outside Chicago. It is the reason that I chose a study abroad program which accepts less than fifty students each semester that no one from my college had ever attended. It is also the reason that I hold leadership positions in a number of organizations. My individuality also accounts for my somewhat eclectic interests. I am a pacifist who debates and boxes her dad, an avid reader whose favorite writers include everyone from John Donne and Ayn Rand, a hopeless romantic who watches war movies and M*A*S*H, and a theatre geek who is good at biology. All of these interests highlight another personality trait evident from my memory of fifteen years ago.

I value learning and I like exploring new things. I have read books and watched educational TV since I was young. In college I have taken several classes outside of my major because of their interesting topics. I even use the "Useless Trivia" and "365 Interesting Books" page-a-day calendars. I enjoy learning from people around me as well. At seven years old, I learned that some people will not understand you if you are different from them. Now, at age twenty-two, I know that the freedom to think a different way or hold a different opinion from those around you is part of what makes this country exciting and great.

I believe that both of these traits make me a good law school candidate, and there are several reasons I would like to attend law school. I would like to learn about the history and development of law in this country as well as international law. I want to study the concepts and theories of law and legal practices. And I would like to use the education that I will gain during the next three years to become a lawyer who represents people with a wide variety of ethnic, socio-economic, and political backgrounds. I am interested in criminal law with the prospect of becoming a public defender or a district attorney; I also want to learn about human rights law perhaps to formulate government policies; and I plan on taking international law classes to help me become a more informed member of the global community. I believe that my desire for knowledge and genuine interest in discovery of new ideas make me an ideal law student. I also believe that I will do well in a field that requires analytical thought and creativity. I trust that I would be an asset to The University of Alabama School of Law, class of 2010.

LINDSEY C. BONEY, IV

Lindsey was SGA President as an undergrad. He lived abroad in China for two years. He is married and worked for a Christian non-profit for several years before law school. He is also an Algernon Sydney Sullivan award winner (outstanding male graduat

Stats
LSAT score(s): 159/165
Undergraduate GPA: 3.53
College attended: Auburn University
Year of college graduation: 2001
Hometown: Mobile, Alabama
Gender: Male
Race: Caucasian

Admissions information
Law school attended: University of Alabama, Class of 2008
Accepted: University of Alabama
Denied: University of Virginia, Georgetown University, Vanderbilt University
Waitlisted: University of Texas, Washington and Lee University

General personal statement

Unconventionality has marked my life. As a child diagnosed with asthma, doctors advised me to stop running competitively. My heart failed to listen. By the end of my high school years, I was a seven-time state champion and double state record holder. College experiences took me along the same path. As an ambitious college freshman eager to get involved and make a difference on campus, I bucked conventional wisdom by turning down a bid from a well-connected fraternity to remain "independent." Three years later, I had built a network across campus, been elected Student Government Association President, and given my time to a myriad of activities despite a lack of Greek affiliation.

It was this unconventional streak that led me to China. As my classmates headed to Atlanta, Birmingham, and Nashville for lucrative jobs or graduate school, my wife and I surveyed our lives and decided to take a bold risk. Having each spent a summer studying abroad in China, our love of its mysteriously unique culture and our passion for international travel convinced us to pack our bags, leave our families, and move to China to study Mandarin. Our time there helped define who I am and what I want to become.

China opened my eyes to a world much larger than the United States. Initially, it was a cynical glance at the world—the pressing crowds and throngs of people filling the sidewalks grew tiresome. Once novel stares began to annoy. As the romance of a foreign land wore down, I began to loathe the cultural differences I was experiencing. Eventually, though, as we lived abroad longer and began to adjust culturally, I realized my limited worldview and relative perspective. Conversations with my Chinese friends about politics, religion, cultural tradition, and history helped me recognize my classic American tendency to see the world only through a limited cultural lens. I began to value the differences inherent in culture and to consciously consider the global implications of law and U.S. foreign policy while evaluating international reaction to world events. It was a slow, difficult mindset shift—and one that is not complete.

In many other respects China instilled in me compassion and vision. After living in a country where millions of people fight for scant few jobs and socio-economic status is visibly polarized, I could not return home unchanged. Witnessing unemployed laborers come to blows over the opportunity to carry a bookcase up twenty flights of stairs for a dollar and a half has softened me. Playing Santa for children at a local deaf and blind school reminded me of the immense treasure of a smile.

China also shaped my desire to study law. As I saw the influx of western business, the opportunity to help those corporations understand the unconventional Chinese market became increasingly compelling. When signing contracts for rental property, I realized the difficulty of enforcing such contracts in what is mostly an extrajudicial legal environment. Contract disputes, intellectual property regulation enforcement, and the definition of personal liberties will continue to impact the integration of China with Western markets. In such an evolving business environment, the need for American, Chinese-speaking attorneys will only grow in my lifetime.

Finally, my affinity for the unconventional has taken me to the non-profit sector, in religious work. This setting has been fulfilling but has confirmed my desire to study law—I have relished roles that require me to develop compelling arguments that demand action and to deliver them with passion and conviction. I have also seen a glaring need for legal expertise in the non-profit community as *pro bono* legal counsel.

Though my journey to law school has been atypical of aspiring law students, I do not believe the transition is far-fetched; rather, I believe my unique life experiences have prepared me well for the rigors of a legal education and would add rich diversity and an international perspective to the University of Alabama School of Law class of 2009.

UNIVERSITY OF ALABAMA

MICHAEL DAVID WATERS, JR.

Michael graduated magna cum laude *from Huntingdon College where he received the English Award. He was a member of Phi Eta Sigma and Alpha Beta honor societies in addition to the Film Society, Outdoor Recreation Club, and Women's Center. His short stories were published in the college's literary magazine and newspaper, and this helped him greatly with his writing. In terms of work experience, Michael worked as a runner in two different law firms. Because there are several lawyers in his family, he is well acquainted with the lifestyle of law.*

Stats
LSAT Score: 157
College GPA: 3.97
College: Huntingdon College
College Graduation Year: 2006
Hometown: Montgomery, Alabama
Gender: Male
Race: Caucasian

Admissions information
Law school attended: The University of Alabama, Class of 2010
Accepted: The University of Alabama
Denied: None
Waitlisted: None

Personal Statement

Though it has taken several forms, I've always had an inherent interest in the concept of justice. As a child, I idolized colorful superheroes for their commitment to fairness and equality; they fought ceaselessly to preserve order in a world besieged by chaos and crime. I desperately wanted to emulate these fantastic warriors and devote my life to fighting for my beliefs. Then I grew up.

Nevertheless, my aspirations haven't changed significantly. Though my career goals no longer involve donning brightly tinted spandex and wielding supernatural powers against evildoers, I believe more fervently than ever in the preservation of justice, order, and law. My intellect and reason have matured with age and I possess a greater grasp of these somewhat abstract concepts.

Exactly what is justice? This is a question I feel all who seek their profession in law must ask, and I have arrived at my own personal answer. Justice is what ensures that all people are given impartial treatment, and penalty, under the law. In a just legal system, none may stand above anyone else, regardless of extraneous factors such as race, class, or creed. Justice is what separates a democratic form of government from despotism; I believe with every confidence that it is worth fighting for. In a world that continuously appears to be descending into madness and despondency, the notion of justice gives me the greatest hope for the future.

I will never be a superhero, but I can and will fight for my ideals if afforded the opportunity. This fight is what I long to devote my life to, for it is among my strongest convictions, and it is why I sincerely wish to attend law school. Over the course of my college career, I have devoted myself to academic growth, and I anticipate with great enthusiasm the prospect of challenging myself further.

As an attorney, I will be able to fight for what I hold dear as well as give aid to those in need. Because I have been granted many gifts in life, it is my responsibility to help others in every possible capacity. I believe this is part and parcel of justice. In an effort to reduce my personal environmental impact on our world, I have become a vegetarian, eat an organic diet, and recycle as much as I can. This is a natural extension of my beliefs regarding justice.

I was a teenager the first time I volunteered for a local soup kitchen. This experience and many others like it made me realize how truly blessed I am. It is the responsibility of those with opportunities as I have to use them for the benefit of mankind. Such is my goal, and I will work ardently to ensure that my life and potential are not wasted.

My mother, as the former director of Legal Services Corporation of Alabama, worked for years in the field of public interest law, and I've witnessed first hand what this occupation entails. Though she was often depressed by the squalor and desolation she'd seen in many of her clients, my mother was content at having the chance to make a difference in the lives of the less fortunate. Her work was vital and rewarding, and I can see myself performing the same service.

As both my parents are attorneys, I am well acquainted with the lawyer's lifestyle, but I do not wish to attend law school because of their experiences. While growing up, in fact, I swore vehemently that I would never become a lawyer. However, adulthood has changed my views and I sincerely believe the law is where my future lies. It is because I believe so dearly in the fight for justice that this is the path I've chosen.

NICOLE ANNE OERTLI

Nicole feels that the diversity of her academic interests (journalism, politics, physics, and forensic accounting among them) were instrumental in the her admissions decisions. Her achievements in those fields, including a position as editor-in-chief of the student newspaper, founder and president of College Democrats, and a finalist at the Intel International Science and Engineering Fair, speak for themselves as to her aptitude in those fields. The greatest single factor in most admissions decisions is not necessarily the achievements themselves but what was overcome to attain them.

Stats
LSAT score(s): 165
Undergraduate GPA: 3.74
College attended: Spring Hill College
Year of college graduation: 2006
Hometown: Mobile, Alabama
Gender: Female
Race: Caucasian

Admissions information
Law school attended: University of Alabama, Class of 2010 **Accepted:** University of Alabama, Emory University, University of Georgia, University of Houston **Other (explain):** Declined to take a place on the waitlist at University of Texas and was subsequently denied.

Describe your most character-building experience.

My most character-building experience has been a continuous process that began at the age of eight, resulting in the character traits of determination, perseverance, and an affinity with victims and underdogs that have become the core values of my character. As a child, I showed academic promise, and was encouraged to skip the second grade. My third grade teacher, however, initially stated that she "[wouldn't] have an immature first grader in her class," and from the very first day of class, assigned me additional work. When I was unable to finish them, she detained me from my gifted writing, reading, and other enrichment classes, as well admonished and humiliated me verbally. I would sit, alone in the room or outside in the hallway, for what seemed like years at a time. During this dark period, I was diagnosed with attention deficit disorder. While the diagnosis may have been disheartening for others, it was encouraging for me, as it meant that my hyperactivity was not a character flaw that would cause me to fail, as my teacher had convinced me, but was a physiological condition that could be medically remedied. I convinced myself that no matter how much hard work it took, I was going to succeed, academically and otherwise, and set out to achieve that objective. A few weeks later, a second setback occurred, making my goal more daunting, when I was rushed to the hospital emergency room suffering an epileptic seizure. When I returned to class, no one would talk to me or touch me, and called me a witch. Many years later, I found out that while I was absent, my third-grade teacher, who didn't understand the scientific basis for epilepsy, had told my classmates that I was "possessed by the Devil." Upon my return, she placed me in a class with a tutor, telling me that I was "stupid", and I was asked not to return to the school in the fall. While some might have expected these disadvantages and societal expectations to constrain me, I have allowed the experience of dealing with them to become part of my identity, which has made me unique.

After being diagnosed, I learned quickly that those who ask for help with disabilities not visible to the naked eye risk being viewed as hypochondriacs, or as lacking in motivation. I did not know it at the time, but this realization was to become my defining moment, because I refused to allow myself to be labeled as lazy or learning disabled, a decision that gave me perseverance and determination to succeed. At the same time, my experiences allowed me to identify with victims and underdogs. Occasionally, the disparaging remarks of people regarding ADD and epilepsy arouse my ire in a manner I cannot express, one ringing example being the middle-school science teacher who asked my mother, "How can she be so smart when she takes so many pills?" However, such comments have only increased my determination to become an attorney and an advocate, without the extra help available to me because of my disabilities. I took both the LSAT and the GMAT without the extended times to which I was legally entitled by the Individuals with Disabilities Education Act (IDEA) and Section 504 of the Rehabilitation Act. Though this required more preparation than if I had relied on extended time, I am prouder of my scores of 165 and 710 than I would have been of scores of 170 and 750 achieved with an accommodation.

My most character-building experience is a continuous process, as I am reminded every day from the moment I wake up in the morning to the moment I go to sleep at night. My perseverance and determination help me rise to the challenge of living with ADD and epilepsy, while my affinity with victims and underdogs draws me to the practice of law, to provide hope for the same chance at success in life for these individuals.

MARK ALLAN PICKERING

Mark graduated with honors from and received the Edwin Smith Hinkley Scholarship at Brigham Young University, where he majored in political science. He worked for three semesters as a teaching or research assistant for his professors. He interrupted college for two years to serve in Frankfurt, Germany, as a missionary for the Church of Jesus Christ of Latter-day Saints.

Stats

LSAT score: 168
Undergraduate GPA: 3.91
College attended: Brigham Young University
Year of college graduation: 2002
Hometown: Arlington, TX
Gender: Male
Race: Caucasian

Personal statement prompt

Mark did not report writing his personal statement in response to any particular question.

There was a time in eighth grade, shortly after the riots in Los Angeles that followed the acquittal of police officers accused of brutality in beating Rodney King, when the school administration decided they needed to call an assembly in order to explain things. I sat obediently through the proceedings and agreed with the condemnation of rioting: "Rioting is just stupid," said one student. But when the police officer speaking to us and responding to student comments off-handedly dismissed the court proceedings that acquitted the officers as obviously flawed, I decided I had to say something. I raised my hand, was called on, and then stood up. In a somewhat feeble voice (there were a lot of people in there), I said, "None of us was at the trial or saw the evidence. I think we ought to trust the courts and not condemn what we haven't seen." Silence and rude glares followed, but no responses came.

My professors, fellow-parishioners, and classmates — if they know me at all — know me as one who thinks for himself. In my tenth grade American literature class we were discussing John Steinbeck's *Grapes of Wrath*. When asked to present commentary on a section that compared Jefferson and Madison with Lenin and Marx, I registered my disagreement. The members of my class were somewhat irritated — you weren't supposed to *disagree* with the author!

Now, I wasn't disagreeing to be disagreeable — I really believed what I was saying. I was disturbed people were willing to believe the book because it was in print. But most importantly of all, it did not bother me that I disagreed. I remained convinced of my view because no one satisfactorily refuted my arguments.

Teachers didn't always like me in High School. I guess I disputed too much. Teachers in college love me — they seem to think no one here disputes enough. Here is an atypical example: a few weeks ago a professor of mine felt obligated to apologize for the Supreme Court's use of the word "imbeciles" to describe mentally disabled people. I told him it was a technical term that specified mental ability according to IQ. He didn't believe me, so I looked it up. He looked it up as well. An imbecile is a person with a mental age of eight to twelve.

Often I find myself to be the only one in a classroom willing to defend an unpopular point of view. Once a visiting lecturer in one of my small classes criticized libertarianism. I found myself sticking up for it. At BYU, I find myself in certain situations to be the only one who is willing to speak for theistic evolution.

I suppose this propensity to think for myself has always existed, but I think my experience in Germany strengthened it. When in Germany, I had the opportunity to speak with an American accountant whom a large German company had hired. He described his difficulty in getting his coworkers to switch to Generally Accepted Accounting Practices (GAAP). I then rejoined, "Then just imagine how difficult it is to get them to believe in the Book of Mormon!" He merely shook his head, stupefied. "I can imagine..." he said.

Sometimes my companion in the mission field and I were the only Latter-day Saints for miles. For hours, days, and weeks on end, we would be unable to find any one interested in listening to us. Occasionally came a shrill rebuke, especially from elderly men, "Why don't you go find something worthwhile to do? You're just wasting your time!" At first it was quite discouraging, but after several months I found myself quite accustomed to acting as only I found appropriate. People ignored me as I tried to stop them in pedestrian zones. It became a challenge to get past barriers people erected to keep out solicitations from strangers.

I found when I returned after two years that this experience had permanently changed the way I dealt with resistance to or criticism of my views. I respond with emotional indifference now. This combined with my previous and current independence of mind has been a gift that has allowed me to think and pursue what I think is right no matter what the opposition.

HILLARY SCHROEDER

Hillary graduated from the University of Wisconsin—Madison, where she majored in creative writing. She was editor of UW's national literary magazine and a book critic for the university's student newspaper. After college, she earned her MA in humanities from the University of Chicago. Between academic programs, Hillary worked at a wildlife rehabilitation center and at a public interest law firm.

Stats

LSAT scores: 168, 170
Undergraduate GPA: 3.36
College attended: University of Wisconsin—Madison
Year of college graduation: 2002
Graduate school GPA: 3.58
Graduate school attended: University of Chicago
Year of graduate school graduation: 2004 (MA in humanities)
Hometown: Oshkosh, WI
Gender: Female
Race: Caucasian

Admissions information

Law school attended: University of Chicago, Class of 2008
Accepted: University of Chicago, Boston College, Fordham University, University of Iowa, University of Wisconsin
Denied: University of California—Los Angeles, University of Texas
Waitlisted: Duke University, Northwestern University

Personal statement prompt

After sending in her initial application to the University of Chicago, Hillary was contacted by an admissions officer who requested that she submit an additional essay. One of the topic options was to write a response to a current best-selling book. She wrote about the use of code and illustration in Extremely Loud and Incredibly Close and was accepted to the University of Chicago within two weeks of submitting this essay.

When America's newest and youngest literary darling decides to tackle September 11 in his second novel, everyone has an opinion. I began reading Jonathan Safran Foer's bestseller, *Extremely Loud & Incredibly Close,* mere weeks after it was released amid a flood of critical debate. Because the book enjoys, or suffers from, such intense journalistic scrutiny, I knew, even before lifting the front cover, that *Incredibly Close* features illustrations, epistolary prose poems and a fourteen-page flipbook. John Updike dubbed these items "textual embellishments" in his review for *The New Yorker.* Some argue that the embellishments result in compelling mixed-media and others insist that they constitute a cheap marketing ploy. Although I initially struggled with the disruptive nature of these literary idiosyncrasies, I eventually came to see them as necessary and moving. *Incredibly Close* explores our diminished capacity to communicate in the aftermath of catastrophe. Words often fail Foer's characters, forcing them to attempt other modes of expression. This book's unusual form, occasionally privileging other media over standard text, is the mirror image of their plight.

The characters in *Incredibly Close* suffer from an inability to disclose their emotional burdens with speech, and they are hard-pressed to find alternatives. Our hero is Oskar Schell, a precocious nine-year-old whose father perished in the September 11 attacks. When Oskar comes home from school on that fateful day, he finds his dad's last words recorded on the answering machine. Instead of sharing these messages with his mother, he hides the machine and makes her coded jewelry:

"What I did was I converted Dad's last voice message into Morse code, and I used sky-blue beads for silence, maroon beads for breaks between letters, violet beads for breaks between words, and long and short pieces of string between the beads for long and short beeps…"

Oskar is a forthcoming and even garrulous child who usually speaks everything on his mind, even to the chagrin of the other characters. It is thus especially revealing that he is unable to disclose his traumatic discovery, hearing his father's last words, to his mother. His need to share is obvious. Why else would he spend a reported "nine hours" creating the bracelet? Oscar's inability to discuss the incident verbally leaves him no choice but to seek an alternative.

The reader learns that Oskar's sculptor grandfather, Thomas, is marked by a similar disability, having lost his capacity for speech after surviving the Dresden bombings. His silence is the result of a mental barrier rather than a physical injury. Thomas explains, "…the silence overtook me like a cancer." Now he primarily communicates by answering questions with "yes" and "no," words that are tattooed on his hands. The thing he most wants to discuss is his pain over the lover he lost in Dresden. Because he cannot, Thomas continually sculpts her likeness. This is another character whose brush with catastrophe renders him unable to express what he holds most dear, except through abstract, nonverbal means. His difficulty resurfaces later in the novel, when the reader encounters several pages filled with numbers. Here, Thomas is writing a letter and is incapable of using words to describe this sorrow. It is easier for him to create a numeric code.

Foer reinforces his point by giving *Incredibly Close* a structure that suffers from the same affliction as its characters. Foer is often uncomfortable spelling out poignant events to the reader. He prefers other channels, such as those infamously labeled "textual embellishments." I found the most affecting example of this to be a letter from Thomas, written to the son he abandoned. Instead of describing the letter, Foer just inserts it, covered in red circles. If I wasn't made previously aware of the son's compulsion to circle typos and grammatical errors with a red pen, I couldn't be sure he read it. The text doesn't offer a narrative account of the son's reaction to this letter, nor does it offer an account of him receiving it. Foer's reader must glean the son's feelings by noting which words receive red circles, which parts of the letter he marks as untrue. The circles are the story. It takes a moment to understand the task at hand, but the letter's significance is quickly understood and Foer's strange tactics do not feel cheap. The book's form echoes the lessons of his characters. *I cannot tell you. Words are not enough to get me through this.*

My reading may not be intuitive to everyone. When taken out of context the codes, use of color, and illustrations appear to be style without substance. Admittedly, many critics disagree with my view. In his review for *The Boston Globe*, Steve Almond wrote, "We don't need gimmicks to keep our attention; we just need the truth." In a Salon.com article, Ruth Franklin had an especially negative reaction to *Incredibly Close's* flipbook sequence, referring to it as puerile. She wrote, "[I] found [it] the book's most egregious example of inappropriate whimsy."

These critics stand in direct opposition to my own beliefs. The flipbook is the final sequence of *Incredibly Close,* beginning where Oskar's words end. It is created from video stills of a man falling from the World Trade Center, but Oskar orders the images backwards, resulting in an impossible ascent. He harbors the childish wish that we might travel back in time, to the pre-September 11 era, and be safe. Seeing the pages had a much greater impact on me than reading about them would have. But even if this were not the case, I could not find the flipbook, or any of the "embellishments," inappropriate, much less whimsical. They are an integral component of Foer's vision of our struggle for connection in the wake of tragedy. He insists that words will sometimes fail us. Instead, we must employ other forms of communication, other types of art. When an artist decides that the shape of his novel and the lives of his characters will be molded by the same principles, the results are in real anger of becoming gimmicky. Fortunately, this is not the case in *Incredibly Close*. This marriage of form and content triumphs in its investigation of the people September 11 left behind. Foer goes head-to-head with an all too recent tragedy. His decision to occasionally favor a visual component over additional explication makes his work feel true. And, as one critic pointed out, this is exactly what a September 11 novel should do.

STEPHANIE LADD

Stephanie attended the University of Colorado—Boulder, where she was a classics major. During her undergraduate years, she worked the overnight shift full-time at a software company to pay her way through school; she also had two years of bookkeeping/accounting experience. In her last year of college, she received a prestigious travel fellowship for archaeological research in Italy. She also noted in her application that she was a first-generation college graduate.

Stats
LSAT score: 161
Undergraduate GPA: 3.5
College attended: University of Colorado—Boulder
Year of college graduation: 2001
Hometown: Santa Fe, NM
Gender: Female
Race: Caucasian

Admissions information
Law school attended: University of Colorado—Boulder, Class of 2005
Accepted: University of Colorado—Boulder, Lewis and Clark College, University of Miami, Washington University
Denied: None
Waitlisted: None

Personal statement prompt

In Stephanie's words, "I used the same essay for each school; the topic for the CU—Boulder essay was simply to write a personal statement on anything we would like the admissions committee to consider. I decided that committee members probably grow weary of endless essays pontificating the virtues of their writers, so I just shared something about myself and my past."

In the summer of 1990 my father, a mechanic for the city of Grand Junction, Colorado, was involved in an accident. He was working on a fire truck engine when his hand glanced too close to the turbocharger. The screen that should have acted as a barrier to such accidents was missing, and a large portion of my father's right hand was instantly consumed. A small financial settlement was made, but it did not correspond to the resulting pain which even now remains present or to the loss of one's sole trade.

Within a few months my father found a job as an auto-electric rebuilder. This was a step down for a master mechanic, but the position was less physically demanding; besides, employment opportunities in Grand Junction were rare. A year and a half later, my father invested everything he owned into his own auto-electric business, Mesa Alternator Service.

My father, mother, eldest brother, and I all worked together at the small shop. I did everything from filing taxes to polishing parts with a bead-blaster. My mother and I spent weekends writing up advertisements, mailing out statements, and tidying up the shop. My father himself worked seventeen-hour days and developed alternators and starters vastly superior to those already on the market. The business was wildly successful; it was out of the red within the first year, and profits rose steadily each subsequent year.

People often tell my father that he has been extraordinarily lucky; I disagree. The individuals involved with the operation of that company sacrificed to ensure its success. The same people often remark that I, a first generation college student, have also been extraordinarily lucky to attend such fine institutions. I have enjoyed many educational experiences during these past years; yet it must be emphasized that I approached them determined to use every method of succeeding. The experience I gained at Mesa Alternator Service facilitated this greatly; when I found it necessary to work full-time while in school, I was able to persuade a company to hire me despite a policy not to hire full-time students. They did not regret their decision.

I have often read that the greatest predictor of success in an academic setting results from growing up in a family with strong educational and professional backgrounds. I suppose this is true to a certain extent, especially in respect to professional programs. Yet a far more important determinant of success is to take measure of how the student resolves to put to use all the resources available at the time. My GPA and LSAT score indicate that I have the potential to succeed at law school. The short chapter of family history recounted above shows why I believe that intelligent resolve to succeed may count for more.

ROBERTO DELEÓN

Roberto started law school almost twenty years after completing his undergraduate degree in electrical engineering. A nontraditional student, he was accepted into the evening program at the University of Houston Law Center and works full-time during the day at a Houston law firm, where he drafts patent applications. Before applying to law school, Roberto worked in the semiconductor, aerospace, electric utility, and oil and gas industries as a computer consultant and design engineer. He is married with two children, one of whom was born the day before his first law school final. Roberto hopes to work as a patent attorney after graduation.

Stats
LSAT score: 155
Undergraduate GPA: 3.10
College attended: University of Houston, Cullen College of Engineering
Year of college graduation: 1983
Hometown: New York, NY
Gender: Male
Race: Latino

Personal statement prompt

Roberto notes that he responded to an open-ended essay prompt.

It's interesting how a day that changes your entire life starts out just like any other. I woke up that fall morning in 1970 and got ready for school just like I always did, walking by the television on my way to the breakfast table as the morning newscaster recited the latest totals of dead and wounded in Vietnam with the monotonous regularity of a metronome. The war had always been there for me, just another part of the background of my life. After breakfast and a brief walk up the hill, I spent an otherwise uneventful day at school.

When I came home from school I entered the house through the garage and into the kitchen and immediately knew something was wrong. My mother was on the phone with a frantic look on her face. She looked at me just long enough to say, "Your father has been in an accident." I stood there in silence, numb with confusion and uncertainty. How was I supposed to feel? Why wasn't I feeling anything? The day turned into a blurred montage of disjoint images. The hospital; my dad with his head wrapped up; my sister crying over the remains of his favorite sweater; the pillow on my bed as I cried myself to sleep.

My father had been in an explosion. He worked for an explosives company making weapons for a war that many people no longer wanted. Someone, it seems, decided to express this feeling with a bomb. Six hundred pounds of Astrolite ended the lives of three men that day and for three days we waited, hoping my father would not become the fourth. "Wake up Monkey" my mother whispered into his ear. I never knew my parents had pet names for each other. And on the third day he heard her. My father opened his eyes and through the wires holding his jaw together he commented, "Lots of pretty nurses around here!" to which the doctor declared that he was on the road to recovery.

And recover he did. Over the next several months I watched in awe as the man that, up until then, I never truly knew taught me what it meant to never give up. Within one month, he was back home. He endured countless surgeries to rebuild his face, his jaw and one of his eardrums. For years after the explosion, he removed splinters from all over his bodies, embedded there by the force of the blast. Yet through all of it, the pain, the hospital visits, the rehabilitation, always there was a smile. My father, and his father before him, always had a wonderful sense of humor. He could always find the lighter side of any situation. The explosion had left him without his right ear, but even this was something he could joke about. "I'll never trust Italians," he told be with a totally straight face one day. "Why not dad?" I asked with the classic innocence of a 10-year old. "Because this guy came up to me and said Romans, countrymen, lend me your ears, and I did and he never gave it back." We laughed together at his silly joke. Dad was OK with it, he really was OK; and if he was OK, I was OK!

My dad eventually went back to work, but as the years went by, the injuries took a toll on him. He had to stop working and over time his life slowed down more and more. But through all of it, there was always that smile, that contagious laugh. He never lost his humor, his desire to always see the people around him happy. And not once did I ever hear him speak hatefully of the people who placed that bomb. He never saw the point in wanting revenge. We never did find out who they were.

This is the inheritance I received from my father: his gift to me of perpetual hope and faith. Throughout my life it has lifted me up and carried me through some of the hardest times of my life. It kept me in college when I thought becoming an engineer was too hard for me. It gave me courage those times when I faced the uncertainty of the many career changes I made. It gave me hope during my divorce when I thought I would never be loved again. And it gives me the strength not just to face the challenges presented by life, but to actively seek them out. Now I face Law School. It is with faith in myself that I take on this challenge, and it is with hope that I look to my chosen future.

It's been eight years since my father passed away. I do miss him, but I know that he is with me always, still whispering his silly jokes into my ear. I know that I will always be able to face the challenges that await me and that even when I do not fully succeed in overcoming them that I will still walk away from them that much wiser and always with a smile on my face. It's all about the attitude that you keep in your heart.

By the way Dad, I'm still OK. Thanks.

UNIVERSITY OF MICHIGAN

ANONYMOUS

As an undergrad, this student worked roughly 20–25 hours a week at assorted jobs in addition to her regular course load. She still made time to tutor high school students in Harlem, write for Barnard's news magazine, and actively participate in a couple of student organizations. After graduating from college, she completed a year-long policy research fellowship at a non-profit that promoted sustainable homes, workplaces, and communities and worked closely with the executive director on a wide range of environmental advocacy issues. After the fellowship, this student took about five months off to travel throughout Europe while studying for the LSAT and completing law school applications.

Stats
LSAT score: 158
Undergraduate GPA: 3.4
College attended: Barnard College, Columbia University
Year of college graduation: 2007
Hometown: Atlanta, GA
Gender: Female
Race: Caucasian

Admissions information
Law school attended: University of Michigan, Class of 2012
Accepted: University of Michigan, Columbia University, University of Texas at Austin, Washington University in St. Louis, University of Georgia, University of North Carolina
Denied: None
Waitlisted: University of Virginia, University of Pennsylvania, Northwestern University, Duke University

Personal statement prompt

This student wrote this in response to an open-ended essay prompt.

I grew up within walking distance of East Lake Meadows and the East Lake Golf Club, and the proximity of both has influenced the direction of my life as much as they shaped the character of my neighborhood. East Lake Meadows, a public housing complex of derelict apartment towers, was nicknamed "Little Vietnam" by city officials because 86% of the residents were unemployed and the crime rate was 18 times the national average; it was the only neighborhood that the mayor of Atlanta refused to drive through alone. Many of the worst characteristics of East Lake Meadows permeated the neighborhood – rampant drug trafficking, violent crime, an undeniable disregard for community, and the pervasive perception that there were few viable opportunities available. I was exposed to little outside my neighborhood beyond what I read in books, and although I could see that some neighborhoods were cleaner, and others had much bigger homes, I was largely ignorant of how poorly my neighborhood compared to others. It was only when I enrolled in a private high school on the other side of town that I began to explore other neighborhoods in depth.

There were many things I could have envied about my new classmates' lifestyles, but the only thing I coveted was their neighborhoods. My friends lived in safe places where children went trick-or-treating and played in the local parks; their families left their cars to linger over meals that were brought to them at a table; culture—in the form of art galleries, theaters and concert halls—was everywhere; there were multiple grocery stores, and they were all clean and stocked with fresh produce. Eventually, I came to realize that the amenities were the superficial manifestation of what was truly appealing—limitless opportunity and possibility. A desire to attend college, backpack around the world or hike the Appalachian Trail was never questioned in their neighborhoods in the way that it was questioned in mine. I began to understand that there were so many connections between where you live and your understanding of your place in the world around you.

Across the street from East Lake Meadows was the East Lake Golf Club. The private golf course country club was famous as the location of the PGA Tour Championship and as the home course of the legendary golfer Bobby Jones. Unfortunately, the glory of the East Lake Golf Club was declining in direct proportion to the rising infamy of the neighborhood, and the country club seemed destined for closure. Instead it was sold, and the new owner spearheaded a coalition of partners—including the City of Atlanta and private developers – that began an extensive campaign to revitalize the neighborhood. The public housing was razed and replaced with mixed-income housing, a YMCA and a charter school. Over time, the crime rate plummeted, middle-class couples began moving into the neighborhood and renovating houses, the charter school was held up as a model of success and, nearly ten years later, the neighborhood is beginning to be considered a trendy urban community.

As these changes evolved, so did my perception of the built environment. Cities, with their tall buildings and miles of concrete, had always been fixed entities in my mind. Learning that they were in fact malleable, and that positive changes in the built environment can spur positive changes in the lives of its residents made me recognize the potential of urban planning as a tool for social change. It was while I was studying the built environment at Barnard College and while working at a non-profit that promotes sustainable homes, workplaces and communities that I began to see the many legal dimensions to building strong and healthy communities. I learned of the legal battles that surrounded the demolition of East Lake Meadows as I was researching eminent domain; writing my thesis required me to understand the process of rezoning New York's industrial waterfront; incorporating sustainability into community development introduced a component of environmental law. This process of discovering and exploring my personal and professional interests in urban planning, community development and sustainability led me to law school because the law stands out as a tool that significantly impacts all three.

Statement of Diversity

"We seek to admit students from different academic, cultural, social, ethnic, and economic backgrounds. If you choose to submit this essay, tell us how you think you would contribute to the intellectual and social life of the law school."

I have had many disparate life experiences that set me apart from others. I was born and raised in the South, where I was first educated at an inner city public school and then at a private international school. My education then led me northeast to a women's college in New York City. My family of ten was poor, but I have been very privileged to attend some of the best schools to study precisely what I am passionate about – largely cities and sustainable development. I am a liberal feminist, which conflicts regularly with my conservative Mormon upbringing. My gender and ethnicity have been omnipresent factors as well. These experiences will contribute to the diversity of the student body at ___ Law School in two ways. On a very fundamental level, they have shaped my perspective of the world, which will influence the conversations I have with my peers and professors throughout law school. In addition to offering diversity, these experiences have given me the ability to bring together people with divergent backgrounds and actively facilitate meaningful interaction among them.

I have had the uncommon opportunity to meet and to befriend people from a wide variety of socioeconomic, social and cultural backgrounds, which has shaped my understanding of and desire for diversity. I have found people with unconventional backgrounds to be open minded and accepting of my own complex, and at times contradictory, background. For example, one friend—a conservative, gay Black man—understood more readily than others that a Black Mormon could also be a liberal feminist. A second beneficial byproduct of diversity has been greater intellectual stimulation. Discussions with people who hold an array of political opinions are simply more interesting than discussions where homogeneous viewpoints are reiterated over and over again. It is because of these benefits of diversity that I actively seek out people with disparate histories, motivations and viewpoints. My experience interacting with people with a broad array of life experiences has equipped me with the skills necessary to bridge the gaps among them. It is thus that I both offer diversity and facilitate diversity.

DANIEL MARTIN

Dan graduated from SUNY—Geneseo with a major in sociology. He lived or traveled abroad during most of his post-college years; during this period, he visited more than twenty countries and studied several languages. He started his own company in Japan; backpacked around Asia for two years; and enrolled in a Chinese university to study Mandarin before returning to the United States start law school.

Stats

LSAT score: 173
Undergraduate GPA: 3.14
College attended: State University of New York—Geneseo
Year of college graduation: 1995
Hometown: Liverpool, NY
Gender: Male
Race: Caucasian (Dan notes, however, that he "always checked the 'decline to answer' ethnicity box" on his law school applications)

```
Admissions information
```

Law school attended: University of Michigan, Class of 2005
Accepted: University of Michigan
Denied: Columbia University, Harvard University, University of Virginia, Yale University
Waitlisted: Duke University, University of Chicago, Vanderbilt University
Other: Dan's law school application history is as follows: In 1997, Dan applied to Columbia, Harvard, NYU, Stanford, University of Chicago, University of Michigan, University of Pennsylvania, Vanderbilt, and Yale. He was denied admission to all except Vanderbilt and University of Pennsylvania, both of which Waitlisted him. Then in 2001, Dan applied to Yale alone and was denied admission.

Personal statement prompt

Dan notes that he submitted this essay to all of the schools to which he applied. The application for the University of Michigan had the following prompt: "Michigan's talented student body is one of the Law School's richest resources. Each entering class of Michigan law students is composed of exceptionally accomplished people who bring a vast spectrum of experiences and perspectives to the law school community. To aid in constructing such a diverse and interesting class, Michigan's application for admission requires a personal statement. This statement provides applicants an opportunity to demonstrate the ways in which they can contribute their unique talents and experiences to the law school.

"The required personal statement should be well organized and well written; apart from that, the form and content are up to you. Successful applicants have elaborated on significant personal, academic, and professional experiences, as well as meaningful intellectual interests and extracurricular activities. In general, the personal statement should not be a mere catalog of accomplishments and activities, but a thoughtful explanation of what those accomplishments and activities have meant to you."

Also included is an optional additional essay for the University of Michigan.

"I'd like to see the world, for the whirligig of men is, as it were, a living book and as good as any science."

—Gogol, Dead Souls

I remember the day clearly—it was day number six of an eleven-day Vipassana ("Insight") silent meditation course in Dharamsala, a Tibetan refugee village in Northern India—after some fifty hours of meditation, six days since my last spoken words, I decided that I was ready to go to law school. Hundreds of monkeys screamed in the trees above me, and the sky was ethereally blue.

I left the US over a year ago, to travel throughout much of Asia, in search of adventure, a bevy of unpredictable experiences, and insights into a world of multifarious ideals—I have encountered all three on various levels. But while traveling has had innumerable benefits to me as an investment in my future self—challenging many of my opinions and world-views—I am now ready to begin my career, among some of the world's brightest objective thinkers.

Because my ideas and plans have changed so frequently over the past six years, I am not sure where my career will lead; I would like to work internationally, perhaps serving as a corporate liaison between cultures. A law school education will open many doors, but I am most interested in interacting with intelligent peers, and learning how to improve my ability to think objectively on a number of levels.

My strong interest in objective analyses first manifested itself two years ago, in thoughts and discussions about reading. I was working as a night security guard at a public nursing home—since most of the residents posed only a minimal flight risk in the middle of the night, and the building was equipped with a state-of-the-art security system to thwart unauthorized entry, my official duties were few. I am grateful for my curious younger self's vigilance in performing a self-imposed duty: reading widely, across disciplines. An average of five hours per night, I read mostly academic journals or textbooks, spending roughly equal time studying neuroscience, genetics, sociology, philosophy, psychology and literature. I would read three books at a time, so as to spot patterns and similarities in the different fields.

In the last year, I have read countless books on innumerable bus journeys or train rides, and held many interesting conversations with people from many countries. I have learned the worth and the sacrifices inherent in probing the minds or hearts of people from different cultures. I will bring a valuable form of diversity to law school, in my exposure to different cultures and the perspective which objective analysis of my experiences has given me. I have spent four of the past five years abroad, visiting thirty countries. But I was not always reading a book or debating the nature of dreams or emotions while I was riding buses or trains...

In Laos, fate put me on a truck with no headlights, driving slowly up a mountain dirt road after five days of monsoon rain—after a flat tire, several hours of slogging through mud, and a brake problem, I found myself sitting on the roof of the cab with a Vietnamese man, illuminating the road with our flashlights so the driver could see it. In Indonesia I woke up at 2AM on an overnight bus to find a machine gun in my face—all of the other men had been taken off the bus. It turned out to be a standard military checkpost in an unstable region—after showing my passport to the soldier and trying to explain in Indonesian that my visa was not expired, I went back to sleep.

My serious interest in travel was born shortly after I moved to Tokyo in 1996. Japan is a fun place, full of mysteries and the strange idiosyncratic trends of 110 million people. I was a conversational English teacher for a year, and I left that job to start my own company—my company was very small, as I was the only employee! I was an English Consultant for Hikari Tsushin, Inc., a mid-size telecommunications distributor—as such, my duties were "anything and everything related to English," including Business English lessons to executives; "Survival English crash courses" for Directors and the President; and writing English public relations materials, such as a bond underwriting proposal or the annual report.

In Japan I met many travelers on their way around the world—it was primarily their stories which peaked my interest, convincing me to leave Japan in search of self-education and funny stories. One of my most surprising yet disturbing lessons learned is that much of the rest of the world's people understand America and American interests, at times quite intimately. I have had discussions on American politics in the jungles of Sumatra, small villages in Northern Thailand, and in the mountains of Nepal. Our overall lack of knowledge about the rest of the world is a dangerous vulnerability which, in my opinion, needs to be addressed. Though budget traveling around the world does not pay the bills, and entails many emotional sacrifices, I honestly feel that I am a better person because of my experiences. I feel that I would be a valuable member of your entering class, and I respectfully hope that you concur.

Dan wrote this essay in response to the following prompt: "Applicants are also invited to submit, at their discretion, two additional 250-word essays. . . . The second optional essay should reveal, in a way that an LSAT score or a grade point average cannot, something about the way you think. For example, you might choose to discuss an intellectual or social problem you have faced or a book or film that has particularly affected you."

*Culmination of Research, Travel and Thought, 1996–2001

"Through conscious beings the universe has generated self-awareness."

—V.S. Ramachandran

Humankind is an eyeball, which perceives itself through the lens of its internally generated conception of a self-image.

The human body is a complex jumble of incalculable intricacy, housing untold numbers of competing desires, thoughts, proteins and parasites, imprisoned together in the dense jungle of Self. Our memories, antibodies, dreams and genes lay the groundwork while our consciousness forges the path, examining detailed interpretations of the present course.

Similarly, every human society is composed of competing, yet symbiotic, cells and organs: its members and the institutions to which they relate. All human cultures, through the actions of their members, effectively promote or discourage certain behaviors, emotional states, and family structures, in line with a core set of values and ideas through which they are defined at the macro level. Most societies, like all organisms, seek to reproduce and expand their influence.

How cultures interact with one another, how people within a given society interact, and how the individual cells and desires within those people do the same, is the essence of the study of people—one of my core interests—an integration of the fields of biology, neuroscience, psychology, philosophy, physics, religion, anthropology, sociology, and laws which unite, divide, and define them.

Going one step further, I believe that the Earth is alive, and that a diverse humankind is one of its most important organs—taken as a whole, we are the self—conscious mind struggling to understand its place in the universe, the organ of planetary self-awareness.

ISRAEL MOYA

After graduating from college, Israel worked as a sixth-grade teacher at an inner-city school in Los Angeles. Other work experience he has had includes manual labor jobs and a position in university outreach helping low-income students prepare for and apply to college. As a Peace Corps health volunteer in Central Asia, he gained experience in community organization, small project development, and health care advocacy and he emerged with "a deeper understanding of international human rights concerns."

Stats
LSAT score: 158 (first score cancelled due to testing center problem)
Undergraduate GPA: 3.4
College attended: University of California—Los Angeles (transferred from Bakersfield Community College)
Year of college graduation: 1998
Hometown: McFarland, CA
Gender: Male
Race: Mexican American

Personal statement prompt

Israel notes that he responded to the following prompt in writing this essay for his application to the University of Michigan: "Michigan's student body is one of the law school's richest resources. Each entering class is composed of accomplished people who bring a spectrum of experiences and perspectives to the law school community. To aid in constructing a diverse and interesting class, we require a personal statement. This statement provides you with an opportunity to demonstrate the ways in which you can contribute your talents and experiences to the law school. Successful applicants have elaborated on significant personal, academic, and professional experiences; meaningful intellectual interests, and extracurricular activities; factors inspiring them to obtain a legal education; and significant obstacles, challenges, or disadvantages met and overcome. The form and content of the personal statement are up to you. (For ease of reading, please use double-spacing and at least eleven-point font.)"

Several years ago I sat at home and wondered what to do. My mother had come home crying. She had been fired from the convalescence home where she worked cleaning and doing laundry. It was the best job she had had since arriving in "*el infierno*", as she referred to McFarland back in 1987 when we first moved there from Los Angeles. For her it *was* hell. There, in the small farming town in California's San Joaquin Valley, the weather was unbearably hot and our poverty took a different face. The primary work that was available to uneducated and non-English speaking people like my parents was in the fields, and that's where my mother worked, until she found the job at the convalescence home several years later. She had been so happy with her job as a cleaning lady that she felt that it was like heaven. Of course, it was terrible to see my mother crying after she had been fired, but it was worse to feel that I could do nothing about it. I sat angry and wondered what to do, but in the end did nothing. This was a great and painful shame. I was glad to know that my sister went to the director's office to ask for my mother's job back, but I knew that I should've done more. My mother returned to the fields where she picked grapes in the summer and pruned frozen grapevines in the winter. It was bruising work. She had an accident in the fields some years later and ended up on disability with a damaged spine. Although she later found justice by returning to volunteer at her former place of work, it would take me a while longer before I could excuse my lack of action during my mother's time of need.

I now realize how experiences such as my mother's have helped define the purpose of my life. Concerns of the poor and disadvantaged, be it in education, employment, immigration, housing, and social services have always been personal matters. Although my third-grade educated parents weren't able to give me a literary education they were able to instill in me lasting virtues that have allowed me to lead a meaningful life. By the sixth grade I was already helping my father pick onions, dragging the full buckets back and forth from the field to the bin, tallying one more dollar for every load. I was just a child, but I understood that while some work was thankless, it was necessary. I always felt a need to carry my own weight working throughout college and university and during nearly every school vacation, up until the summer after my graduation from UCLA, when I sorted and bagged carrots at a processing plant in Bakersfield. This lifelong experience combined with the encouragement that I found in books like *The Grapes of Wrath* and *The Autobiography of Malcolm X* had a powerful effect in my life. This is manifested in my love for and dedication to my community, and in my steadfast concern for the social, economic, and political well being of the poor.

In the summer of 2000 my desire to further understand my community led me on a daring adventure. With a small budget and an ambitious itinerary I aimed to travel for half a year, studying social and political movements in Mexico. My solitary five months trekking across Mexico led me to discover strength and beauty that I didn't know existed in my culture. I became a strong new person as a result of the trip, and I developed a further understanding of the difficulties of living poor. This understanding would serve me well in my roles at work and in my community, but also, the trip to Mexico gave me the confidence to go places and do things that where unheard of in my community.

Today I am a Peace Corps volunteer. From this side of the world, in Uzbekistan, I see my home back in America from a unique perspective. Justice, economic freedom, and civil liberties are concepts that have new meaning to me now that I can more clearly see how their lack of protection affects people's lives. Here, in my village in the Ferghana Valley, there are regular examples of how people can become demoralized when they have no way of challenging the problems that affect their lives. When my friends' salaries go unpaid for months, and they still show up for work, lest they lose any chance of ever being paid, I am reminded of how many years ago my mother cried after being fired. There is no doubt that American society offers more recourse than tears, but this is something that seems unknown in many of the poorest pockets of America. This motivates me to take on the challenges of the poor back home. I know that as I go on to become a public interest lawyer I will find much strength and encouragement from the insight I've gained here in Uzbekistan.

My life's experiences have undoubtedly shaped my mind and eyes into critical and compassionate instruments of social analysis. Even so, I expect that the greatest intellectual leap of my life still awaits me at The University of Michigan Law School. My concerns for the poor will find new practical forms of expression as I learn jurisprudence; furthermore, I intend to shape my legal education with the firm commitment that I will not allow my thoughts and objections to go unheard. These are not resolutions that will pass with the day, but determinations which are rooted in a lifetime of experimentation.

BARRY BERENBERG

Before applying to law school, Barry worked as an aerospace engineer, engineering consultant, and technical writer for thirteen years. This work experience, he writes, "not only contributed to my admissions decision, but has also been valuable during my first year of law school." During his second year of law school, Barry served as a staff member on the New Mexico Law Review and as president of the IP Matters student organization. He remains active in the Society for the Advancement of Material and Process Engineering and serves as the community representative on New Mexico's Newborn Screening Advisory Committee.

Stats
LSAT score: 168
Undergraduate GPA: 4.3/5.0
College attended: Massachusetts Institute of Technology
Year of college graduation: 1988
Graduate school GPA: 4.8/5.0
Graduate school attended: Massachusetts Institute of Technology
Year of graduate school graduation: 1991 (MA)
Hometown: Minneapolis, MN
Gender: Male
Race: Caucasian

Admissions information
Law school attended: University of New Mexico, Class of 2007
Accepted: University of New Mexico
Denied: None
Waitlisted: None

Personal statement prompt

The University of New Mexico requested a longer essay (three to five pages) than do most law schools. Barry responded to the following prompt: "The personal statement is an important part of your application. It is your opportunity to highlight important information not apparent in your application that may affect the Admission Committee's decision. Consider including general autobiographical information (family history, educational experiences, work experiences, achievements, obstacles overcome, extracurricular activities) and your reasons for wanting to study law in New Mexico."

The baby monitor woke me up some time after midnight. Ethan was eight or nine months old at the time. Although he would usually fall back to sleep after playing by himself for a bit, I decided to check on him anyway. As I stumbled into the room, still half asleep, he looked at me from his crib and said "Dad-dy." It didn't consciously register for a few moments: that single word, with a distinct pause between the two syllables. Like he was saying "Hey, I know who you are."

Thirteen years earlier, I could not have understood the importance of that event. I had just graduated from what is arguably the top engineering school in the world. A five year internship program had given me the experience to land a job with Orbital Sciences Corporation, a small company which had just launched its first rocket into orbit. On my first day at work, I was put in charge of structural development for the Taurus vehicle, a new, 100-foot tall rocket. At any other aerospace company I would have been analyzing bolts and other minor components for my first few years. Orbital, though, gave its young engineers a lot of responsibility: Taurus would never fly if I failed in my assignment.

I dove right into the job on my first day, learning about new technology, reading design reports and ordering the equipment and software I would need. (I would also meet my future wife, Lisa, that day, though at the time she was just another engineer on the program.) Over the next three years, I would learn the practical aspects of designing and building a rocket from scratch – from "art to part," as engineers like to say. I would travel around the country, managing manufacturing subcontractors and running full-scale structural tests. I would find that written and oral communication is critical to successful engineering, as I argued for my ideas and participated in design reviews. And I would be in the control center on March 13, 1994, as the first Taurus roared into orbit. At some point during those three years, Lisa and I would also find the time to get married and enjoy a short honeymoon.

Taurus lacked a second contract, so the original engineering team was disbanded. I worked on some new business proposals and smaller projects for the next year or so. In the summer of 1995, I was offered a job as the manufacturing engineer for Aurora Flight Sciences, a small company that builds unmanned aircraft (UAVs). I was to be in charge of building the Theseus UAV. With a wingspan greater than a 747's, it was designed to set new altitude records. The job offered a lot of responsibility for an engineer my age. Many of the skills I learned at Orbital carried over to the new job, but I also found myself more closely involved in day-to-day management and business development. The work was both challenging and fun, but both Lisa and I were having trouble adjusting to our new location. When my college intern employer called with an offer, we decided to take the opportunity to move back to New Mexico. I worked right through moving day, so I could ship out the last Theseus component.

We stayed in Los Alamos for a bit over a year, then we moved to Albuquerque when we both found aerospace jobs at Kirtland Air Force Base. We eventually settled in to a nice house in the East Mountains, and Ethan was born just under a year later. At first we both worked part time, but when Lisa was offered a promotion, she had to go back to work full time. I already had some small consulting jobs, so we decided I would quit my salaried job to take care of Ethan and work part-time as a consultant.

The job changes were to take place in October of 2000, right before Ethan's first birthday. That would turn out to be a difficult month, for many reasons. The day I quit my job, the contract I had been counting on for the bulk of my income was cancelled. Lisa's salary and my residual income would cover our expenses, but we would have to be careful. Later that month, we found the first indications that something might be wrong with Ethan. At the time, however, it didn't seem like a serious problem, and we had other concerns that at first seemed more pressing.

Because I was spending more time at home, I started to notice a lot of cracking in the walls and floors of our house. I called a structural engineer, who discovered some major settling problems. The repairs put a serious dent in our savings, but at least they stabilized the house. This also began my first real encounter with the legal system. The engineer had found clear evidence that the settling had been an ongoing problem that had been improperly repaired by previous owners. I began talking to some lawyers and quickly learned that having the facts on our side did not necessarily mean we could win a lawsuit, and that even if we did, the costs would likely exceed any award. Coping with Ethan's increasing medical problems also made it difficult to concentrate on anything else. We had decided to absorb the repair costs as an expensive lesson when – just a week before the statute of limitations was set to expire – our insurance company threatened to terminate our policy.

We felt we had no choice at that point and filed a negligence suit against our pre-purchase inspector, because he had missed obvious signs of the earlier repairs. Several months later, just a few days before the initial arbitration hearing, the inspector would turn over reports clearly showing he had diagnosed the same settling problems for the previous owners. Although the new evidence immensely helped our case, it was still a shock (to both us and our attorney) to learn that the inspector and the sellers had so blatantly withheld information from us. We ended up winning in arbitration, and the case is now waiting for trial on the inspector's appeal.

Although the entire process has been somewhat stressful, as our attorney warned it would be, I also found it to be challenging in the same way I am challenged by engineering projects. My structural engineering background gives me a deeper understanding of the facts in the case, even though rockets are not made with drywall and nails. More importantly, my general engineering skills – the ability to think logically, a close attention to detail and effective communication with a wide range of audiences – seem to be the same skills a good lawyer needs, and have enabled me to help our attorney analyze the evidence and testimony in our case.

During this time, as taking care of Ethan began to require more of my normal working hours, I began to shift my jobs from aerospace consulting to writing and Internet development – jobs I could more easily do in the middle of the night, when necessary. In covering the composites industry as a journalist, I became more aware of the complex intellectual property, patent and antitrust issues surrounding the technology. In many cases, these legal issues pose more of a challenge than the engineering development. As an Internet developer, the limitations of the legal system when dealing with issues of copyright, trademark, privacy, software patents and even telecommunications regulation in the new online world have become all too apparent. As I look at transitioning back into full-time work, I believe my technical background combined with a legal education will allow me to help shape policy in these areas.

Despite my intellectual interest in these issues, and my desire to take a more active role in developing policy, it was my experience as a parent that drove my final decision to pursue a legal career. Back in October of 2000, when I was dealing with the uncertainty of self employment and massive home repair bills, Ethan's pediatrician started a series of tests to determine why his motor development was delayed. A month later, a routine eye exam would reveal a rare defect that was the symptom of an even rarer disorder: GM2 Gangliosidosis. Tay-Sachs Disease, as it is more commonly known, is a degenerative neurological disorder that is always fatal by age five. At a time when most parents are planning for kindergarten, I find myself instead dealing with home health aids, physical therapists, feeding tubes, suction machines, multiple seizure medications, adult-strength laxatives and fluidized air mattresses.

Handling these purely medical issues gives me something to focus on. I have been able to use my technical and research skills to help our doctors find treatments for Ethan's symptoms. Dealing with the health care system, however, has by far been the more difficult task. Although we have good private insurance through Lisa's employer, it does not cover all of our major costs. We learned early on that Ethan was eligible for the Medically Fragile waiver under Medicaid, but bureaucratic and legislative obstacles made it both difficult to apply for and then be accepted into the program. I pushed my way through the system, meeting with the governor and state legislators, and even testifying before the state Health and Human Services Committee. We got Ethan into the program, but I still wonder how many other families would simply give up after encountering so much resistance.

Before Ethan was accepted into the program, we had to deal with denials from our insurance company. Often a simple letter from Ethan's doctor would solve the problem, but once, when a piece of equipment was denied, we had to go through the appeals process. I researched the particular benefit carefully and prepared a detailed document explaining why the item should be covered and how it met the definitions of a benefit given in our plan. Although the plan's medical board appeared to listen to my presentation, they rejected the appeal without responding to any of my arguments, simply repeating the original denial. I was in the process of preparing the next appeal when Ethan was accepted into the Medically Fragile program, which then covered the item. Still, the appeal was not in vain: several other families have used the documents I prepared as the basis for their own appeals.

I would only hear Ethan say "Daddy" two more times before he finally lost the ability to speak. Last October, just after his fourth birthday, he lost the ability to eat, his last remaining skill. All we can do for him now is to keep him as comfortable as possible. By studying family and children's law, however, I hope to help improve the lives of other children in the state. UNM's Community Lawyering Clinic offers a unique opportunity to work in this field before graduation, similar in many ways to the internship program I found so valuable in my engineering career. Although I do not expect family law to be the sole focus of my legal career, law is perhaps the only profession where I can work on both highly technical problems and social issues. The events of the past several years have gradually pushed me down this new career path, and I now look forward to beginning my studies at the University of New Mexico.

J. E.

J. E. is a nontraditional law student with fourteen years of work experience as a certified electrician. He attributes his admissions success to not only his broad life experiences, which stem from being a mature student, but also in part to his community work with the Red Cross. J. E. is a member of the Golden Key International Honour Society and has graduated with honors in political science from the University of British Columbia.

Stats
LSAT score: 150
Undergraduate GPA: 83 percent
College attended: University of British Columbia
Year of college graduation: 2005
Hometown: Vancouver, British Columbia, Canada
Gender: Male
Race: Caucasian

Admissions information
Law school attended: University of Ottawa, Class of 2008
Accepted: University of Ottawa, University of Manitoba, University of Saskatchewan
Denied: Dalhousie University, Queen's University, University of Alberta, University of British Columbia, University of Calgary, University of Victoria, Windsor University
Waitlisted: Western University

Personal statement prompt

J. E. reports that he wrote this essay, which he submitted as part of his application to the University of Ottawa, in response to an open-ended prompt.

Becoming a lawyer was never my intent. It was only through a series of personal transformations and experiences that I found my path leading towards the field of law. The experiences gained throughout my upbringing, global travel, undergraduate studies and community service have contributed in countless ways to my character and instilled in me an intrinsic sense of empathy and fairness, two attributes that will serve me well in my legal career.

As a child, I lived amidst the paranoid delusions of a schizophrenic and single parent. The reality of this disease was traumatic; it took a long time for me to understand that my mother was ill and that her frequent invective was merely symptomatic. For years we lived on welfare where hunger was a daily reality. Unable to cope with the responsibility of a child, my mother effectively left me to fend for myself. This lack of care culminated when I was abused by a person with whom my mother had entrusted me—a person she hardly knew. I quickly learned to become self-reliant but the emotional toll of my life led to behavioural problems and I was consequently expelled from school. It was at this point that I began taking responsibility for my future; I was thirteen years old.

Though young, I decided that an education was important to me and registered at a local alternative school. After completing grade ten, I chose to leave the alternative system and commit to the regular program for my final two years. When I was sixteen years old, I moved out on my own and successfully obtained my diploma in 1990. With high school completed, I decided to pursue a career as an electrician. I moved to Victoria and completed the requisite four-year apprenticeship and received my Canadian Inter-provincial Electrical Trade qualification in 1995.

Following my certification, I headed overseas to travel and work throughout Australia, New Zealand, South-east Asia, Europe, and southern and eastern Africa. My travels throughout the developing world have provided me an education no institution can parallel. I prefer the Third World because it imbues in me a strong sense of compassion and perspective. Unless witnessed first hand, a system devoid of rule of law is impossible to fathom. After observing the unjust and malignant politics of Africa, I returned to Canada determined to pursue a direction I would not have contemplated earlier—a career in the legal profession.

Considering my experiences abroad, it is not surprising that I hope to work within the practice-area of international law. While this desire largely stems from my travels, it is also linked to my education and my involvement in international humanitarian law. I chose to study Political Science because I felt it could provide some insight into the many issues I've encountered during my travels. In observing the different political systems across the globe, I have been able to see how international lawyers participate in the advancement of human rights. Similarly, my current internship with the Canadian Red Cross has further fuelled my desire to enter the realm of international law. I am presently working with the Red Cross on a project to raise public awareness of humanitarian law including its development, limitations, and future prospects. Actively working in the international humanitarian field has given me a different perspective on the realities of law in the international sphere, and I am eager to involve myself in the process.

My decision to pursue a legal education entailed considerable sacrifice. After ten-plus years in the construction industry, I walked away from a secure and substantial salary to re-enter the classroom and compete with fellow students who have never left the sanctuary of school. Despite this unusual decision, I have succeeded in my post-secondary studies in Political Science, achieving a grade point average of 83% over the past four years. I have demonstrated that I can research and write upon a wide variety of subjects and have honed my ability to analyze critically. I feel that my willingness to embrace these significant changes, despite the financial sacrifices and my educational history, is a testament to my unfaltering drive to pursue a legal career.

One limitation that may stand out on paper has been the Law School Admissions Test (LSAT). Admittedly the occasions I have written the exam have been amidst a rigorous honours curriculum and a time where narrow devotion was challenging. While I dedicated all free time towards succeeding on the LSAT, the fact remains that my results do not reflect my efforts. However, I strongly believe that my life experiences, my academic record, and my proven desire to pursue a legal career far outweigh any reservations that my LSAT results may instigate.[1]

I am applying to the University of Ottawa for numerous reasons. Aside from its favourable location and proximity to the Supreme Court of Canada and Parliament, the University of Ottawa offers one of the strongest international law and human rights programs in Canada, subjects congruent with my interests. Moreover, the opportunity to become involved with the Human Rights Research and Education Centre, Legal Aid, and other distinguished affiliations make the University of Ottawa my foremost choice. I ask that the University of Ottawa Law faculty consider my application under the general or mature category for the 2005/2006 academic year. In return I assure the Law faculty that my dedication to academic excellence will be unsurpassed and that I will embody the high standards any law school would proudly claim their own.

---

[1] Philip Shelton, president and executive director of the Law School Admission Council (LSAC), admits the LSAT is "good but not that good."(a) Further, Shelton states that "the [LSAC] now finds itself in the schizophrenic position of downplaying the usefulness of its own product."(b)

ELIZABETH HOROWITZ

Elizabeth graduated magna cum laude *with a major in child development; she was placed on the Dean's List every semester at Tufts. She was also a four-year starter on the Tufts University varsity women's lacrosse team, and her teammates elected her captain her senior year. That same year, she also led a seminar for freshmen and acted as a peer advisor to the fourteen students in the class. She worked in a law office during the summers.*

Stats
LSAT score: 168
Undergraduate GPA: 3.63
College attended: Tufts University
Year of college graduation: 2002
Hometown: Westbury, NY
Gender: Female
Race: Caucasian
Admissions information
Law school attended: University of Pennsylvania, Class of 2006
Accepted: University of Pennsylvania, Boston University, Fordham University, Georgetown University
Denied: Harvard University, New York University
Waitlisted: Columbia University (ultimately denied)

Personal statement prompt

Elizabeth submitted this essay as part of her application to Columbia, Fordham, Georgetown, and NYU. According to Elizabeth, "Basically, these schools requested that you simply share any information that might help them to make their decisions."

People, for the most part, can be divided into two groups—chocolate people and vanilla people. You may find an occasional strawberry but they are rare and, for the most part, unheard of. I am, without a doubt, a chocolate person. Be it ice cream, candy, or cake, I always opt for the chocolate choice.

I inherited this preference from my father, who suffers from a slight obsession with the flavor. My mother is quite the opposite; her loyalties lie with vanilla. I suppose that the chocolate-lover's gene is dominant. My passion for the flavor, however, is not solely a result of my genealogy. My ever-so-dedicated father has always been a source of encouragement regarding the pursuit of my interests, and the development of my sweet tooth was no exception.

My mother always worked during the day, but for a time during my grade school years she had to work one night during the week as well. My older brother and I were left in the hands of my less than health conscious father. Maintaining our balanced diets of three squares a day had always been my mother's terrain. With my father treading upon it, however, it was not long before "Mom's Work Night" was transformed into "Chocolate Night."

My mother would leave for the office and my brother and I would anxiously wait to hear my father's key turn in the lock. We were always prepared, having cleaned off the coffee table in the den to make room for the pile of sweets he would bring. I remember climbing up onto the counters, searching the cupboards for the tallest glass I could find. (I never checked the sink; washing a dish wasn't an option.) I would fill the glass until it was brimming with milk, threatening an overflow at the slightest disturbance. After all, there was nothing worse than having to go upstairs for a milk refill while my selfish brother continued to greedily eat in my absence. Once filled up with my dairy fuel, I would slowly make my way down the den stairs, where I would sit in anxious anticipation of my father's arrival.

Finally, he would appear! After putting down his briefcase and taking off his coat, he would descend the stairs with the treasures of the night tucked under his arm in a brown paper bag. One by one, he would take out the assortment of savory sweets. The exotic bars always impressed me, or at least, at the time, I thought they were exotic. These were not the everyday Hershey Bars and Baby Ruths that I was used to buying with my left over lunch money. These curious candies had names I could not even pronounce; we feasted on Toblerone, Godiva and Bacci—this was classy stuff.

So, with a fleeting glimpse of the stomachache that was sure to follow, Chocolate Night began. While trying to ration my milk, I proceeded to eat an obscene and downright unhealthy amount of chocolate. My father would tell us facts about each bar, where it came from, and what made it unique, most of which I don't remember. What I do remember, however, is the weekly tradition that we created. I remember looking forward not only to the appeasement of my confectionery cravings, but also to the time I spent with my greedy older brother and my hard-working father. Don't misunderstand me, the chocolate was a plus. In reality, though, it was merely a vehicle that my father used to bring us together around the coffee table; to bring us together at all. While fostering my growing sweet tooth, he fostered sweet memories as well.

I can also recall, quite vividly, the feeling of contentment that consumed me (no pun intended) while we sat on the rug, chewing on our chocolate treats. I felt whole, as if I belonged nowhere else but in that spot, milk in hand and chocolate in mouth.

It was that same feeling that motivated me to apply to law school. My father claims that he knew it all along and he was just waiting for me to figure it out for myself. In the end, however, it was that perfect-fit-feeling that made my decision so clear. Opting for law school felt as natural as opting for rocky road over butter pecan. The thought of pursuing a career in law stirs the same sense of completeness that I felt while sitting around the coffee table. Though I'm not sure how law school will measure up to Chocolate Night, I am expecting great things, and I know I will not be disappointed. Chocolate night always left me feeling full and contented; I expect that after digesting my education in law, I will feel quite the same.

PRISCILLA JAYNE

Priscilla graduated from the Leventhal School of Accounting at the University of Southern California, where she majored in accounting. As a National Merit Scholar, Priscilla was invited to enroll in the freshman honors curriculum, Thematic Option. While at USC, Priscilla was a member of the professional, business fraternity, Delta Sigma Pi, in which she served as the New Member Educator for one semester. She was also a member of Gamma Phi Beta sorority and the Accounting Society. Priscilla volunteered with the Joint Educational Project and the Alternative Spring Break. After college, she worked as an accountant, first for two years in public accounting at Deloitte Touche Tohmatsu and for four years in private accounting at Ingenio, Inc., an Internet/telephony-business. Priscilla's interests include music and creative writing. She volunteers with Planned Parenthood of Southeastern Pennsylvania.

Stats

LSAT score: 171
Undergraduate GPA: 3.8
College attended: University of Southern California
Year of college graduation: 1998
Hometown: San Francisco, CA
Gender: Female
Race: Caucasian

Admissions information

Law school attended: University of Pennsylvania, Class of 2008
Accepted: University of Pennsylvania, New York University, University of California—Los Angeles, University of Southern California
Denied: Stanford University
Waitlisted: None

Personal statement prompt

Priscilla submitted this personal statement to the University of Pennsylvania. She notes that she responded to the following prompt: "The Admissions Committee requires that every applicant submit an original example of written expression. You may wish to describe aspects of your background and interests—intellectual, personal, or professional—and how you will uniquely contribute to the Penn Law community and/or the legal profession. Please limit your statement to two pages." Also included here is Priscilla's statement of diversity.

When I was eight years old, I made my mother trade in a used violin and twenty-five dollars for a scratched-up, army-issue trombone. Precociously aware that I had little musical talent, I thought that the trombone's single moving part looked simple enough to master. I wanted to be *in the band*—which, for an eight-year-old, is as close to musical glamour as one can get.

It was not long before reality hit me: in sixth grade I was winning regional math competitions and participating in mock trials, but I was definitely not moving up to first-chair trombone. I gave in to my practical nature and quit the band. Years later, my talent for numbers and logic led me to make the epitome of practical choices, and I majored in Accounting at the University of Southern California, aiming to earn my CPA at a Big-Five firm—goodbye glamour.

While I could not escape my natural talents (or lack thereof), I could also not ignore my natural passion for music. In college, I volunteered as security to get into the priciest concerts—the Rolling Stones' "Bridges to Babylon" tour and Fleetwood Mac's "The Dance" reunion concert. After graduation, I moved to San Francisco, a center of the swing music trend. I quickly met many local bands. Through my contacts, I earned free tickets to shows several nights a week; I also developed insight into the issues faced by up-and-coming musicians. At the same time, my new job at a Bay Area dot-com put me in proximity to the biggest revolution in the music industry since MTV: Napster. I had the opportunity to meet Shawn Fanning, Napster's creator and founder, at a charity event. Talking with Fanning expanded my understanding of digital replication software, and showed me, contrary to the majority of press coverage, how this technology could be positive for the music industry.

The more I learned about the music industry, the more I wanted to become involved in music professionally. One evening, watching Norah Jones open for Willie Nelson at the Fillmore West, I realized how deeply I wanted to help bring that kind of beauty into the world. It was a concrete ambition, I realized, which I was willing to pursue with a specific plan of action. Having spent so much time in the company of musicians, I knew that there was one way I could make a unique contribution. I could work as a lawyer and advocate.

I plan to become an entertainment lawyer and manager so that I can provide talented artists with the tools they need to succeed in the music business. From my observation, talent is rarely the only obstacle to a musician's success. Rather, artists fail because they lack a sound knowledge of their contractual rights, they make poor business decisions or (true to the stereotype) they squander their earnings. My ultimate career goal is to provide a full-range of professional services to entertainers through a single firm that would offer legal counsel and management services, as well as tax advice, estate planning, and general business consulting. Most of the local bands I know attempt to survive by selling self-produced CDs at small-venue shows, while making little money for their performances. I am convinced that the skills I will acquire through a JD/MBA program, such as the one at University of Pennsylvania, will allow me to help musicians find a more sensible, direct, and effective way of earning a living.

Thirty years ago, a business background, a love of music, and a few connections might have been enough to be successful in music management. While I have offered casual advice on business organization and tax requirements to my musician friends, I know that there are changes afoot in the industry that I will be able to understand fully only with a JD/MBA. The current controversy around music copyrights makes this an exciting time to study entertainment law, and today 'entertainment law' is truly at the intersection of serious developments in both intellectual property law and our society's relationship to mass-distributed art. Primarily, digital media replication is questioning the boundaries of an artist's intellectual property. In some cases, artists are fighting to keep tight control of their intellectual property; in others, artists recognize a benefit from disseminating their music as widely as possible.

For their parts, the courts have made clear their stance by forcing the shutdown of Napster. Nevertheless, Napster has sent an important message to the music industry: digital replication will be the next major distribution channel for music. If the music industry does not control this medium, the public can maintain it without them. At the same time that digital media is a threat, it is also an opportunity: free file sharing increases artist popularity even as it decreases album sales. Record companies will need to find creative ways to capitalize on that demand while incorporating a new approach to distribution and intellectual property.

A wide-ranging understanding of intellectual property principles will be a crucial factor in my success as an entertainment attorney; so will knowledge of contract law and a firmly grounded conception of business practices. A strong joint JD/MBA program will help me develop the legal knowledge and business skills that artists depend on in their representation while giving me the skills to be an advocate for change. Studying in proximity to New York City will allow me to continue to build entertainment-industry connections that will be pivotal in my post-graduate career. Most importantly, choosing a school that offers a variety of entertainment law and management classes, balanced with extracurricular opportunities in entertainment law, will focus my knowledge. For these reasons, University of Pennsylvania is the ideal school for me.

Once again, I have decided I will join the band—through a JD/MBA at University of Pennsylvania.

Diversity Statement

Mountain climbers often have trouble judging how far they have climbed because they are always facing forward and unable to look back down the mountain. As I too focus on progressing towards my goals, it is a surprise when I recall all that I have overcome to get to where I am.

I remember looking towards college graduation and a professional career from an early age; now that I have reached those goals, I realize that my ascent offered few easy footholds. My parents divorced when I was six. My mother initially supported my sister and me on child support checks and welfare, but recognized that she would have to finish college in order to provide for us sufficiently. For most of my elementary-school years, she held two jobs while working towards her degree.

On our family's income, private school was not an option. Fortunately, my sister and I tested into the Rapid Learner accelerated program offered at a public elementary school across town. By sixth grade, I was learning pre-algebra, studying world geography, reading Shakespeare, and taking the SATs. Due to my mother's busy schedule, I had little help with this work, and therefore received an additional lesson in self-reliance. At the same time, her perseverance and focus on her own goals made her the perfect role model.

Beyond dealing with a difficult workload, I was also learning to deal with the stigma of poverty. Almost as quickly as I learned that I was a 'latch-key kid,' or that my classmates did not also qualify for $.45 lunches, I learned to hide these facts about myself. Ironically, when my mother remarried and we moved to Southern California, our house was on the border of Pomona, a primarily Hispanic city; there, I was isolated in high school from being less economically disadvantaged than my classmates and from not being a minority. At a school-wide rally, a Student Council skit suggested glibly that I wear a "White Power" t-shirt to show more pride in my race. Nevertheless, by becoming more involved in extra-curricular activities and getting to know more of my classmates, I worked past those racial and social barriers. My election as Student-Body President senior year attested to the fact that I had fully overcome their misgivings.

In addition to serving as Student-body President, I was also the Varsity Cheer Captain, the JV Soccer team goalie, and the lead in "Hamlet" my senior year. By my seventeenth birthday that January, I was looking forward to my college acceptance letters, Prom, and graduating as Valedictorian. Five days later, those plans were interrupted: I was diagnosed with Guillain-Barré Syndrome, an inflammatory disorder of the peripheral nerves which causes accelerating paralysis. For two weeks, I was incubated in intensive care. As soon as I had recovered enough to speak, I begged the doctors and nurses to tell me when I could be released. Finally, one nurse allowed begrudgingly that I would not have less than four-to-five weeks of physical therapy. Her estimate was good enough for me—GBS hospitalizes victims on average for six months. I checked out after eight weeks. With the support of my family and friends and the help of my high school teachers I fully recovered and returned to high school to graduate as Valedictorian. I even wore heels to my Prom!

Like a mountain climber, I don't dwell on the distance I've covered; I am more interested in the distance ahead. Yet I know that what I have accomplished so far has been meaningful and has affected my approach to life. I think that my resilience, open-mindedness, and optimism will be an asset in law school and in my career beyond it.

B. B. LIU

B. B. attended Stuyvesant High School in New York City and graduated magna cum laude *from Columbia University. During her undergraduate years, she was vice president of the Student Education Advocacy League at her university, mentored pre-teens from households in which domestic violence occurred, and worked as an intern at both Smith Barney and the Advocates for Children. After graduating from college, she taught fifth grade at a public elementary school in the New York City neighborhood of Chinatown. B. B. also worked as a certified lifeguard, bartender, and approved mediator. She attributes her admissions success, at least in part, to her demonstrated passion for working with kids, as expressed in her essay, which "tied together all the disparate threads of my life into one whole picture. My family background, professional and personal experiences, and areas of interest, taken together, complemented one another" and illuminated "a candidate who seemed unique to the admissions committees."*

Stats	
LSAT score: 166 (first score cancelled)	
Undergraduate GPA: 3.74	
College attended: Columbia University	
Year of college graduation: 2001	
Hometown: New York, NY	
Gender: Female	
Race: Chinese	
Admissions information	
Law school attended: University of Pennsylvania, Class of 2008	
Accepted: University of Pennsylvania, Northwestern University	
Denied: Harvard University, New York University, University of Chicago	
Waitlisted: None	

Personal statement prompt

B. B. submitted this essay to all of the schools to which she applied. The prompt, she writes, "was something along the lines of, 'Tell us about your-self and why you want to study law.'"

Thirty pairs of eyes stare at me in surprise. Finally, Felix breaks the silence. "But... *why*?" he asks. I flounder. "Well.... I... it's just..." I know what I want to tell my fifth grade class, but I suddenly realize that I cannot give them a simple answer as to why I am leaving teaching. How can I convey to them in one minute what it has taken me years to understand?

Through their eyes, and through the eyes of most people, being an elementary school teacher and being a lawyer are completely unrelated. Yet I have always been drawn to both teaching and law, because, at their cores, they are the same. Both deal with the interactions between human beings, and understanding humans in all their passion and complexity; both involve entering the world of ideas and relating those thoughts to the situations around us; and both include ultimately framing and presenting those concepts to others.

When I graduated from Columbia University three years ago, I was hungry for some experience out there in the "real world." Thus I began to teach full-time at a public elementary school in the heart of New York City's Chinatown. Although I have been deeply touched and influenced by my experiences in the classroom, teaching has—ironically—made me certain that law is the field where my skills, interests and values coalesce.

Working as a teacher has been like holding up a mirror to my life and the lives around me. Never have I seen the world with such startling clarity. On the surface, I spent my time interacting with students and lessons—but within me, questions that had previously drifted around the periphery of my life suddenly took center stage in my thoughts. New ones arose every day, every minute—questions about my role, and the role of the school. For example, should I follow my principal's philosophy to focus my time and energy mainly on my neediest students, or should I also be concerned with challenging my top students? As time passed I realized that fundamentally, these all came down to a question about *values*, about what we valued as individuals and as a society. I found many questions and few answers. I also discovered that while busy keeping our heads above the proverbial water, my colleagues and I never had time to explore these larger issues which arose in our day-to-day work.

Not only did I interact with my students, but I was also privy on a daily basis to the realities of their entire families' lives. During parent-teacher conferences, I would see the overwhelming tiredness on parents' faces if I suggest they help their kids with math at home. They are just struggling to survive and have little time for tutoring. It was not one single incident, but all these accumulated stories that allowed me to develop, through the months, a deep and genuine respect for the struggles of the kids and their families, for how hard families worked to not only to feed themselves, but to do right by their loved ones.

My work as a mediator, both at P.S. 124 and at the Safe Horizon Mediation Center, has been incredibly eye opening. Witnessing the disputes between well-intentioned people of various ages made me wonder how it was that we human beings even manage to live together as peacefully as we do, given that we are all so different and do not necessarily share a common morality. I finally came to a single conclusion: law.

Law is the common language that unites us all. It is these rules of human behavior (as codified into a set of laws) that help us to live together despite our overwhelming differences. In our darkest hour, when we seek protection from our own neighbor, it is to the law that we turn. Law is also the great equalizer. The illiterate immigrant and the CEO of the New York Stock Exchange are both equal when they face each other in court.

Not only do I find the concepts of law to be fascinating, but I also saw in my own life the need for social change on a broad scale, particularly in the lives of immigrants and other Americans who have limited understanding of the protections afforded them by the laws in our society. They are the people who most need an advocate on their side. Because my mother did not speak fluent English for most of her life, she faced many difficulties when confronted with situations that required legal expertise. When she filed for her divorce from my father in 1985, for example, she was unable to afford an attorney and thus did not end up with alimony. A few years later, my father stopped making his child support payments and despite the efforts of several government agencies, we never did track him down. Last year, when my mother was the victim of a (minor) hit-and-run accident, she had an extremely difficult time finding a Mandarin-speaking attorney who had experience as a litigator. Working in Chinatown every day, I have also seen the need for immigrants to become more involved in the political and legal processes of our country.

As a second-generation Asian-American, who has divorced parents and now works on a daily basis with children and families, I am in a unique position to empathize with the struggles of families and immigrants, and also to share with them my knowledge and expertise. Taking my students on trips to the local Supreme Court and enacting mock trials in class was one way of helping immigrants to begin to appreciate and utilize the legal processes of this country. As an attorney, I would be able to serve as a bridge between immigrants and the legal systems in our country, and affect a larger degree of change. Not only could I represent my clients and educate them about the opportunities and rights afforded by U.S. law, but I also believe I could bring to their attention programs which they may not have considered, such as Divorce Mediation or the Sandcastles program, which provides free but highly effective therapy for the children of divorcing couples.

I am particularly intrigued by the issues and conflicts at the core of Family Law, for nothing impacts our personal lives so fundamentally as the relationships we have with our families. The questions at the heart of family law are concerns that burn deeply in each of us: What is the role of the family versus the role of the state, particularly in matters of caring for children? How do we weigh the rights of an individual versus the obligations he has towards the people who depend on him? What can the law do (which is not currently being done) to support the family structure in our society without infringing on the family members' right to choose their own lives? Law is a powerful tool, for just as it could protect families, so too could it tear them apart. At the University of Pennsylvania's Law School, courses such as *Family Law* and *Anatomy of a Divorce* would allow me to gain a deep foundation in the theories behind family law. I will also be able to continue to my work with children and families through your Inter-Disciplinary Child Advocacy and Mediation Clinics.

Most of us spend the majority of our lives seeking meaning and hoping to affect others' lives in a way that matters. Thus far I have engaged with people and their stories as a teacher, as a counselor, as a mediator. Law school is the natural next step for me and practicing law will allow me to continue my intimate involvement with people and their lives. Rachel Reimen stated it perfectly: "It is not about changing a world I cannot change, but about touching the lives that touch mine in a way that makes a difference." I am already doing this, and I now make the choice to continue doing so in a different way. But I will be touching those lives just the same.

ANONYMOUS

Anonymous won two writing awards in college and held a number of leadership positions in extracurricular activities, including Greek life and several philanthropic organizations. She also worked as a research assistant for professors. Additionally, Anonymous participated in two unique internship experiences, one of which became the subject of her personal statement.

Stats

LSAT score: 164
Undergraduate GPA: 3.8
College attended: Emory University
Year of college graduation: 2003
Hometown: St. Louis, MO
Gender: Female
Race: Caucasian

Admissions information

Law school attended: University of Pennsylvania, Class of 2006

Accepted: University of Pennsylvania (placed on wait-list before being accepted), American University, Emory University, Fordham University, The George Washington University, Saint Louis University (full scholarship), Washington University ($45,000 scholarship), Yeshiva University ($60,000 scholarship)

Denied: Columbia University, Harvard University, New York University

Waitlisted: University of Pennsylvania (ultimately accepted)

Personal Statement Prompt

Anonymous notes that she "just wrote a general personal statement" that she submitted to all of the schools to which she applied.

My first job interview never happened—the interviewer did not show up. Despite the inauspicious start and perhaps out of pity on the part of my gracious and apologetic interviewer, I was hired to be an intern with Urban Strategies, a sister company of Mc-Cormack Baron & Associates. MBA is a for-profit residential development and management company, dedicated to reviving depressed inner city neighborhoods. Urban Strategies provides human and social services to the residents of these neighborhoods and acts as an intermediary between MBA and residents.

The focus of my work with Urban Strategies was a North St. Louis City neighborhood called COVAM (Carr Square, O'Fallon Place, Vaughn High Rise Apartments and Murphy Park). After a spate of violent crimes in COVAM, residents felt a need for a structured community summer program for high school students. Their vision was a youth group structured around neighborhood pride and a sense of community that would make crime and other destructive activities undesirable.

My job was to assist three graduate students who were organizing and implementing the COVAM Summer Youth Program as part of a social work credit-based practicum. The result of our planning was a three-part program designed to provide the students with paid community work within the neighborhood, social activities and life skills education.

Three weeks into the eight-week program, the graduate students elected to finish the duration of their practicum at a different site. Their frustration and ultimate decision to abandon the project was largely a result of negative interactions with community members who were resentful of our presence. As one COVAM resident put it, "We wanted a way to teach our kids to love their neighborhood. You brought people outside of the neighborhood to do it." Despite the initial community disapproval and the departure of the grad students, Urban Strategies decided to continue the program with me as the primary director.

People often ask me if the program "worked" or if the students were "saved" from their troubled neighborhood. I am not sure how to respond to questions like that. I think people are looking for a concrete answer—so I can give them the statistics. The good: Two are going to college and three are continuing their community work throughout the school year. The bad: Two failed to finish the program (one due to chronic tardiness and the other for attacking a visiting speaker) and two dropped out of high school (one to enroll in a cosmetology class; the other, a 16 year old, due to an unplanned pregnancy). But, these statistics cannot adequately describe the successes and failures of the COVAM Summer Youth Program, nor does the question address the situation, needs, and goals of the program's participants.

After analyzing this question, its implications became clear. The question infers that I had the ability to "make" or "break" these students—that if I did a good job with the planning and implementation of the summer program, the students would all be college-bound, community-minded, organized, self-respecting, upstanding, contributing members of society. And if I failed, the students would be left to decay in a cesspool of crime and degradation.

These assumptions are problematic for a number of reasons. First, they make unfair and untrue suppositions about the COVAM community. Second, they imply that life transformations and successes and failures can be identified and accomplished in eight weeks. Lastly, and most importantly, these assumptions suggest that I could, in some way, change the fate of the COVAM kids so that they could achieve my definition of success.

Truthfully, my involvement in the lives of the 20 participants of the COVAM Summer Youth Program was likely not a crucial, life-changing experience for them. What I did was bring new experiences to each student, but what they did with those experiences depends on them. Whether or not each succeeds comes from within each student, not from me. It comes from the degree to which they internalized their experience, how relevant each felt the lessons learned were to their lives, their attitudes about the program and effort they put into it, and the extent to which they have the desire and resources to achieve their goals. Most importantly, it depends on how each defines personal success. Ultimately, only the students can determine the success of the COVAM Summer Youth Program.

What did I take away from this experience? Again, the hard facts. The good: I successfully created the program, organized five field trips, brought in interesting and effective guest speakers, supervised the students at their work assignments, and ultimately gained the respect of the COVAM kids. And the bad: The majority of the neighborhood thought of me as an obtrusive, self-righteous, privileged outsider who sought to exploit their children. Two community supervisors quit in the middle of the program leaving nine students without work assignments, and I often felt that when I discussed my work with my friends or family, they could not understand why this internship was both challenging and exciting to me.

But, just as the COVAM kids were more than statistics, I too gained more than can be quantified in a job performance report. This real world experience allowed me to see where I fit in the larger community—how I relate to "cultural others", what I might have to offer them and what they can (and did) offer me. I gained appreciation of the processes and methods of social change. These self-realizations increased my security, confidence and knowledge of the ways of the world and provide direction to my future. This self-actualization is my success.

LARS JOSEPH NELSON

Lars graduated summa cum laude *with a degree in advertising from the School of Journalism and Mass Communications at the University of Minnesota. He was a member of Phi Beta Kappa. During college, he also worked part-time in a divorce-law office. His community service involvement included working as a high school public-speaking coach for two years.*

Stats
LSAT score: 159
Undergraduate GPA: 3.9
College attended: University of Minnesota—Twin Cities
Year of college graduation: 2003
Hometown: Roseville, MN
Gender: Male
Race: Caucasian

Admissions information
Law school attended: University of St. Thomas, Class of 2007
Accepted: University of St. Thomas, Hameline University, University of Minnesota, William Mitchell College of Law
Denied: None
Waitlisted: None

Personal statement prompt

Lars writes: "I used the same essay for all the schools to which I applied. I only changed the last couple of paragraphs."

I scanned my thesis questionnaire and looked up at my surly Alaskan interviewee. "My final question," I said. "Would you let your daughter date a journalist?"

"No." He laughed. "And, definitely not a journalist like you."

I laughed too. With a B.A. in Journalism-Strategic Communications (a.k.a. advertising), I often have to correct this misconception. "Sorry. I'm not a journalist. I'm an advertiser."

"Oh! I wouldn't let an advertiser *near* my daughter. You can't trust advertisers."

Whether I am in Alaska or Minnesota, I hear these sentiments. Although most people allow me at least in the general proximity of their daughters, they characterize advertisers as immoral manipulators and slick salespersons. Lawyers, unfortunately, do not fare much better. According to a 1999 Gallup poll, 41 percent of Americans believed lawyers are dishonest. So, as an advertiser, would my acceptance into law school represent a marriage of two dishonest professions?

Yes or no. Yes, if I wanted to use a law degree to swindle people. No, if I am seeking a legal education to pursue my goal of empowering others. I have never fancied sales or Madison Avenue; rather, I have used my advertising skills to help others become better communicators. It is this aspect of my advertising training that I want to integrate with a legal education at the University of St. Thomas (UST) School of Law.

I realized early in my education that advertising is about more than salesmanship. It is about helping people solve their problems. Usually, advertisers solve problems with an ad that demonstrates how a product is a solution. For example, an ad for the Swiffer™ mop conveys how the mop helps someone who needs clean floors before the arrival of his or her judgmental in-laws. But what happens when someone's problem is not solved by a product? This was the challenge that I faced with James.

For James, a teenager with cerebral palsy, his problem was that he wanted to be funny. I met James while coaching competitive public speaking at Roseville Area High School. I was drawn to coaching because it was an opportunity to use my skills to help students become better communicators. But James posed a challenge. Sometimes his S's were slushy and his gestures were stilted by his palsy. As a result, James found the public speaking world—a world that values enunciation and poise above all else—an unwelcoming place.

I realized that no product would solve James' problem. Further, I knew that giving James funny lines to recite would not empower him because the words would not be his own. I challenged James to find his own words. Together we wrote and edited a humorous speech about society's hypersensitivity toward cerebral palsy. Thus, rather than being hindered by his condition, James found inspiration in it. His speech earned him the laughs he wanted and a second-place trophy at a national speech tournament.

Society has many problems that products do not address and advertisers cannot solve. I witnessed this dilemma firsthand while working on cases as a legal secretary in a divorce law office. Some cases were petty, such as one couple's battle over who kept the can openers, refrigerator magnets, and house plants. Other cases were serious, such as a Somali immigrant who was struggling to assert her independence from her abusive husband. Although these cases may not have reflected society's most significant problems, they were significant matters for the parties involved. And, my employer's effectiveness at resolving them reinforced my conviction that the legal profession is uniquely empowered to resolve challenging conflicts for which there are no material solutions.

I am the type of person who meets challenges head on. Thus, I am not deterred by society's perception of lawyers because this perception can be changed. Just as James was frustrated by a world that did not embrace him, so too is our society frustrated by a legal system that intimidates the layperson with its fine-print jargon, systems, and processes. Just as James' problem was solved with the help of a guide, so too is society's perception of lawyers fixable with the help of individuals who understand communication and who will serve as honest guides for others.

A legal education from UST is a natural continuation of my mission to empower others. This mission is embodied in UST's integration of faith and reason within its curriculum; in its requirement that law students engage in community service; and in its recognition of the relationship between legal and social problem solving within its Center for Counseling and Legal Services. It is this mission that I want to be part of. And, with the marriage of my proven academic and career-developed skills and a UST legal education, I will not only be able to contribute solutions to society's problems, but, also, I will continue to empower people such as James.

My convictions are strong and my reasons are clear for pursuing a law degree at the University of St. Thomas School of Law. However, if any reservations remain about trusting this advertiser, consider that I am just pursuing jurisprudence. It is not as though I am asking to date your daughter.

ANONYMOUS

Stats
LSAT score(s): 163
Undergraduate GPA: 3.8
College attended: Concordia College
Year of college graduation: 2004
Hometown: St. Cloud, Minnesota
Gender: Female
Race: Caucasian
Admissions information
Law school attended: University of St. Thomas, Class of 2010
Accepted: University of Minnesota, William Mitchell College

Personal statement

A group of eleven American students, including myself, have just arrived at Siddharth Village, a non-governmental organization in India. We are waiting to speak, through translators, with about thirty Indian Dalit women. My ears are filled with soft snippets of conversation in many languages and my skin prickles at the cool breeze that urges the women to wrap their saris over their shoulders. I see the women pointing discreetly at Kate's eyebrow ring and making faces of surprise at one another, saying "Look at that!" In return, we American women point indiscreetly at their nose rings and make similar smiling expressions. True bonds were formed when I lifted the hem of my shirt to reveal my navel ring.

Akka was one of the women who cemented that November Thursday very clearly in my mind. Though we did not speak the same languages, we communicated through smiles and awkward gestures. In fact, I never learned her name, and only called her Akka, a term of respect meaning "elder sister." I framed the picture I took that day and it is the first one I put on the wall each time I move. The expression of pride and dignity on Akka's face is extremely humbling to see, because Akka, like most of the women I met at Siddharth Village, is a Dalit.

Dalits have historically been viewed by Indian society as impure and worthless. Horrible atrocities are committed against the Dalits in the name of punishment for so-called crimes like accidentally hearing sacred scripture being read, or taking water from the wrong well. Since a person's caste is determined by his or her ancestry, many people in India can tell if a person is a Dalit simply by looking at them. However, Akka's expression and posture in this picture defy her inherited caste. Akka is a woman who radiates dignity.

Akka and her colleagues lived for about two months at Siddharth Village with a mission to search out their collective identity as Dalit women and to educate themselves on their rights as Indian citizens. Siddharth Village was founded by other Dalit women with help from the Women's Initiative for Development Education (WIDE), a local NGO committed to empowering Dalit women.

There are protections for Dalits in the Indian constitution, though few people are aware of them and fewer people heed them. Because of their collective lack of formal education, Dalits are not able to stand up for themselves legally. With help from WIDE, however, Dalit women are learning how to demand the same rights as other Indian people.

Looking back, it is clear to me that my short stay at Siddharth Village generated in me a desire to practice public interest law. I met a group of strong, confident women who had demanded dignity from a society that deemed them worthless. It would have been virtually impossible for the women of Siddharth Village to confidently make such demands without the assistance they had received from WIDE. WIDE was able to offer them information, mostly relating to Indian laws, that can only be gained through formal education, something these women have been denied for generations. However, once they had the tools they needed, the women were able to create voices for themselves to prove their worth to their communities.

Because of my desire to practice public interest law, I spent a year volunteering as a Legislative Assistant for Lutheran Immigration and Refugee Service (LIRS) in Washington, DC. During that year I learned a great deal about the United States' legislative systems and had the opportunity to influence changes in our laws. I helped draft amendments to major bills and was often a resource for Congressional staff on matters of newly introduced immigration legislation. I looked forward to work every morning and truly began to understand the importance of having a law degree when working in advocacy.

The experiences I had at LIRS and in India are two of the main reasons I am pursuing a law degree. These experiences have also made it clear to me that the University of St. Thomas School of Law is the right place for me. I am very impressed with the work being done at St. Thomas and with the University's obvious commitment to public interest law.

This commitment is evidenced through the Legal Services Clinic, and I am especially interested in the Immigration Law Practice Group. I am also very attracted by the public service requirement, and would appreciate attending a law school with so many fellow students who are willing to volunteer their time. I graduated with degrees in Religion and Political Science, and am very interested in the intersections of law and religion, so the presence of the Terrence J. Murphy Institute for Catholic Thought, Law and Public Policy is very appealing to me.

The opportunity to study law that comes with my talents and social status also implies a responsibility. Given my personal opportunities and interests, I will fulfill this responsibility by receiving a law degree and subsequently using my understanding of law to give voice to those who have been unjustly silenced.

Since returning from India I have forgotten how to put on a sari and my taste buds can no longer handle spicy food. My immune system is back to normal and I have stopped wearing bindis. There are elements of my experience in India, however, that will never leave me. I make time for a warm cup of tea each day and I can cook a *channa masala* that even my host mom would enjoy. More powerful than these, I came home with a stronger sense of who I am and my duties in the world. There is no doubt in my mind that now is the right time, and the University of St. Thomas School of Law is the right place, for me to receive a law degree. I only hope that I can give one person the sense of dignity that WIDE helped Akka cultivate.

ASHLEY STREET

Ashley's primary extracurricular activity was a local pre-law fraternity, Beta Alpha Rho, in which she served as an officer for two semesters. She was also a member of Alpha Phi Sorority and competed in mock trial tournaments. She held part-time jobs as a messenger for the Texas State Senate during her junior year and as a Felony Court clerk during her senior year. She also worked as a summer intern with the Bush for President Campaign. Ashley served as a community supervision (probation) officer for Travis County after her graduation from UT.

Stats
LSAT score: 179
Undergraduate GPA: 3.63
College attended: University of Texas at Austin
Year of college graduation: 2001
Hometown: Albuquerque, NM
Gender: Female
Race: Caucasian

Admissions information
Law school attended: University of Texas at Austin, Class of 2005
Accepted: University of Texas at Austin, New York University, University of Southern California
Denied: Stanford University
Waitlisted: None

Personal statement prompt

Ashley writes that the crux of the essay prompt was as follows: "Your personal statement should give the admissions committee insight to your character and experiences."

My grandfather passed away during my sophomore year of high school. Oddly, the one thing I remember clearly about his passing is writing the obituary. As my mother and I sat and tried to write a statement that could sum up my grandpa's seventy years on earth in fifty words or less, we could not think of the words to describe the adversity he had overcome in his lifetime. Grandpa was survived by seven children and twenty grandchildren, of which I was the youngest. As a child, I looked up to my grandpa more than anyone else, and I admired his courage. I was *his* baby girl.

To this day, no one in our family really knows where our family came from. Grandpa worked in the coal mines as a child alongside his father. When he was thirteen years old, the mine collapsed killing his father, my great-grandfather. Shortly thereafter, my great grandmother abandoned her children. She left my grandpa, as the eldest child, to raise the others. Grandpa refused to talk about his mother. The only thing he would ever say was that she was an "ole' Indian squaw." Because he had to raise his brothers and sisters, grandpa received little formal education; yet, he eventually would own his own landscaping business. I respect my grandpa's adaptability and resourcefulness. He never had a lot of money, nor did my parents when I was young, but I never knew that because they always made sure I had whatever I needed to succeed. They were never afraid, or at least they did not show it. Their courage is something I respect, envy and strive to emulate.

As mentioned earlier, my grandpa was survived by twenty-seven people. Among all twenty-seven plus my dad's family, I am the first to graduate from college. I am certainly the first to pursue a graduate degree. Being the first has its advantages and disadvantages. One definite advantage is that whenever I accomplish something new, whether it is making the Dean's List or getting an internship, my family is excessively proud. Also, I have never been pressured to follow someone else's path. I am free to pursue my own goals and interests and no one else can judge me or claim that they did it better. On the down side, my entire college career has been filled with unknowns. I feel like I am constantly walking in shadows. In *The Hollow Man,* T.S. Elliot wrote "Between the idea/ And the reality / Between the motion/ And the Act/ Falls the Shadow." It is that shadow, that unknown which is the biggest obstacle I faced when applying to college, during my undergraduate years and now applying to law school.

I began noticing the difficulty of being the first when I started applying to undergraduate programs. Neither my parents, nor anyone else I knew had gone through that process before, so they were unable to offer much advice. To make things more confusing, I moved from Texas to New Mexico during my junior year. My counselors did not know me well, and I did not feel comfortable asking teachers I had only known for a semester for recommendations. While filling out the applications I was a nervous wreck. I had never even heard of a personal statement before and did not know how to go about trying to actually write one. Throughout college I had other similar experiences. I was moving hundreds of miles from my parents, and I did not even know where I was going to live until three weeks before I moved to Austin. I was not aware you had to apply for on campus housing before you were even accepted to the University. Once classes started, I felt all alone at a very large school, so I decided to become involved in some student organizations. I quickly went from knowing no one to feeling like the campus had 5,000 students instead of 50,000. After four years, I finally graduated. Preparing for graduation was stressful. One of the best parts of my life was coming to an end. I had more family in town than most of my friends because everyone was so excited for me. The actual day of graduation was both stressful and wonderful, because I was the first.

I love having the recognition of being the first to do something, yet it often makes me feel pressured. I know my family is counting on me to succeed and to make the most of the opportunities I have been blessed with. However, I know my grandpa is always watching over me and guiding me wherever I may go. He always knew that I would excel at whatever I tried to do and was always encouraging. Although the challenges I face are nothing in comparison to the hardships of his life, I know he would be proud that I graduated from college and even happier to hear that I am going to go to law school. After all, he was the one who always told me I argued too much.

After law school, I hope to use my degrees and talents to continue stretching the boundaries. After working with the Travis County Felony Courts, I have decided to pursue a career in criminal justice. When I was younger I wanted to be the first female Attorney General. Janet Reno beat me to it, but there is always something new to accomplish. The most important thing I have learned in college is to always push myself. If I would have followed the easy road or only done the bare minimum, I would never have accomplished all that I have. I thank my Grandpa and my parents for teaching me that and demonstrating the courage that it takes to achieve more than what is expected.

DAVID GREENE

David served as the president of the Kite and Key Society, the oldest and largest student group at the University of Pennsylvania. He was also elected to the Undergraduate Assembly, Penn's student government. He conducted research in psychiatry and political science during the summer after his junior year. David graduated in 2002 with a double major in political science and engineering.

Stats
LSAT score: 164
Undergraduate GPA: 3.69
College attended: University of Pennsylvania
Year of college graduation: 2002
Hometown: Newtown, PA
Gender: Male
Race: Caucasian

Admissions information
Law school attended: University of Virginia, Class of 2005
Accepted: University of Virginia, The George Washington University (with one-third scholarship), Northwestern University
Denied: Columbia University, Harvard University, New York University
Waitlisted: Georgetown University, University of Pennsylvania

Personal statement prompt

David reports that he did not write his personal statement in response to a specific prompt.

I was commanded to walk quickly and keep my arms at my sides. Any sudden movements may evoke agitation from the patients, I was told. I followed a few steps behind my advisor, unsure what to expect as he pushed open the doors leading to the clinic. On my first day with the Unit for Experimental Psychiatry, I found myself in the psych ward at the Hospital of the University of Pennsylvania.

I had expected to work in a computer lab crunching numbers for my independent research; instead, I observed institutionalized patients who were spending weeks in the ward. I investigated a typical lab where a patient would be deprived of sleep in order to test reaction times at various levels of sleeplessness. My study, along with other work in the lab, would benefit NASA and the armed forces; astronauts and soldiers receive only six hours of sleep per night on average, and my results, part of a long-term project, would help determine if such limited hours would reduce their performance.

My first attempt at independent research involved writing an original computer program analyzing over one million points of data, and I found the task daunting. Facing the prospect of putting together over one thousand lines of computer code required me to find new approaches to intricate problems. The only way I could begin to tackle the project involved breaking the complex end-task into a number of smaller, easier-to-obtain goals that I could manage individually.

My work in the Unit for Experimental Psychiatry ward taught me valuable problem solving skills. I believe that both my engineering education and my experience applying it to research will prove valuable in the study and practice of law. Both research questions and legal problems have numerous possible answers, and choosing the proper initial course for my research showed me all the directions in which it could progress. In my study, I had many options for a number of variables: What computing language should I use? How should I structure the program? When I wrote guest opinion pieces arguing on behalf of social and political issues in the University of Pennsylvania's student newspaper, I had to carefully construct a logical argument using relevant information to support my point of view. My analytical ability, developed through an engineering education and improved through practical applications, will be helpful in a legal career.

My experience with the Unit of Experimental Psychiatry was a lesson in "crash courses:" first, how to walk through the Psych ward safely, and, secondly, how to work, define, and eventually solve a complex problem. While I do not expect a legal career will require the first skill I learned through my research, I feel confident that I will benefit from the problem-solving skills I acquired as I study and eventually practice law in ideally a business or technological setting.

JANALEE SUE KRASCHNEWSKI

JanaLee participated in the Miss America system and received awards at the local, state, and national levels. Her undergraduate honors included induction into Phi Beta Kappa during her sophomore year, honors in her major (Spanish language), Dean's List, and graduation with distinction. She grew up in a rural environment and was actively involved in 4-H, a program that allows young people to raise animals, participate in a variety of craft projects, and compete against others at county fairs.

Stats

LSAT score: 166
Undergraduate GPA: 3.94
College attended: University of Wisconsin—Madison
Year of college graduation: 2003
Hometown: Burlington, WI
Gender: Female
Race: Caucasian

Personal statement prompt

JanaLee notes that her essay was a response to an open-ended prompt and that she "particularized just the last few sentences for each school."

Gardening 101

The resume I have included with this application is not complete. The section that lists my employment history is missing one item. For the past three years, on my days off of other jobs, I have been mowing my parents' lawn for five dollars an hour. Despite having seven acres of lawn, I'm not getting rich off this job, but merely filling my gas tank. One would think that a partially college-educated woman of the twenty-first century would demand more than less-than-minimum wage, but my current pay is a huge raise from what I was receiving a few months ago: Nothing. Lawn mowing, whether with compensation or pro bono, is something that must be done in order to maintain a presentable appearance of the home. Most people just mow the lawn to keep the grass short. Each time I hop on that rider mower, though, I carve into my back yard a different design, ranging from the simple smiley face to the intricate and difficult treble clef. Maybe I should ask for another raise, because my parents are certainly getting more than their money's worth. You can either mow the lawn, or you can mow the lawn with pizzazz.

Mowing the lawn is similar to attending law school in many ways. Both activities produce results. Both are seen as necessary steps in a process—one to a nice-looking abode and the other to a legal career. Both can tell a lot about the executor of the activity. Before I was old enough to operate our fifty-inch mower, my father was Chief Gardener. "Jeff," my mother would frequently cry to the man who lacked attention to details and aesthetics. "You didn't do the trim again!" Since I took over, the trim gets done, the design gets created, and the hand shearing of individual grass blades from around the tree trunks gets done. My attention to detail, commitment to quality work, and extra effort to make everything I do special and unique will serve me well in law school.

These characteristics have been more than beneficial in my scholastic career thus far. My academic record reflects each of them, but the flare that makes my transcript truly me comes in my Senior Honors Thesis, *Pluma en pata*. A Political Science major typically does a research project of some sort for his or her thesis, so I chose to write mine for my other major, Spanish Language, which allowed me much more liberty. *Pluma en pata* is a novel, written in Spanish, telling the life of the seventeenth-century Spanish painter Diego Velázquez as seen through the eyes of his pet dog. Because of the uniqueness of my project, I was awarded a grant to produce it, as was a young lady working on stem cell research and a young man studying certain marine life extinctions. To my knowledge, only one Spanish thesis was ever chosen to receive the grant.

As a multi-lingual lawyer, I know I will be better able to help disadvantaged clients who are even further disadvantaged because they cannot speak English. One day, I hope to earn a judgeship so that I can hold multilingual court. After all, everyone in America has the right to a fair trial, and how fair can a trial be that is gibberish to the parties?

Being a judge will not be a completely new experience to me. As Chief Justice of the University of Wisconsin's Student Judiciary, I have heard cases as simple as by-law discrepancies and as complex as the controversial viewpoint neutrality in student segregated fee disbursement. This experience has helped me hone my leadership skills as I presided over the whole Student Judiciary. It also introduced me to the heart-ache that can come with making a ruling against a good friend. More importantly, I have learned the warmth that starts in the pit of the stomach and spread when deciding something that upholds the constitution of an organization, the very framework of the group.

The University of Michigan Law School is everything anyone could hope for in a law school. The top-notch education, the quality and diversity of course offerings, and the close proximity to the Wendy's in the Michigan Union lead me to believe I would be an excellent fit for its incoming class. I have been blessed with talents that have given me the tools necessary for academic success. The greatest gift God gave me, though, was a heart big enough to hold all the drive and determination to make my dreams come true and the creativity to do it differently than everyone else. After all, you can attend law school, or you can attend law school with pizzazz.

L. KATIE MASON

Katie double-majored in English and social change & development at the University of Wisconsin—Green Bay. She graduated summa cum laude *and was a member of three undergraduate honor societies. She also worked at a law firm during her college years.*

Stats
LSAT score: 164
Undergraduate GPA: 3.95
College attended: University of Wisconsin—Green Bay
Year of college graduation: 2003
Hometown: Cedarburg, WI
Gender: Female
Race: Caucasian

Admissions information
Law school attended: University of Wisconsin, Class of 2006
Accepted: University of Wisconsin, Marquette University, University of Notre Dame, University of Illinois, University of Iowa, University of Minnesota
Denied: None
Waitlisted: Northwestern University

Personal statement prompt

According to Katie, she wrote this essay in response to the prompt for the University of Wisconsin, whose admissions office requested the following: "Please include a personal statement on a separate sheet. A carefully prepared personal statement telling us about yourself and reflecting upon our admissions criteria, which are described in our publication Law at Wisconsin, *is very helpful to the Admissions Committee. Include any special factors, problems, plans, explanations, or additional information that you think may help the law school in acting on your application."*

* Name has been changed.

"I hope this won't take long. I have a night class to get to," I said to the emergency room nurse who was monitoring my breathing.

"It shouldn't be too long, unless, of course, you need to be admitted," she replied, smiling reassuringly as she made a notation on my chart.

I sat back, relieved. There was no way I'd have to be admitted, I thought. After all, I'd been walking around like this for days, attending classes, giving presentations, and staying up late to work on papers. I wouldn't even have been in the emergency room if it weren't for the increased difficulty breathing I'd been experiencing that day. I certainly didn't have time for a visit to the emergency room, much less a stay in the hospital.

It was almost the end of the semester, and I had so many papers due in the coming two weeks, not to mention exams just around the corner. Three days earlier, while sitting on the couch, I'd suddenly been overcome with a crushing pain in my chest and left side. I should have gone to the emergency room right away, but I really didn't want to miss class. In fact, even though my condition seemed to getting worse, I considered putting off this emergency room visit until the following morning, just to avoid missing my night class.

I'd just found out a few months earlier that my friend, Lisa*, with whom I'd ridden and shown horses since the age of thirteen, had been diagnosed with leukemia. Her chemotherapy wasn't working, so her only chance for a cure was a bone-marrow transplant. Even then, the doctors told her that there could be complications because it would be practically impossible to find a donor who was a perfect match. Sitting in the hospital, terrified, all I could think about was how scared Lisa must have been when she was waiting to find out what was wrong with her.

"Well, we know why you've been having trouble breathing," the emergency room doctor said gravely as he came into the room. "Your left lung is collapsed, and we're not sure why. We'll be able to fix it, but you'll have to stay in the hospital for about three days."

The entire hospitalization process was very frustrating; at first, the doctors were unable to give me any definitive answers about my condition. Worse yet, no matter how many times I explained to the nurses that I had classes to attend, they refused to sneak me out of the hospital. So I did what I could: I read a novel for an English class, I taught myself a chapter's worth of Spanish, and I copied notes that friends brought to the hospital.

Three days turned into ten, and I was eventually referred to a heart and thoracic surgeon after the initial treatments didn't repair the hole in my lung. During our first meeting, I asked the surgeon so many questions about my upcoming surgery that he inquired if I had ever thought about going to medical school. I told him I hadn't, that I was planning on law school, and jokingly noted the fact that law covers all kinds of areas, including medicine. The more I've thought about this, the more I've come to realize how true it is and how much it represents the reason I want to study law: There are so many areas of legal study, each one presenting its own unique set of challenges and possibilities.

My surgeon's comment about medical school, combined with my own and my friend's recent medical problems, have added health care law to the ever-growing list of areas of legal study that have captured my interest. I am particularly excited about the prospect of participating in the University of Wisconsin Law School's Center for Patient Partnerships. I can think of nothing more rewarding than helping people in the same position as my friend. There is no more helpless feeling than being sick or watching someone who is sick and not being able to do anything about it. Your clinical program provides an opportunity to work toward a better situation for those who are ill, and, while I cannot claim to know what area of law I will ultimately focus on, I do know that the Center for Patient Partnerships is something of which I would like to be a part.

Despite all odds, my friend was able to receive a bone-marrow transplant from a donor who was an exact match; it's been nine months since the transplant, and she is getting better every day. I am convinced that she is the strongest person I will ever know. The time I spent in the hospital was torture enough; I don't know how she was able to tolerate month after month of hospitalization during what should have been the prime of her life.

Lisa and I were both lucky because our insurance companies unquestioningly paid for the procedures we needed. But as bill after bill arrived at our home, detailing the cost of each and every procedure and test that I underwent in the hospital, I realized that I could have been in lifelong debt had my insurance company refused to pay for my medical expenses. I was only in the hospital for a little under two weeks; the cost of more serious illnesses and injuries must be unfathomable. This experience made it clear that health care law has an intense impact on individuals and society as a whole.

My studies at the University of Wisconsin—Green Bay, as well as my experience as a volunteer at the Golden House Family Violence Center have also greatly aided me in thinking about the role of law in society. One class in particular, Law and Society, was especially helpful in this respect. This class helped me understand that laws are not simply abstract concepts to be discussed in the classroom; laws affect real people with problems, interests, and dreams. The discussions we had in class repeatedly focused on not only court decisions themselves, but also the implications such decisions could have on a wide range of people from various walks of life. Dealing with children from homes where domestic violence was prevalent during the course of my work at the Family Violence Center also helped put a human face on some of the issues with which the legal field deals. The news reports of domestic violence are no longer about "other people;" they are about the children I baby-sat, some of them not much older than infants, and the tired, frightened women who came to the center.

My collapsed lung made me realize how important it is to have support during times of crisis; I was lucky enough to have my parents to lean on during this difficult time, but not everyone is so fortunate. I would like to think that my stay in the hospital helped further develop the compassion necessary to deal with people who are at a low point in their lives, as those seeking legal counsel so often are. Ultimately, my condition turned out to be a blessing in disguise, adding more depth to my understanding of the role of law in society and of the human condition in general.

I fully recovered from my collapsed lung and even managed to maintain my grade point average for the semester. It was ultimately determined that my lung collapsed due to an undetected birth defect; luckily, no future problems are anticipated. The success I achieved in maintaining my grades after missing so much school has made me more certain than ever that I will succeed in law school and in legal practice no matter what surprises are thrown my way.

ANONYMOUS

After graduating from the University of Chicago, Anonymous returned to his hometown and worked for two years as a technical writer. He then enrolled in journalism school at the University of Oregon, from which he earned a master's degree in 1998. He was granted membership in the national honor society Kappa Tau Alpha. Anonymous worked briefly during journalism school as an associate editor for a trade magazine and, after graduating, as an editor for a small publisher of financial books and periodicals.

Stats
LSAT score: 164
Undergraduate GPA: 3.1
College attended: University of Chicago
Year of college graduation: 1995
Graduate school GPA: 3.9
Graduate school attended: University of Oregon
Year of graduate school graduation: 1998
Hometown: Eugene, OR
Gender: Male
Race: Caucasian

Admissions information
Law school attended: Vanderbilt University, Class of 2005
Accepted: Vanderbilt University, Case Western University, Emory University, Tulane University, University of Oregon
Denied: Duke University, University of Notre Dame, University of Virginia
Waitlisted: College of William and Mary, Washington and Lee University, Washington University

Personal statement prompt

Anonymous notes that he did not write his personal statement in response to a specific prompt.

Question: "What do you get when you cross the Godfather with a lawyer?"

Answer: "An offer you can't understand."

It is perhaps impertinent of me to begin my personal statement with a joke about lawyers, But I do so to illustrate an important point: most students begin law school woefully unprepared for training in legal writing, having little knowledge of English grammar, correct usage, and proper style. And after three years of reading convoluted opinions and statutes, most of these students finish law school with the notion that good legal writing requires an impenetrable, jargon-filled style.

I came across a fine example of this recently. An oversight committee in Maryland, charged with the unenviable task of interpreting many of that state's more perplexing statutes, came across this monstrosity:

> The Board may appoint, discharge at pleasure, and fix the com-
> pensation of the secretary and such clerical force as from time to
> time in its judgment may be necessary in the administration of this
> subtitle if it has funds available for the payment of such persons.

("It means" said the committee, "that the Board may employ a staff in accordance with the state budget.") It seems that impenetrable writing is not just common in the legal profession, but a requirement. I recently saw an advertisement placed by a business law journal seeking applicants able, in part, to "produce verbose, 1st-draft material under tight deadlines"!

I can tell you that professional writers in the field in which I work—stock and commodity market investment—labor under the same delusions. I see it every day in my job as an editor. Recently, my company's lead writer—a New York University graduate with nearly 20 years of experience—handed me his latest article to edit. I turned his three pages of convoluted, wordy prose into less than a page of lucid, concise writing. When I presented him with the edited version, his complaint was immediate: "The article sounds far less impressive the way you have it written." I asked him to provide me with an example. He pointed to one of his original sentences, which he was quite proud of(!): "Prognostications of prominent investment-house analysts and other well-known pontificators provides an ominous picture for the stock market's future, making it less inviting than bonds." "Here," he said, "is a sentence that *sounds* important—one that immediately grabs the reader's attention and holds it firmly."

This all-too-common misjudgment among writers—and the source of most bad writing, I believe—is the *desire to impress* the reader combined with the writer's *dearth of literacy.* This was the case here: the former was apparent in the writer's complaint to me; the latter was evident in the original sentence:

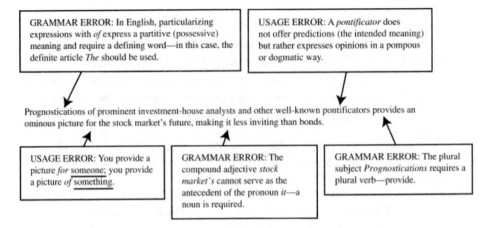

GRAMMAR ERROR: In English, particularizing expressions with *of* express a partitive (possessive) meaning and require a defining word—in this case, the definite article *The* should be used.

USAGE ERROR: A *pontificator* does not offer predictions (the intended meaning) but rather expresses opinions in a pompous or dogmatic way.

Prognostications of prominent investment-house analysts and other well-known pontificators provides an ominous picture for the stock market's future, making it less inviting than bonds.

USAGE ERROR: You provide a picture *for* someone; you provide a picture *of* something.

GRAMMAR ERROR: The compound adjective *stock market's* cannot serve as the antecedent of the pronoun *it*—a noun is required.

GRAMMAR ERROR: The plural subject *Prognostications* requires a plural verb—provide.

When I pointed out to my friend just some of the errors in this sentence, his confidence in its virtues vanished. He agreed that my edited sentence—"Many analysts predict a general decline in the stock markets; if these analysts are correct, the bond markets will rise"—was better.

I am not suggesting that highly literate writers always write well or that grammatical prose is invariably well-written. To write well requires a *high degree of literacy* and *good judgment about the written word.* Much of the strength of my candidacy for admission to Vanderbilt Law School lies in the fact that, as a skilled and experienced writer and editor, I have both: I achieved a high degree of literacy by earning a two-year journalism degree (and graduating at the top of my class); I attained good judgement about the written word by working for two years as a technical writer and five years as an editor. My knowledge and experience in this area, combined with the education I received at the University of Chicago, provide strong evidence of my ability to succeed at the study and practice of law.

BRYAN KETROSER

Bryan double-majored in East Asian studies and linguistics at Brandeis. He completed an internship with the housing unit of a legal services agency during his senior year of college. While Bryan worked in the cafeteria part-time during his first year, as a Japanese language tutor part-time during his second and third years, and as a temp full-time during the summers, he had no extracurricular activities, save the occasional game of tennis or chess with a friend.

Stats

LSAT score: 180
Undergraduate GPA: 3.89
College attended: Brandeis University
Year of college graduation: 2002
Hometown: Minnetonka, MN
Gender: Male
Race: Caucasian

Admissions information

Law school attended: Yale University, Class of 2005
Accepted: Yale University, Harvard University, University of California—Berkeley, University of Chicago
Denied: None
Waitlisted: Stanford University

Personal statement prompt

According to Bryan, his "personal statement was not tailored to the individual law schools; they all got the same thing."

Determination. If you are truly interested in my personality, there it is. This is not to say there is nothing else to me, it is just that determination is what seems to stick out most. Nor is it to say I am a perfectionist. Perfectionism places too much emphasis on results, at the expense of the process. I always strive for the best possible outcome because it is the best way to enjoy the journey, not just because it leads to better results (though, of course, this is a perk).

Oddly, this has a great deal to do with a disorder I only began to understand at the age of fourteen. Around that time, friends and teachers began commenting on facial twitches that I was exhibiting with increasing frequency. I had coped with minor tics so long that, by then, I was only vaguely aware of their existence. But then they started getting worse, forcing my consciousness to deal with them. My father—ironically, a neurologist—gave me his diagnosis: Tourettes Syndrome. This was soon confirmed by another physician.

The symptoms are primarily a collection of omnipresent and ever-changing tics. It is difficult to adequately explain what a tic feels like to one who has never experienced it, but if the reader has not had the "pleasure," the best analogue would be to imagine having an itch. While no actual feeling of skin irritation accompanies a tic, the impulse which leads to a tic is much akin to feeling the need to scratch an itch.

My case of Tourettes has been neither so mild as to be readily ignored nor, in my opinion, so severe as to warrant medication. But no matter where I go or what I do, it is always in at least one corner of my mind, for like the urge to scratch an itch, it *is* possible to suppress a tic. Learning to live with Tourettes has thus helped me in two ways. First, it has taught me patience; tics are constantly waxing and waning, and when they are bad, they have a tendency to require more attention to maintain the same level of control. This generally becomes aggravating, which in turn worsens the tics. The only way to avoid such a cycle is by being patient, and not letting the extra difficulty get to you. The other thing I have gained from the disorder is, as I mentioned before, an aversion to giving up. Tourettes is with me 24/7 and, while I pause every now and then to think how fortunate I am that I did not get a more disabling version, it is something that requires constant effort.

One of the first tests of my patience and resolve presented itself during my final year of middle school. I had been moderately overweight for several years, but as I grew older I began crossing the line distinguishing "chubby" from "obese." At around 5'6", my weight had crept up to over 180 pounds, and was still rising. My parents occasionally suggested that I take steps to lose the weight, but I hated exercise, and one can no doubt imagine just how thrilled the average 12 or 13 year-old boy would be to go on a diet. I was aware of the problem, but uninterested in putting forth the effort needed to rectify it.

And then, it happened. At some point, I just said to myself, "I know I can do it, so why in the world *haven't* I?" I have been a different person ever since. On the spot, I resolved to lose weight. I played tennis virtually every day during the spring and summer, and in the months I could not play, I used a treadmill. Perhaps more importantly, I forever changed my eating habits. The changes were difficult; there were many days when I spent two hours on the treadmill, only to sit down to a dinner that was considerably smaller (and greener) than my body desired. Still, I never questioned my decision to stick with it. Completion of the task was simply a given. Within nine months, I shrank from over 180 pounds to an even 140 pounds. By consistently making the right dietary choices and getting enough exercise, I have stayed between 140 and 145 pounds for the past seven years.

I have also harnessed my determination when it comes to my academic interests. A fascination with the people and culture of Japan led to my enrollment in an intensive Japanese language summer program at the University of Minnesota at the end of my junior year of high school. In eight weeks, I learned the equivalent of a year's worth of Japanese. Whereas seven years of Spanish classes had me doubting my foreign language-learning abilities, those eight weeks showed me that I could succeed in even my weakest areas if I put my mind to it. And put my mind to it I did. The class met for five hours a day (in addition to over an hour of commuting time), Monday through Friday, and often required another five hours of homework or more per night. The first surprise was that I was doing well, but the big surprise was that I was having the time of my life. Throughout my college career, I made certain that I put this level of determination into all my academic endeavors, and found that it invariably lead to greater enjoyment of each and every one. The fact that law is my chief interest will be the supreme bonus in the three years to come, and this makes me even more excited to dive headfirst into the law school experience.

As for Japanese, I continued my studies throughout my senior year of high school, taking evening classes at the University of Minnesota after my high school classes. I went to Japan for six weeks the summer preceding my matriculation at Brandeis University, then continued to study the language both there and at nearby Wellesley College. I am currently translating the second of two short stories from Japanese into English for an honors thesis in East Asian Studies. And I'm loving every minute of it.

SIMON Y. MOSHENBERG

Throughout college at Columbia, Simon was active in working for a number of political causes. During the summers, he interned with various nonprofit organizations. After graduating summa cum laude, he spent two years working as a labor rights monitor for a nonprofit organization in Central America. Following this experience, he worked for one year in Washington, DC, for a women's rights organization. He was married in October 2004.

Stats
LSAT score: 175
Undergraduate GPA: 3.97
College attended: Columbia University
Year of college graduation: 2001
Hometown: Alexandria, VA
Gender: Male
Race: Caucasian

Personal statement prompt

Simon's personal statement was not written in response to a particular question. Also included is a second short essay, which Simon submitted as part of his application to Yale.

I had never visited Latin America before 2001, when I was selected for a research internship that sent me to a banana-producing valley in rural Honduras where bananas were no longer produced. Dole and Chiquita owned most of the best farmland, which they left untilled. But the companies still vigorously asserted their property rights and would call the army to evict unemployed banana workers who trespassed on the farms to grow beans or plantains for their subsistence.

Honduras had always been part of the global economy, its bananas ending up on breakfast tables around the world. After the banana industry collapsed, the garment factories moved in. Suddenly it was women, not men, whose wages sustained their families. Women garment workers in the export-processing zones were earning more than ever. But they were getting sick and they were getting hurt, and it was rare to find a garment worker over the age of 25.

The Jesuit priests for whom I worked were interested in documenting workplace health violations, but they also wanted to help the workers stop getting sick. So we organized community trainings. We began with the principle that occupational health is the responsibility of every worker, and that this responsibility includes confronting unhealthy and unsafe labor practices. Reading Honduran labor law, the workers found that the law extended them rights about which they had never been informed. But they also saw that when individual workers demanded these rights, they were often fired, and the process for challenging unlawful firings was inaccessible. The workers decided collective action was the best way to demand their rights.

In Honduras, I learned that human rights are not something government automatically bestows upon its citizens. An individual can only enjoy human rights when she is aware she has rights and she knows how to make claims upon them. Human rights come into being not when they are codified into law, but when people and communities begin to use them and demand them.

I spent the following two years in El Salvador, researching and writing about the legacy of a civil war whose last shots rang out over a decade ago yet still reverberated in the ears of many. While the Salvadoran tourism board has sought to promote an image of the country as a successful post-conflict democracy, the realities of political violence and human rights abuses I observed suggested to me a very different story. I felt this story was one that needed to be told, especially at a time when most Americans had their attention turned east rather than south.

Traveling the Salvadoran countryside, I encountered many of the same conflicts of rights that I found in Honduras. The property rights of landowners conflicted with the subsistence rights of landless peasants. The right of some citizens to live free from the fear of gang violence conflicted with the right of other citizens to live free from police violence. When government stepped in to arbitrate these conflicts, it inevitably favored the interests of the powerful.

But I also met groups of people building power through active use of the democratic process. I visited rural and urban communities that organized their social and economic life around their understanding of justice as articulated in the Salvadoran constitution or in the Bible. I learned that law is not the set of rules that government imposes upon people, law is also the structure by which people organize their own social, political and economic interactions.

As part of my job in El Salvador, I coordinated international monitoring of the 2003 local elections. We documented and tried to prevent acts of fraud by ruling-party supporters whose audacity would make Viktor Yanukovitch blush. In one town where the mayor won re-election by fewer than 100 votes, hundreds of opposition-party ballots were invalidated by ruling-party elections officials. Even when the law is just and impartial, I realized, a contest between two groups is not balanced unless both groups have equal access to the legal machinery of justice.

Returning to the United States in 2004, I helped organize the March for Women's Lives. With 1.15 million people in attendance, it was the largest reproductive rights march in U.S. history. My job was to bring people from 18 states, all without leaving my office in Washington. I could not recruit door to door in neighborhoods and on campuses in California, Iowa and Minnesota, so I had to identify leaders and help them organize their communities. Working in leadership development helped me to develop as a leader. It taught me about the different reasons that spur people to mobilize in defense of their rights, and the different ways that they do this.

I also served as one of the march's principal liaisons with city and federal agencies. Organizing the first major march on Washington since Sept. 11, 2001, we knew we were operating in a new regulatory environment. After researching the agencies' regulations, I coordinated the design of the logistics plan. I presented the plan to the agencies and negotiated to win their approval. This experience provided me a crash course in navigating the time, place and manner restrictions that make up the real context in which people in the United States exercise our rights to freedom of speech, freedom of assembly and freedom to petition the government for a redress of grievances.

I bring to Yale Law School my experience as a researcher, writer and social communicator, both in the field and in my studies. Moreover, I bring the perspective of the communities in which I have worked, from Honduras to El Salvador to Washington. I hope to study how legal principles and practices apply to different communities, their differing access to the law, and how the law is continually reshaped by their struggles for access. I look forward to contributing to the study of human rights and the clinical practice of public interest law at Yale.

As groups of people struggle to gain access to human rights, they further develop the rights that we all enjoy and change the legal machinery of justice which we use to claim these rights as ours. I aspire to be a public interest lawyer, working for the development of human rights by supporting women and emerging communities in their struggles to gain equal access to and make claims upon the law.

Question 7 Response (250-Word Essay)

"I've traveled all over Central and South America," a Brazilian priest once told me. "But I never truly understood Latin America until I stood in the checkout line at the Pathmark in Jersey City."

If the Western Hemisphere is more integrated than ever before, it is because of migration, not free trade. For example, more than a quarter of El Salvador's citizens live in the United States, and more Salvadorans live in Los Angeles than in San Salvador. 65 percent of the country's external revenue comes from remittances: dollars sent home from the United States by mostly low-wage workers.

Even the language spoken in El Salvador has changed as a result. Fifteen years ago, most colloquial expressions came from the indigenous Nahuatl. Today, many come from Mexican prison slang, brought back by deportees from California. Meanwhile, second-generation immigrants in the United States have developed a new language, Spanglish, that mixes English and Spanish dialects spoken in dozens of Caribbean and Latin American countries. In El Salvador, "cora" is the word for a twenty-five cent coin; it is pronounced just like "quarter" in Brooklynese.

Race reflects how a group identifies itself and is identified by others. For the U.S. Census Bureau to drop the category of "other" in an effort to force Latinos to identify as black or white would thus be to ignore emerging linguistic and cultural transformations in Latino communities. For many second-generation immigrants, Hispanic describes their ancestry, but Latino describes who they are in the United States.

ABOUT THE AUTHOR

Eric Owens is a proud graduate of Loyola University Chicago School of Law. He currently serves as an American diplomat.

NOTES